THE POLITICS OF GOD

BY JOSEPH R. WASHINGTON, JR.

Black Religion: The Negro and Christianity in the United States
The Politics of God

THE POLITICS OF GOD

By JOSEPH R. WASHINGTON, JR.

BEACON PRESS : BOSTON

To David, our beloved teacher of the trinity—that it is not the only model for a people whose life is expecting the unexpected.

PREFACE

MANY READERS of my *Black Religion: The Negro and Christianity in the United States* have urged me to suggest constructive ideas which would provide for those who accept the critical analyses of that book some sense of direction, some goals. Since for the foreseeable future institutions of religion dominated by Negroes will continue to exist in segregation, the challenge seemed worthy of response.

In the preparation of this book two basic facts emerged. First, if there is a uniqueness in the religion of the Negro it is to be found in their history and has its highest expression in the Negro spirituals. Second, Negroes and whites are generally optimistic about the developments of their relationships because of an unwarranted belief in the reasonableness of men. My fundamental presupposition, based upon Negro spirituals and the experience of Negroes in America, is that reason, like good will, is a necessary but insufficient means for creative change. Reason may well determine the attitudes and behavior of an elite, but it tends to be of merely academic significance to the general will of the people—in the daily grind, where it counts.

Thus, *The Politics of God* is an attempt to understand the creative possibilities for dynamic change in the historic religion of Negroes, as distinguished from the western tradition of reason found in both humanism and Protestantism. In this way, it is hoped the distinctive function of the Negro in the struggle between black and white Americans will be found and its meaning, relevance, and purpose will prove to be creative in our complex society.

Part I is an exploration into some basic questions and answers vis-à-vis Negroes and Caucasians posed by scientific rationalists, Christian rationalists, and rational moralists. Each of these perspectives is significant and indispensable. Their solutions are criticized for being paraconclusive insofar as the irrational dimension of man and the unique role of the Negro do not enter their equations. Rationalists have helped us to know what is right, but have not helped us to do what is right.

Part II adds to the rational perspectives the real and fundamental evil which leads to the demonic attitudes and behavior of whites when they believe that Negroes should be separated from them, psychologically and socially, if not spatially. White Christian ethicists perceive the issue as religious blasphemy. However, since all human failures are due to what they call "original sin" or the "fall" of man, the distinctiveness of Negro-white tensions is blurred and Christian ethicists are unaware that they share the same myopia which afflicts their secular counterparts. These thinkers have helped us to do what is right, though they have not helped us to know what is right.

Part III combines knowledge of the right with doing the right. This section is the heart of the book. Instead of centering attention upon the white power structure or the oppressor, the Negro victim is called forth as the singular human resource for bringing this malaise to an end. The greatest weakness of the Negro and, paradoxically, his greatest strength is his respect for and support of ministers and churches. These sentimental favorites are offered a theology, a mission, and urged to a self consciousness so that Negroes can perceive the depth of their plight and discern their task.

If the convictions which motivate this book are revolutionary, it may be due to the fact they are informed by the Bible and Negro spirituals. Admittedly, both of these historical sources are radically revolutionary in content and intent. They also happen to comprise the deepest resources of American Negroes. But they need to be recognized as such, re-connected to present experience, and re-understood.

Joseph R. Washington, Jr.
Albion, Michigan
November, 1966

ACKNOWLEDGMENTS

WERE IT NOT for my wife Sophia's comforting care and her release of the guilt amassed during hours shut up in my study away from her infectious presence, this work could not have come to fruition. I do owe my son, Bryan, this apology for spending these past months writing instead of being a father. My good friend, Mrs. Marilyn Schmitt, made valuable suggestions for which I am deeply indebted. And a special word of appreciation is due Mrs. Henrietta Seibert, my very able secretary, who virtually alone can decipher my handwriting, for typing the manuscript.

I am grateful to the Presbyterian ministers, Negro and white, who so freely and critically reviewed these ideas with me as they were being worked out at the Johnson C. Smith Institute in Charlotte, North Carolina, July 1965; and I particularly wish to thank Daniel G. Little of the Home Mission Board of the Presbyterian Church, U.S.A., and Herman Counts of Johnson C. Smith, who made this encounter possible. A word of gratitude is also due the Reverend Mr. M. B. Meekins of McKeesport, Pennsylvania, and the Reverend Mr. W. C. Johnson of Denver, Colorado, for arranging ecumenical encounters with their colleagues.

The author gratefully acknowledges permission to reprint passages from the following copyrighted works: "A Professional Radical Moves in on Rochester," by Saul D. Alinsky, copyright © 1965, by Harper's Magazine, Inc., excerpted from the July 1965 issue of *Harper's Magazine* by permission of the author; *The Concept of Race*, by M. F. Ashley Montagu, copyright © 1964, reprinted with permission of The Macmillan Company; *Southern White Protestantism in the Twentieth Century*, by Kenneth K. Bailey, published by Harper & Row, Publishers, Incorporated; *The Fire Next Time*, by James Baldwin, published by the Dial Press Inc.; *The Protestant Establishment*, by E. Digby Baltzell, published by Random House; *Race: Science and Politics*, by Ruth Benedict, copyright 1940 by Ruth Benedict, all rights reserved, reprinted by permission of The Viking Press, Inc.; *The Negro Revolution in America*, by William Brink and Louis Harris, published by Simon and Schuster, Inc.; *Dark Ghetto: Dilemmas of Social Power*, by Kenneth B. Clark, published by Harper & Row, Publishers, Incorporated; *Minorities and the American Promise*, by Stewart and Mildred Cole, published by Harper & Row, Publishers, Incorporated; *Black Folk: Then and Now*, by W. E. Burghardt Du Bois, published by Holt, Rinehart and Winston, Inc.; *The Wretched of the Earth*, by Frantz Fanon, translated from the French by Constance Farrington, copyright © 1963 by Presence Africaine, published by Grove Press, Inc.; "Urban Lag" by Ben A. Franklin from *The New York Times* of August 8, 1965, © 1965 by The New York Times Company, reprinted by permission; *The Negro Church in America*, by E. Franklin Frazier, published by Schocken Books Inc.; "Negroes and Jews: The New Challenge of Pluralism," by Nathan Glazer, published in *Commentary* of December 1964, reprinted from *Commentary* by permission, copyright © 1964 by the American Jewish Committee; *The Accidental Century*, by Michael Harrington, reprinted with permission of The Macmillan Company; *The New Equality*, by Nat Hentoff, copyright © 1964 by Nat Hentoff, all rights reserved, reprinted by permission of The Viking Press, Inc.; *Protestant, Catholic, Jew*, by Will Herberg, copyright © 1955, 1960 by Will Herberg, reprinted by permission of Doubleday & Company, Inc.; *Community Power Structure*, by Floyd Hunter, published by The University of North Carolina Press; *Racism and the Christian Understanding of Man*, by George D. Kelsey, published by Charles Scribner's Sons; *On the Road*, by Jack Kerouac, all rights reserved, reprinted by permission of The Viking Press, Inc.; *The Pastor and the Race Issue*, by Daisuke Kitagawa, published by The Seabury Press, Incorporated; *America as a Civilization*, by Max Lerner, published by Simon and Schuster, Inc.; *From State Church to Pluralism*, by Franklin H. Littell, copyright © 1962 Franklin Hamlin Littell, reprinted by permission of Doubleday & Company, Inc.; *Seeking to Be Christian in Race Relations*, Benjamin E. Mays, Friendship Press, New York, copyright, 1964; "Our Guilt for the World's Evil," by Arthur Miller, reprinted by permission of Ashley Famous Agency, Inc., copyright © 1965 by Arthur Miller, originally appeared in *The New York Times Magazine*, January 3, 1965, © 1965 by The New York Times Company, reprinted by permission; *The Spoil of the Violent*, by Emmanuel Mounier, reprinted in *Cross Currents*, Vol. XI, 1–3, 1961; *An American Dilemma*, by Gunnar Myrdal, Harper & Row, Publishers, Incorporated; *Challenge to Affluence*, by Gunnar Myrdal, published by Pantheon Books; *God Is No More*, by Werner and Lotte Pelz, copyright © 1963 by Werner and Lotte Pelz, published by J. B. Lippincott Company; *A Profile of the Negro American*, by Thomas F. Pettigrew, copyright 1964, D. Van Nostrand Company, Inc.; *The Kingdom Beyond Caste*, by Liston Pope, Friendship Press, New York; *Christian Ethics and the Sit-In*, by Paul Ramsey, Association Press; "The Negro in American Religious Life," by Harry V. Richardson, in *The American Negro Reference Book*, edited by John P. Davis, published by Prentice-Hall, Inc.; "The Chicago Protests," by Stephen Rose, *Christianity and Crisis*, Vol. XXV, No. 13, July 26, 1965; "From Protest to Politics," by Bayard Rustin, published in *Commentary* of February 1965, reprinted from *Commentary* by permission, copyright © 1965 by the American Jewish Committee; "Johnson So Far: Civil Rights," by Bayard Rustin and Thomas Kahn, published in *Commentary* of June 1965, reprinted from *Commentary* by permission, copyright © 1965 by the American Jewish Committee; *The Negro Leadership Class*, by Daniel C. Thompson, © 1963, by permission of Prentice-Hall, Inc., Englewood Cliffs, N. J.; *Democracy in America*, Vol. I, by Alexis de Tocqueville, published by Schocken Books Inc.; and from *To Be Equal*, by Whitney M. Young, copyright © 1964 by Whitney M. Young, Jr., used by permission of McGraw-Hill Book Company.

CONTENTS

PART ONE
THE RATIONAL WORLD

CHAPTER I
RATIONAL SOCIETY AND RATIONAL RACISM

DESPITE SOME MOST PECULIAR RESULTS, the *idea* of western society as a fundamentally rational one is largely unquestioned, and this generally exclusive emphasis on the rational is due as much to the faith of those who are committed conservators of this strain in our tradition as to its reality. In an age of scientific rationalism this thrust tends to set the patterns for both social intercourse and problem solving. Even in interpersonal conflicts the results are frequently computerized programs. Today the way that problems of natural science and technology are defined and solved through the rational process has become the preferred and imitated way in interpersonal and intergroup problems and issues. So strong is the reigning scientific rationalist faith that it has usurped, for all effective purposes, other alternatives in the sphere of human problems. Clearly what has occurred is an awareness of social problems almost unaffected by either religion or humanism. The social sciences have been nurtured and promoted as scientific methods comparable to natural science, promising the same exactness of results. The promise, if not the success, of today's social science is visible in its virtually unchallenged ideology as the way to human progress, an accepted faith that people, problems, and issues—attitudinal and behavioral—are significant insofar as they are rational. Issues are to be defined and solved by rational methods informed by scientific description and prescription. Events can be planned after the scientific model of prediction and control and it is said that this is the way to develop the kind

of society planned by choice, to accomplish what western human-
ists have idealized and for which religionists have prayed.

Understandably, therefore, antirational thought, problems,
and solutions are simply proven to *be* antirational, i.e., against
the mainstream of our scientific and rational humanist tradition.
Issues labeled antirational are either dismissed or translated into
rational issues. However, by not meeting irrational problems on
rational terms, the rationalist-humanist-scientific complex gives
neither serious attention to the effective, popularly held irrational
beliefs, nor appreciably changes the destructive irrational attitudes and behavior born of antirational beliefs. It is on the popular level that the majority of people act and react and therefore
impair human relations, especially among those who are disadvantaged, disinherited, and disengaged. Moreover, even the rational elite are victims of irrationality, particularly in their daily
existence outside their studies and laboratories since the irrational
tradition of western civilization which continues in the present as
the past, does affect the world in which they live.

The success of a society formed and guided by persons singularly attuned to a rational method is unmistakable in its natural
science and to a lesser degree in its social science. What is also
evident is the gap between the two levels of science. The rationalist faith of social scientists and indeed most of the elite of the
nation is that this gap between the natural and social sciences will
rapidly narrow as social science proves itself indispensable and
is looked to as the method for achieving a rationally planned
society. But the gap between a scientifically planned political
economy and popular behavior patterns is the most glaring of
all, although there are thinkers who have the faith that this too
will pass away and that in time there will come a unity of attitudes and values throughout the various divisions of our society.
The basic assumption here is that social science will be as universally accepted, respected, and used as is the natural science-
technology complex.

If reason contended only against anti-reason, all thought and
action not of reason could be so exposed and then ignored by the
reasonable men who control and dominate power structures. To

identify and then ignore anti-reason for the sake of conserving thoughtful energy for methods of reason and science appears reasonable. But western man, like all men, is more than a rational-political-social-economic animal with productive-consumptive-creative needs. He is also that type of animal called human being who encounters the irrational—a third force other than reason or anti-reason. The irrational may be many things; certainly the irrational is the form in which holy presence discloses itself. The irrational is also the most convincing form of "religion," but religion is not interchangeable with holy presence. Often religion is a distortion of holy presence, a response to the demonic which is sometimes deliberately misrepresented as holy where it is not mistaken for that presence. Nevertheless, the irrational in the form of religion is an inevitable dynamic of the human equation and the irrational cannot be understood, determined, or even encountered through the process of reason. Reason is powerless to eliminate the irrational. By ignoring the irrational and consequently genuine or distorted religion, the reason- and science-oriented elite who influence the non-interpersonal spheres of human life do not affect irrationality as much as they are affected by it.

To ignore the irrational neither sends it away nor makes it ineffective in human events. By opting for the rational as opposed to the irrational, instead of engaging both, the scientific-humanist tradition controlling our society improves the material resources and formal procedures of life but ignores too many humans who are victims of distorted religion, which can be a demonic misrepresentation of the holy irrational.

This demonic irrationality is most devastatingly present in the increasing conflict between black and white in America. Racism has been on the uprise during the preceding two centuries and has yet to reach its climax. The creed of racism, and its resulting antirational or irrational attitudes and behavior, has developed precisely because our scientific society provides an occasion for pseudoscientific ideology. On the assumption that the doctrine of race hatred is fundamentally antirational, racism has been attacked by scientists with rational methods and rational racism has been disproved by reason and science. Since social scientists have been placing an increasing number of Negroes on the economic escalator, it cannot be denied that the rational humanist tradition has gained a measure of success in combatting rational racism.

But if rational racism is on the sharp decline, irrational racism is on the uprise and it is this irrational racism which is the most effective dehumanizing phenomena in twentieth century relations between Negroes and whites in America. Irrational racism is a demonic religion, ignored by rationalists for the most part because of their indifference to and antipathy for religion.

Clearly the rationalists' proof that racism is a myth does not prevent racism from being the determining force in Negro-white relations in America. Indeed, the rationalists' insistence upon proving racism a *myth* is indicative both of their attitudes toward religion and of racism's religious or irrational nature. There is a sense in which the elimination of rational racism without the concomitant elimination of irrational racism leaves our society subject to increased racism. There is an applicable parable in which Jesus states our condition succinctly:

> When the unclean spirit has gone out of a man, he passes through waterless places seeking rest, but he finds none. Then he says, "I will return to my house from which I came." And when he comes he finds it empty, swept, and put in order. Then he goes and brings with him seven other spirits more evil than himself, and they enter and dwell there; and the last state of that man becomes worse than the first. So shall it be also with this evil generation (Matthew 12:43–45, RSV).

Racism is persistent, like all demonic forces. Clean-swept though rational racism may generally be, irrational racism has found a dwelling place in the dry and deserted depths of religion among a majority of white Americans and a minority of reacting Negro Americans.

Ethnocentrism is the disposition of people to consider their family, society, culture, or "race" superior in values, worth, goodness, and rightness. Ethnographers have discovered ethnocentrism to be an inclination of human groups of universal long standing. In the popular mind, ethnocentrism is viewed as a widespread tendency which inevitably leads from intergroup conflict of various permanent character to racism. Ethnography has shown conclusively that the various attempts of a people to justify their superiority are subject to modification if not elimination in the process of interaction with different groups. Consequently, the ethnocentric residual is not necessarily damaging to or preventive of intergroup engagement. Ethnocentrism is generally a means that keeps alive the healthy and enriching diversity of peoples, justification taking the form of pride in and gratitude for one's heritage. Ethnocentrism is a malleable human condition which to the degree that it is healthy, is indispensable. It is not necessarily strife producing. Ethnocentrism is not identifiable with either group conflict or racism, nor does there exist a linear movement from ethnocentrism to group conflict and racism. External forms may appear identical to the popular mind, but the motives, intentions, methods, and consequences are not the same among these three patterns.

Intergroup conflict is similar to ethnocentrism in that it is universal and of long standing in human history. The justification or motive of intergroup and international conflict is the claim of superiority and rightness. The intention is to prove and make this so-called superiority permanent. The method for gaining hegemony has varied among intellectual-cultural-political-religious power coercives, often beginning with war and ending in enslavement. The consequences have been group hostility and personal inferiority-superiority complexes. Thus intergroup conflict differs from ethnocentrism in being the hatred and aversion to a group resulting from cultural, political, and religious differences. Ethnocentrism gravitates around the exclusive pole of aversion but not the aggressive pole of hatred. The tendency of intergroup conflict is toward the exclusive and aggressive pole of hatred which wants to realize the thought of superiority in deed. Ethnocentrism bears no special relation to the special strife between Negroes and whites. But when one seeks to understand the roots of racism (and particularly Negro-white conflict) from the perspective of rationalists and scientists, intergroup conflicts provide a helpful background.

In the history of the West, cultural differences between peoples has been an important factual base supporting the desire of various political groups to be dominant over others. A number of societies have viewed themselves as culturally superior and have even tried to develop theses to prove their superiority. One of the first documented instances of this is found in the fourth century B.C. The Greeks were at their height in cultural development during this period and entered into relations with Asiatic foreigners whom they dubbed inferior along with that "out group" labeled barbarians. The Greeks considered themselves the "in group" of superior achievement. In order to rationalize the Greek in group hegemony, Aristotle set forth a bold hypothesis in his *Politics* that *people are born slave or free.* Aristotle's intellectual defense of dominance over people of different culture and skin color provided a precedent for the justification of slavery and the apparent beginnings of racism in the West. It is clear that Aristotle was making some kind of claim to innate and unchangeable human characteristics. Nevertheless, we are assured by scholars including Ruth Benedict that the superior Aristotelian in group versus inferior out group thesis was a cultural claim as opposed to a racial dogma. Aristotle was merely stating in the extreme the cultural claim that "I belong to the Elect," people who are destined to enrich and preserve civilization. The "fair skinned barbarians" were culturally inferior. Ruth Benedict determines that Aristotle is not making a racist argument because in his references to innate slavery and freedom in *Politics,* he meant only the barbarians and Asiatic peoples *as* Asiatic peoples, not the cultural attainments of the Hellenized Asiatics. Ruth Benedict is the foremost proponent of the position which states that the key to racism is a requirement that group "blood" not be mixed, a thesis she claims to be foreign to Aristotle:

His pupil Alexander, in the course of his conquests, advocated intermarriage, and ten thousand of his soldiers took wives from the natives of India. Alexander himself married two Persian princesses.[1]

If Aristotle's affirmation that *some people are born to be free* and *others are born to be slaves* is taken seriously, the actions of Alexander may not so much disprove a racist strain in Aristotle as it does indicate the development of a thinker turned actor, informed by his experiences and the natural tendencies of soldiers serving extended duty in occupied territories. However, Ruth Benedict is making two claims. The in group–out group antagonisms are cultural limitations which have been historically modified through intermarriage, an acceptable pattern which is unacceptable to modern racists. Further, as we shall see, racism is defined as a pseudoscientific dogma demanding "race" groups be kept "blood" pure.

The Romans continued the Greek tradition of in group superiority as evidenced by the low esteem in which the citizens of the Roman Empire held the out group peoples they conquered. Unlike the soldiers of Alexander however, members of the Roman militia were not encouraged to intermarry with barbarians because the Roman "cake of custom" explicitly approved of marriages only between Roman citizens. On the other hand, conquered territories became provinces and eventual inheritors of citizenship as well as "in group" privileges and advantages. Even more, Romans did not discriminate against aliens on the basis of race or culture but wisely used indigenous leadership on behalf of the Roman Empire, thus instituting a laissez faire policy "in regard to the folkways and cultural life of the provinces." [2] Ruth Benedict thus sees ancient group antagonisms as caused by cultural rather than racial pride:

> Aristotle's attitude was characteristic of Europe in ancient times, and the Roman Empire therefore did not have to free itself of racist doctrines in the building of its great cosmopolitan state.[3]

[1] Ruth Benedict, *Race: Science and Politics* (New York: Modern Age Books, 1940), p. 159.

[2] *Ibid.*, p. 161.

[3] *Ibid.*, p. 159.

A second historical cause of group antagonism is politics. Even the cultural claim of in group Greek superiority is intertwined with politics. Fundamental to political hegemony was slavery. Even the Greeks found it necessary to justify enslaving people; we have seen this in the writings of Aristotle. Although Greek and Roman views of cultural superiority may flow from the former to the latter, Aristotle's doctrine of innate slavery among some people finds no counterpart among Roman philosophers of comparable stature, of which Cicero may be typical:

> Men differ in knowledge but all are equal in ability to learn; there is no race which, guided by reason, cannot obtain virtue.

Among the people conquered and subjugated by Greeks were Negroes, but white people in Ancient Greece composed the vast majority of slaves and were treated the same as the Negroes. Similarly, the Roman Empire knew Negro slaves as well as those from Asia Minor and western Europe. It is clear that the distinction between those free and enslaved was made on the basis of cultural-political dominance, rather than on the basis of "race" color and physical features, and "blood." Ethnographers are unanimous in stating that Negroes were enslaved for political rather than racial reasons in European antiquity; in this they did not differ from white slaves.

The earliest record known of political discrimination and the Negro comes from the Pharaoh Sesotris III, who lived from 1887 to 1849 B.C.:

> Southern Boundary. Raised in the eighth year of the reign of Sesotris III, King of Upper and Lower Egypt, to whom be life throughout all ages. No Negro shall cross this boundary by water or by land, by ship or with his flock save for the purpose of trade or to make purchases in some post. Negroes so crossing shall be treated with hospitality but no Negroes shall hereafter forever proceed by ship below the point of Heh.

As Du Bois points out, Egyptian sculptors and painters described Negroes as having kinky hair and thick lips, "as a slave and captive, as a tribute-bearer and also as ruler and official." [4] Du Bois takes the position that slavery as an ancient system of making captives supply labor for the leisure of women and the freeing of men to fight was not substantially different among conquerors:

> Greece and Rome had their chief supplies of slaves from Europe and Asia. Egypt enslaved races of all colors, and if there were more blacks than others among her slaves, there were also more blacks among her nobles and Pharaohs, and both facts are explained by her racial origin and geographical position. The fall of Rome led to a cessation of the slave trade, but after a long interval came the white slave trade of the Saracens and Moors, and finally the modern trade in Negroes. [5]

Modern slave trading as a political reality commences with the conquests of Africa by the Mohammedans, who along with African barbarians first threatened African culture. Caught between Mohammedan conquests and the intertribal wars of Negro kingdoms and tribes which came into power finding "the slave trade lucrative and natural," Negro slaves became "the incident of African Wars."

One further cause of intergroup antagonism affecting Negro and white relations, finally, is religion. The hegemony of the West passed from Greece through Rome into the hands of the Roman Catholic Church. It is in the religious wars fought by Christians that we find the beginnings of "alien races" as compared with the more ancient and less rigid notion of alien cultures. Roman Catholics first persecuted, then warred against Jews, pagans, and Moslems, and finally enslaved them. The basis for this hostility which yet permeates Christians of the West was neither cultural nor political differences; it was that Jews, pagans, and Moslems refused to be converted to Christianity, the one issue about which Roman Catholics were totally intolerant. The Crusades were motivated by an attempt to convert or annihilate these enemies

[4] W. E. Burghardt Du Bois, *Black Folk: Then and Now* (New York: Henry Holt and Company, 1939), p. 24.

[5] *Ibid.*, p. 130.

of the faith. From the First Crusade to the fifteenth century, Roman Catholics seethed with hostility against non-Christians and sought to force their religious perspectives on people identified as members of "alien races." Thus the Portuguese, Spanish, and Italian merchants of the fifteenth century voyaged to new lands and found new peoples whom they sought to convert to Christianity and make equals through assimilation. The idea of perpetual servitude and racism was a later development.

When Europeans journeyed to Africa, hitherto unknown to them, they found (as Christianizers) common ground with Moslems in the enslavement of Africans for religious reasons. The practical result for the African slave was not the same, given "the Moslem enmity toward the unconverted" and the "Christian attitude toward heathen":

> In Mohammedan countries there were gleams of hope in slavery. In fiction and in truth the black slave had a chance. Once converted to Islam, he became a brother to the best, and the brotherhood of the faith was not the sort of idle lie that Christian slave masters made it. In Arabia black leaders arose like Antar; in India black slaves carved out principalities where their descendants still rule.[6]

The best scholarship, critically accepted by scientists and men of reason, has decidedly demonstrated the universality of ethnocentrism as mild human pride. Intergroup conflicts are also discovered to be universal and injurious to group relations, but generally amenable through association and intermarriage. The most recalcitrant intergroup antagonism—religion—tending to reject wholesale the out group, is increasingly less adamant. However, the in group superiority of religions sowed the seed of total dismissal of whole out groups, a dimension which is no longer dominant in religions but has given form to racism. The key to religious aggression is persecution, which gives rise to hatred that thrives on a simple appeal to objective and inalienable "rightness."

Social scientists have taken the trouble to disclose racism as

[6] *Ibid.*, p. 132.

the most dangerous development in western cultural history. It is generally agreed that racism is neither a universal nor an inevitable phenomenon. It is a devastatingly western scientific heresy. As we shall see, racism is a unique and independent western heritage, one that poses the most serious threat to scientific hegemony and rational social planning. Though unique and independent, racism is not an autonomous heritage but one which owes its existence to a leap in the continuum from cultural superiority, through political subjugation and religious persecution to human annihilation, with no higher court of appeal (i.e., cultural assimilation, political acquiescence, religious conversion). Moreover, this western heresy is spread abroad with the European enterprise. That is, the discrimination by Indians of Africans in Africa insofar as Indians are seen as the Jews of Africa by Africans is due to the attitudes Indians gained from Europeans, along with their economic prowess.

Racism's foundations are a continuation of cultural-political-religious aggressive persecution. Its immediate modern beginnings are in slavery. The distinctiveness of modern slavery is in what Du Bois calls "trade in men." Slave trade as slave trade is typically modern in being a lucrative and natural source of luxurious living. Historically, slaves were gained through war captives and the supply was strictly controlled by the fruits of victory. To be sure, slaves were no less used for purposes of labor; but with the Mohammedan conquests of Africa there commences a slavery which is supplied by other than the results of war. There is for the first time slave trading in the sense of slaves being bought by wealthy Mohammedans as luxury items to perform the duties required in harems, as servants and porters as well as soldiers. The reason Africa was victimized by the buying and selling of Africans beyond the previously normal pattern of capturing people in war and enslaving them is significant:

> Remembering that in the fifteenth century there was no great disparity between the civilization of Negroland and that of Europe, what made the striking difference in subsequent development? European civilization, cut off by physical barriers from further incursions of barbaric races, settled more and more

to systematic industry and to the domination of one religion;
African culture and industry were not only threatened by
powerful African barbarians from the west and central regions
of the continent, but also by invading Arabs with a new religion
precipitating from the eleventh to the sixteenth centuries a
devastating duel of cultures and faith.[7]

Thus, warring African barbarians created rivals which not only
disrupted African culture but in intertribal wars slaves were captured and sold for handsome rewards to Mohammedans, thereby
draining African culture of its creative potential. Among the
Mohammedans there was the desire for war captives and conversion of the heathen blacks, both of which encouraged enslavement of Africans. Consequently, Africa was fragmented not only
culturally but religiously as well. In time there was added to enslavement via victories in war the desire to convert the uniquely
modern factor of enslavement for the purposes of economic gain.
Enslavement became general throughout Africa with the seventh
century Moslem beginnings joined by Europeans in the fifteenth
to the nineteenth century—without doubt the most extensive and
extreme rape in human history.

In this African chaos came the Europeans in the fifteenth
century. To the old factors of cultural-political-religious antipathy, and the new factor of economic exploitation, the Europeans
added the unprecedented element of color prejudice or racial
hatred. Clearly, the systematic and doctrinaire racist ideology of
"blood" did not take its present form in the fifteenth century, but
its promulgation in the eighteenth and nineteenth centuries would
not have been possible apart from the early color prejudice as
hatred of an entire race.

In the beginnings of European slavery, conquests in war were
not the source: this was a Mohammedan contribution, aided and
abetted by African intertribal wars. Like the Mohammedans, Europeans justified their enslavement of Africans on the basis of
saving the heathens through domination and conversion. Slave
traders, accompanied by missionary Christianizers, began with
Portugal as early as 1450, became dominated by Spain prior to

[7] *Ibid.*, p. 130.

the Pope's Bull of Demarcation in 1493, became institutionalized by the Dutch in 1579, and was wrested from them by the English in the seventeenth century (though the English traded in slaves on a non-systematic basis as early as 1562). Slave raiding was disallowed by the Spanish government for Spanish ships in 1493, but it was allowable to gain slaves via contracts with Portugal until 1600, the Netherlands until 1640, France until 1701, and England until 1713.

European Christianitizing and colonizing of Africa, America, and India became a racial issue as early as 1550 when one Spaniard reinstituted the Aristotelian innate slave-free hypothesis for the purposes of defending Spanish slavery. It was said that "Indians are as different from Spaniards as cruelty is from kindness and as monkeys are from men." This perspective may have been as much culturally as racially based, since Spaniards, like the French and Portuguese, did not hesitate to first convert and then intermarry with the Indians in America, although the pattern of intermarriage never became effective in Africa or any other territory conquered by the English or Dutch. This is a significant and somewhat mysterious element in the history of racial prejudice based on color.

While race prejudice was known among Spanish-Portuguese Europeans of the fifteenth and sixteenth centuries who early dominated slave trading, color prejudice was not an acute malaise among these people. Max Weber's *The Protestant Ethic and the Spirit of Capitalism* is the classical study of the interconnections between Protestantism and the profit motive. In this study Weber does not connect racism with the religion of Protestants and the capitalist mentality. But there is common agreement on this matter among scholars attempting to pinpoint the rise of color prejudice. It is narrowed down to the rise of capitalism dominated by the profit motive, with little special attention given to Protestantism. This rational explanation of color prejudice does not claim a connection between racism and Protestantism, but rather between racism, capitalism, and western civilization. The argument states that color prejudice is not absent from lands colonized by the Latins (Spain and Portugal), but it is decidedly less rigid and heinous in these countries than in those dominated by European Protestants. Spain and Portugal remained under the dominance of the Roman Catholic Church in the sixteenth century, the period in which capitalism broke forth in full measure among the Protestant nations of Northern Europe. The religious spirit pervading these Latin countries and affecting their attitudes toward slavery was one of conflict between believer and unbeliever. This spirit along with the anticapitalism of the Roman Catholic political and economic authority resulted in the universal objectives and purposes of the Church, the religious criterion of equality taking precedence. Nations were not only encouraged by the Church to convert those enslaved but were not inhibited by either the Church or the political authorities from intermarriage with those people of different races who were converted. The basic criteria for intimate association was oneness in Christian allegiance.

It is further argued that the most intense affinity between color prejudice and capitalism arises in those countries which are not under the influence of the Roman Catholic Church. Spirited capitalism and profit seeking in Northern Europe became the national aim and purpose of the Anglo-Saxon and Germanic countries oriented toward Protestantism—Britain, the Netherlands, and the United States for examples. The answer to the question of why color prejudice is so evil in these countries is that the drive for great profits and low wages became the dominant concern of the industrial revolution. Karl Marx puts the matter succinctly:

> Slavery is an economic category just as any other. Direct slavery is the pivot of bourgeois industry, just as are machinery and credit, etc. Without slavery there is no cotton; without cotton, there is no modern industry. Thus, slavery is an economic category of the first importance.[8]

> Under the influence of the colonial system, commerce and navigation ripened like hothouse fruit. Chartered companies were powerful instruments in promoting the concentration of

[8] Quoted in *Ibid.*, p. 138.

capital. The colonies provided a market for the rising manu-
factures, and the monopoly of this market intensified accumula-
tion. The treasures obtained outside Europe by direct looting,
enslavement, and murder, flowed to the motherland in streams,
and were there turned into capital.[9]

With the slave trade as the basis for the great industrial expansion of Protestant Europe and particularly England in the seventeenth century, African slave labor became indispensable because
it was cheap. Not only were African slaves a cheap source of
labor supply, the slaves became "treated as capital goods and
not as human beings." It is thus concluded that the economic
necessity of slavery for industrial imperialism and national pros-
perity not only made slavery the father of western industrialism
but so imperative as to justify it first on the basis that slaves
were war captives or condemned criminals and persons who sold
themselves into slavery, then on the basis of economic necessity,
and finally, when humanitarian protest against their inhuman
treatment became vocal, the justification was the sub-humanity of
Africans, who need not be treated as human beings. In a word,
slave trading led to color prejudice and then to racism, resulting
from the social and economic system of capitalism.

This rational explanation of color prejudice fails to account
for the change from religious persecution until conversion to the
unacceptableness of Africans, who were not sought after for religious conversion, or when some became Christians why they
were still unacceptable. It does not follow that color difference
should lead to casting Africans out of the human race for the
sake of economic profits. We have seen that the Mohammedans
engaged in African slave trading for twelve centuries—as compared to the Europeans for four centuries—without determining
that Africans were not human beings worthy of brotherhood once
converted, and of marriage thereafter. The French, Portuguese,
and Spanish intermarried with Indians, if not Africans. But the
English intermarried with neither the American Indians nor the
Negroes who became Christians. Instead of intimate association,
the English in America, like their brethren and the Dutch in

[9] Quoted in *Ibid.*, p. 141.

Africa, isolated both Indians and Africans, where they did not eliminate them. This is the mysterious element in the interconnection between Protestantism and capitalism which is not explained by rational capitalistic-profit hypotheses. It is important to see capitalism as the new "religion" of Protestants, replacing the universals of Roman Catholicism. We will return in a later chapter to a fuller explanation of this Protestant religion of capitalism which becomes a religion of color prejudice, leading no less a man than David Hume to declare: "I am inclined to believe that Negroes are naturally inferior to whites."

Racial prejudice cannot be understood without facing this mysterious element of color prejudice from which it springs. Even more, color prejudice cannot be understood rationally, whether viewed from the history of intergroup antagonisms or modern reason based on science. Color prejudice is not rational but a demonic distortion of the irrational. But it is no less real. Irrational color hatred and aversion is not like persecution endemic to the great religions of the world. Doctrinaire racism can be explained and understood rational'y, but color prejudice is not identical with racism as most students of racism *qua* racism would lead us to believe. Racism is the effect of the cause we have labeled hatred of colored people. It is also an independent phenomenon of western civilization. It may be traced to its initial and systematic emergence in the rise of capitalism, the profit motive, with industrialism. It may even be possible to state that hatred of colored people is a mental set of attitudes which "causes, supports, or justifies discrimination." But this does not help us to understand or eliminate this mental set as a product of western civilization and Christianity, and most peculiarly it does not explain why it is a dynamic of that section of western civilization and Christianity dominated by white Protestantism. What is there in the Anglo-Saxon–Germanic ethos which produces and sustains antipathy for Negroes? A response which does not include Protestantism's emphasis upon individual and publicly demonstrated achievement (as opposed to Roman Catholicism and the Moslem concern for universal brotherhood) will not be helpful, and it will be an insufficient account of the Anglo-Saxon–Germanic innovation.

If rational hypotheses do not answer the question "Why is color prejudice doggedly espoused among western Protestants?" they do explain its offshoot racism as a doctrine. What is often misunderstood and requires clarification is the statement that color prejudice and racial prejudice are indistinguishable. The distinction between the two is essential, and to claim that both color prejudice and race prejudice are products of a peculiar "social and economic system" is neither true nor helpful.

Racism as a tradition of beliefs based on pseudoscientific presuppositions is defined by Ruth Benedict:

> Racism is the dogma that one ethnic group is condemned by nature to congenital inferiority and another group is destined to congenital superiority. It is the dogma that the hope of civilization depends upon eliminating some races and keeping others pure. It is the dogma that one race has carried progress with it throughout human history and can alone ensure future progress.[10]

According to this definition, when did racism begin? There are those who see hints of it in the Old Testament:

> Cursed be Canaan; a slave of slaves shall he be to his brothers (Genesis 9:25).

This passage, along with many others in the Old Testament, can be understood only as a judgment of faithlessness among people who are called to be faithful to God and the brethren. The faith of Israel did not preclude intermarriage with various human groups or the judgments of faith remaining effective. Both the Aristotelian hypothesis and its repetition in sixteenth century Spain are to be explained by belief in cultural-political superiority, not as racial dogma.

It is the rational scholarly consensus that racial dogma—distinguished here from color prejudice and religious persecution by

[10] Benedict, *op. cit.*, p. 153.

the claim of "purity of blood"—developed out of the eighteenth and nineteenth centuries in western civilization. Roman Catholic persecution of the Jews, pagans, and Moslems was the dynamic which spilled over into justification of the enslavement of heathen blacks. However, the move from religious superiority-inferiority to racial dogma was not fully exploited by expansionists from Roman Catholic countries precisely because missionaries actively accompanied the exploiters of the slave trade for the purposes of conversion, and to that extent Roman Catholic slave traders could not keep Christian Africans as slaves. The missionary tradition was not a Protestant activity during the dominant fifteenth to eighteenth century period of slave trading among those cut off from Roman Catholicism. Why hatred of Africans replaces the religious superiority-inferiority dogma among Protestants is not sufficiently clarified by the appeal to the fact that slaves were turned into capital, for this was also true of the less industrial nations. Protestants were without a religious commitment that stood in judgment upon their political-economic-social activities. Their guide was the religion of profits and individual salvation. Exploiters were held accountable only to their consciences and political-economic charters, which were without moral sensitivity or the Christian understanding of Christian brotherhood. Something else was missing from their conscience, Africans abiding in their homeland as in Spain and Portugal. Without Christian dedication or previous association with colored people and left to their own initiative, white Protestants of Northern Europe gave birth in the fifteenth century to the practical rather than rational notion of sub-human groups as a justification of the inferiority-superiority actuality in those overseas territories they were exploiting for capital gains at home. Color superiority was first justified on purely pragmatic grounds, in the absence of any counter perspective, and took the practical rather than rational form of rigid caste-like separatism among the English. The point to be made is that the later extirpation of native religions and the banishment of those enslaved "outside the pale of humanity, without religion, law, or morals"—to be kidnapped, massacred, or "herded onto reserves"—was an eighteenth and nineteenth century catastrophe of largely white Protestant manipulation.

With this practice in vogue abroad, there arose independently the racist dogma on the European homeland. Unlike color prejudice, racial theories began in class conflicts among whites and can be seen as an extension of religious persecution and other socio-economic problems of discrimination. The initial racist dogma was promulgated by Count de Gobineau in the mid-nineteenth century. This writing was pro-aristocracy, "the doctrine of the innate superiority" of this class. In developing the mythical doctrine of "Aryan" and "Nordic" superiority, Gobineau was concerned to defend the superiority of those people in whatever nation who descended from this lineage. This myth of "Aryan" superiority was an attempt to set up hierarchies of biological and psychological purity within the white European constellation of people. Following Gobineau's attempt to establish an innate class of superiors were attempts to establish innate superiority of nations through such authors as the pro-German Englishman Houston Stewart Chamberlain and America's Madison Grant. None of these writers was concerned with color prejudice but cultural, political dominance.

Subsequently, racist theories were based neither on class nor on nationalism but on social and economic privilege. They grew out of a distortion of Darwin's theory of evolution. Darwin's biological thesis of the "survival of the fittest" was adapted to infer that biological heredity is of sole importance and group heredity is as real as individual heredity. Behind these pseudo-scientific statements is the false belief in a mythical state where human groups existed in "separate races." This false tradition is based on the equally false premise of the "blood theory" of heredity. These pseudoscientific theories of race were given credence in "Social Darwinism" and Herbert Spencer's application of the purely biological theory of Darwin to sociology through the concept of the "survival of the fittest." This "Social Darwinianism" was welcomed by white Protestants mainly as a "scientific" justification of political expansion and economic aggression against Negroes. When applied to this major interest of Europeans, the racist dogmas permitted easy consciences in the gunning down of "inferior peoples" or their enslavement by a superior peoples for economic materialism.

Whether promulgated for the advancement of a class, a nation, or a race, these theories of racial dogma are grist for the rational and scientific mills of scholars. Biological determinism has no basis in scientific fact. Racism is not a product of science, if of scientism. Racism is a rationalization for the desire to replace a supposed inferior group by a superior one. It is the assertion that inequality of groups and cultures is unconditional, absolute, and determined biologically. The scientific response is that race prejudice is simply a "cultural value judgment with no objective basis." Its origin is not in nature but in the propaganda of special interest groups.

Racial prejudice as a theory of racial supremacy can be understood as a result of conflict, political causes, biological differences among people, cultural pride, all in the name of pseudo-science and arising in the West during the eighteenth and nineteenth centuries. The conclusion of the rational scientific argument is that race prejudice prospers because of the fundamental connection between it and the accidental but lethal conflicts emerging from the economic structures which dominate our modern world. Thus it is said that the elimination of race prejudice is directly dependent upon the transformation by society of its economic structures.

The trouble with this explanation is that it tends to equate color prejudice with race prejudice. The assumption is that racial or class discrimination hides a socio-economic antagonism and that color prejudice is but another fact in this broad problem of human conflict. Thus the answer to the problem is for human groups to cooperate, to universalize economic security through political and economic upgrading of all human groups. This may be the answer to anti-Semitism, which is the subject of much racist malignment, but it is difficult to disentangle Jewish hatred from centuries of religious persecution. Racist dogma only supports color prejudice and the elimination of the former may not affect the latter.

The fact is that although eighteenth century race prejudice as a theory has subsequently supported color hatred, color hatred and the disregard for Africans as human beings was a practicing way of life for white Protestants three centuries before the theories of racial dogma were developed on a rational basis. Prior to the pseudoscientific racial mythology which emerged to defend America's "special institution" of slavery, Negroes had long been treated as brutes and persecuted for being black.

It is generally contended today that color prejudice and race prejudice are so inextricably bound together as to make the distinction undiscernible. Yet, racist theories are now insignificant as covert or overt bases of appeal for division among non-Jewish whites in intra- and inter-national conflicts. Some real significance of race prejudice alternates between latent and potent hatred of Jews. Hatred of Jews is fed as much by religious support as emotional disturbance or racist dogmas. It is impossible to rewrite the Gospel of John to eliminate the sixty-six references to the Jews as the enemies of Christ and Christians, or to dislodge the spirit which insists that the Jews killed Christ, or to prevent Christians from accepting Jews as Jews who are not in need of Christianity:

> For you, brethren, became imitators of the churches of God in Christ Jesus which are in Judea; for you suffered the same things from your own countrymen as they did from the Jews, who killed both the Lord Jesus and the prophets, and drove us out, and displease God and oppose all men by hindering us from speaking to the Gentiles that they may be saved—so as always to fill up the measure of their sins. But God's wrath has come upon them at last (I Thessalonians 2:14–16).

If this religious persecution no longer promoted in the name of official Christian religion but in the name of racial dogmas persists, it is difficult to determine whether it is due to an economic class conflict, as rationalists would suggest, or to religious imperialism—perhaps both.

Social scientists, using a mixture of rational scientific method and Freudian psychoanalysis, are convinced to a large degree that if the cause of events can be explained, the problem can be effectively eliminated. Since Negroes are Christians they do not draw the venom of religious persecution as do Jews; rather, the cause of Negro-white conflict is due to historic economic aggression and the unwillingness of whites to allow Negroes a full share of the advantages of industrial-technological America, upon whose body and blood it was built. The scientific rationalist answer to this situation is, as with the Jews, the overcoming of socio-economic and class conflict by providing a well-planned society in which all will gain fuller political and economic shares of the abundant economy.

Although race prejudice vis-à-vis the Jews remains a fundamentally religious problem (which is given little attention because rationalists have generally assumed religion to be irrational or of insignificance in a rational society), color prejudice is enjoined with race prejudice as explainable by socio-economic systems which can be rationally changed. Added to the socio-economic explanation are the psychological and psychoanalytical interpretations which are seen to fit both color and race prejudice, increasing the claim that they lack important differences.

First, racial prejudice exists because of fear. The fear theory states that prejudiced people fear that personal and group privileges may be lost, along with economic security. This cause of prejudiced myths may be eliminated by removing the conditions which give rise to these fears and providing in their stead a sense of personal and interpersonal security which can be measured. *Second,* racism is explained by the "dislike of differences" theory which states that prejudices instinctively issue forth against people who are "different." This theory does not account for stereotyping and the prejudice against persons who are exceptions to the rule as well as to the group as a whole, much less does it explain differences among people which are not the subject of prejudice, or the contradictory statements prejudiced persons express. *Third,* the theory of "unpleasant experiences" as a cause of racial prejudice neither accounts for the good experiences gained with unacceptable people nor the bad experiences with exceptable people. *Fourth,* the "frustration-aggression" or "scapegoat" theory delineates the power of prejudice and articulates the well-known fact that when people are unable or unwilling to handle a tension-producing experience they take out their frustrations aggressively against some scapegoat. The theory fails to signify why Jews and Negroes, for example, become general scapegoats. *Fifth,* the "symbolic" theory states that Jews and Negroes are scapegoats because they have become identified in the unconscious mind with significant values which cannot be consciously expressed but which cannot be repressed, thus Jews and Negroes become the substitute. For example, white boys in the South have for centuries past— as in the present—gained their first sexual experience through intimidating and seducing Negro girls and women. This is a double source of guilt in that the super-religious fervor of the South is opposed to fornication and the Negro is an unacceptable partner for intimate relations. The desire for sex is important as is the religious heritage. The hatred of Negroes is important as is the love expressed with Negro women. The love-hate symbiosis becomes intertwined with the inability and unwillingness to accept the Negro woman as a woman and oppression of the Negro male who, it is believed, seeks revenge either through seduction of white women or violence to white men.

These rational theories for the explanation of prejudice assume not only the real psychological needs prejudice meets but that when scientifically set forth they will in time be eliminated from the life of rational men and women, coupled with its replacement by personal and group security for all.

The great contribution of rational theories to human knowledge is not simply the explanation of racial prejudice. It is also the setting forth of racism as a popular, pseudoscientific tradition of biological race superiority which has spurred on violent and prejudiced behavior so as to make it the most significant prejudice and source of group antagonism in contemporary western culture. It has in this understanding superseded all other forms of antipathy toward whole peoples and become the most demonic-irrational force in the most rational period of human history. Unlike political-cultural-religious antagonisms, which can be bridged, racism declares inferiority of certain groups to be biologically determined.

The question which must be asked of rationalists is whether it is meaningful to associate race prejudice with color prejudice. It has been argued by Ashley Montagu, among others, that there is no such thing as "race" and to honor it as a problem to be solved only perpetuates its credence. Something more is indispensable to the question, however: In the failure to distinguish between color and race prejudice it is assumed that racist biological theories are beliefs widespread and traditional in western society, even though they are largely unconscious beliefs. If they are beliefs then they can be countered by superior beliefs; if they are unconscious they can be brought to the conscious level and dealt with; and if they are a part of the tradition, then traditions can be changed. But what if unconscious, traditional, widespread racist theories are not held extensively by prejudiced people, or, if held, they are vulnerable to demythologizing and therefore are or can be practically eliminated? Does it follow that people are or will be less color prejudiced? What is misunderstood as unconscious belief should be seen as preconscious religion. It is not past or present racist theories which influence people to think in terms of superiority-inferiority dichotomies, for even if they were once and still are articulated by a demonic minority, we cannot thereby account for the mass's prejudice malaise. For at bottom economic aggression, capitalism, profits, fear, dislike of differences, scapegoats, experiences, and symbolic substitutes are not presently conscious or unconscious beliefs but preconscious religion. The issue today is not how to deal with race theories, but with preconscious hatred of Jews and Negroes—and this is a question of religion as much as of reason.

It is important to get rid of race prejudice as a category for what is, in fact, hatred of Jews and of Negroes: anti-Semitism and color prejudice are religious issues of two different orders. Roman Catholics, unlike Protestants, know it to be the case and must be given credit for awareness of their religious culpability in supporting hatred of Jews. Thus Vatican II ended with a declaration which intends to state that the religious issue of Jewish hatred can be eliminated through the teaching, preaching, and consequent living of Roman Catholics. Hatred of Jews is so much a preconscious religion among Roman Catholic and Protestant Christians that this noble effort of Vatican II is bound to be as futile as rational arguments. The only answer is for Christians to become Jews, not Jews Christians, not "Jewish," and affirm this heritage. The trouble is that neither Roman Catholics nor Protestants will take this stand, and it is doubtful whether Jews would welcome Christians. Nevertheless, both the problem and the answer to Jewish hatred is not a question of race but of religion.

If Jewish hatred and prejudice is a Christian-Moslem problem of religious preconsciousness and unwillingness to affirm the root from which they are the offshoot, rather than a question of racial biologism, it is not the same but similar with hatred of Negroes. Hatred of Negroes is especially a Protestant Christian problem in America and the West, though one from which Roman Catholics are by no means exempt. Racist theories and rational explanations neither constitute nor affect hatred of Negroes by whites. It is the case that Negroes and whites have been so intimately involved for generations and the Negroes have been so used and abused until this way of relegating them inferior regardless of their achievements is an independent cause of prejudice which cannot be understood as other than a preconscious religion. The only ultimate answer is for whites, particularly white Christians, to engage in changing the ethos whereby intermarriage with Negroes is not simply permitted but regarded as normal, right, and good. The only problem with this, the only answer, is that the course suggested is most unlikely for whites in general and white Christians in particular—and it is also most unlikely that Negroes would presently find whites acceptable. This issue will be pursued in a later chapter; suffice it here to say that while the initiative for healthy Jewish-Christian relationships lies with white Roman Catholic-Protestant Christians, the initiative for Negro-white relationships lies with Negroes.

The rationalists are invaluable in proving that racism is not innate, universal, or widespread throughout all civilizations. Racism as pseudoscientific dogma is a modern western phenomena originating in class conflict and cultural and national desires for dominance, giving erroneous intellectual arguments for centuries-old hatred of Negroes. Racial myths are antiscientific products of a scientific age which are quickly traversed by science. It is neither racial dogmas nor racial differences per se, nor the fact that actual biological differences in skin pigment lead people to conceive of themselves as different, which is significant in hatred of Negroes. Nor is the actual diversity of cultures and the dominance of western culture over African culture in technological advance—the condition which is so readily obvious to the popular mentality—the cause and effect of Negro hatred and the unwillingness to be enriched rather than divided by cultural diversity. Pseudoscientism is not at all applicable to the hatred of whites by Black Muslims. This is a normal reaction by a segment of the Negro "outcasts" against the racism that has victimized Negroes. Like white hatred of Negroes, Negro hatred of whites in the extreme Black Muslim spirit is not a matter of reason or of unreason but of religion. The socio-economic advancement of Negroes in our society has not affected the truth of the Black Muslim position, whether they increase in numbers or not, Black Muslims can be countered only by a more effective religious force.

Moreover, the rationalist claim that racism is inherently evil and of no value when compared with the healthy, scientific, reasonable possibilities of intergroup cooperation, applies only to race hatred by whites, not by Black Muslims. In a society in which hatred of Negroes is the dominant ethos, the most healthy response is hatred of whites by Negroes. Abnormality alone can deal effectively with abnormality. When a stalemate is reached it may then be possible to move on to the level of reason and cooperation among people who accept themselves and therefore are able to accept others. Further, the Black Muslims have been the most effective force in America dealing with the lumpen proletariat, turning Negroes without pride into productive and creative citizens and family men. Apparently Black Muslims have even effected cures for some of their dope addicts. This should give us pause and teach us to see that a way to deal with un-

healthy white hatred of Negroes—white preconscious religion—
is through unhealthy hatred of whites by Negroes. The latter is
the perfect internalization of pride in one's self and one's group.
It is the necessary process through which Negroes must be reborn
and shows forth the inadequacy of the notion that Negroes can
become healthy-minded in an unhealthy society, or that only
whites need to be changed from unhealthy to healthy-mindedness.
Yet these attitudes are inherent in the rationalist dogma.

By ignoring rational and irrational religion, rationalists have
misunderstood the irrational issue of Jewish and especially Negro
hatred by whites, no less the reverse. This is most clear in that
the answer to the problem of what they call race prejudice lies
along socio-economic changes furthered by psychoanalytic insights. These changes are occurring and Negroes are being es-
calated, albeit slowly and with little change in status or accept-
ableness. We cannot do less than what rationalists urge. We must
do more. Hatred of Negroes is no longer a question of systematic
racism. It is an independent phenomenon of preconscious religious
meaning and value which penetrates western culture and most of
all the United States.

CHAPTER II
RATIONAL CHRISTIANITY AND RATIONAL RACISTS

WHAT IS CALLED "the scientific method" is a virtually monolithic approach to human problems in America today. Our culture is saturated with a dominant belief in "progress through the application of science to human affairs." We are directed from the centers of power by commitment to "rational improvement of our society." Today, this is as true of theology as it is of other disciplines.

In the not too distant past theology boasted of being the "queen of the sciences," but the present scientific rational mode did not constitute the basis for this claim. Presently, theology views itself as the "servant of the sciences," an understanding of its role which has something less than universal agreement, especially among the sciences. The function of theology as "servant" discloses its model for response to the human condition. Like all other ways of knowing and inquiry into human nature and natural realms, theology has as its basic model the prevailing rational scientific one, to which it seeks to contribute unique theological insights. Doctrinal, biblical, historical, and phenomenological disciplines within theology are each patterned after the scientific method.

Thus, it is not surprising to find this model dominating theological ethics. What is unexpected is to find a Christian ethicist who is a Negro combining social scientific rationalism with Christian rational theology in such a way as to add new understanding to the pervasive descriptive-prescriptive or rational approach to racism in the United States. In his *Racism and the*

Christian Understanding of Man, Professor George D. Kelsey of Drew University Theological School has set forth the first serious, valuable, and scholarly treatment of racism by an American Christian ethicist. In this work he reveals a sure grasp of neo-orthodox theology of the Niebuhr-Barth school and a deft knowledge of contemporary social science. The significance of this book as an erudite if belated expression of the best in Christian rationalism and social science is its distinctive focus upon racism, hitherto given no systematic treatment by American Christian theologians. There is no comparable work by an ethicist which shows the strengths and weaknesses of scientific rationalism as a determinant of the dominant Christian response to Negro-white tensions. It deserves extensive and critical treatment.

Scientific knowledge, as we have suggested, is in itself an insufficient force for the elimination of color prejudice. Now we are seeking the awareness of Christian theology to the problem. If it simply reinterprets scientific data in theological terminology it only stultifies itself by identifying the Christian approach with the monolithic rigidity of "progress through the application of science to human affairs."

Professor Kelsey concludes with social scientists that "racism is a modern phenomenon," adding emphasis upon it as an independent

> system of meaning and value that could only have arisen out of the peculiar conjunction of modern ideas and values with the political, economic, and technological realities of colonialism and slavery.[1]

The purpose of the book is clearly

> to provide a Christian criticism of racism as a faith system in all of its facets and tendencies. By and large, Christians have failed to recognize racism as an idolatrous faith, even though it poses the problem of idolatry among Christians in a way that no other tendency does. Racism is especially problematical not only because of the peculiar nature of the racist faith, but

[1] George D. Kelsey, *Racism and the Christian Understanding of Man* (New York: Charles Scribner's Sons, 1965), p. 19.

because it is a "Trojan horse" within organized Christianity and Christian civic communities.[2]

It is Mr. Kelsey's intent to speak out of a Christian context; though it is not always clear whether he is speaking directly to Christian racists only, or also to racists who are inheritors of an historic Christian society. This distinction is important to draw in any attempt to measure the effectiveness of the book upon either the elimination of racism or as a scholarly interpretation of this phenomenon:

> The Christian faith is brought into dialogue with racism for two reasons. First, I am convinced that Christian faith provides authentic answers to the questions which racism poses but to which racism is able to provide only false answers. Second, racism is a phenomenon of modern Christian civilization. By and large, the people who have been the racists of the modern world have also been Christians or the heirs of Christian civilization. Among large numbers of Christians, racism has been the other faith or one of the other faiths.[3]

Racism is described by Dr. Kelsey as the rankest form of human alienation in its hatred of selected human groups *qua* human groups, as distinguished from aversion to peculiar characteristics of diverse human cultures. This worship of one race and the will to the destruction of others is considered a diabolically artificial division of humanity, one which the author can only account for as an idolatrous faith. Racism is a faith in the sense that the racist trusts and values race as an ultimate concern to which he gives supreme loyalty. That is, the ultimate concern is faith in one race as superior to another. The idolatry is its exaltation of "purity of blood" and "racial homogeneity." Thus, the burden of the book is the interpretation of a theological hypothesis of racism as an idolatrous faith, and the racist as a devotee of that faith, through the use of social scientific theory and data.

Since a presupposition of Dr. Kelsey is the inextricableness of Christianity and racism, it will be our task to discover the

[2] *Ibid.*, p. 9.
[3] *Ibid.*, p. 10.

relevance of this "analysis and criticism of racism as an idolatrous faith" for present day Christian or non-Christian racists. We will confine ourselves with the author primarily to Negro-white relations in the United States, although the book seeks to lay the groundwork for larger generalizations. Moreover, it will be useful to determine the value of the scholar's ideal typologies: "racists," "racism," "faith"—white Christians versus Black Muslims—in affecting the reality of racism in society.

Although Professor Kelsey deems it necessary to clarify racism as basically an idolatrous faith, racism would be of very little consequence were it not inherently bound up with and expressed through power politics. He conceives of segregation of the Negro in the United States, for example, as the normal pattern of racism in political action, but its logical conclusion is genocide, as with the Jews in Nazi Germany. Implicit in his Christian faith is the understanding that Christian civilization which both created race hatred and nurtures ameliorative humanism does not tolerate genocide. What is important to ascertain is whether a rationalist Christian response evokes the means for elimination of racism on the one extreme, as well as confining it short of extermination at the other extreme.

But beyond racism as a faith and political power there is the racist philosophy of history, based on biological determinism, which contends that there is a superior white culture which is a precious superstructure granted by God and/or nature. From the Christian perspective that all humans are created equal by God, Kelsey points out that "one part of the primary racist affirmation is the idea that God has made a creative error" in bringing forth "out races." Thus, in addition to the Christian claim of the fall or original sin, whereby all men refuse to return to each other and to God the love He has given in their creation, and cannot be real human beings until each and all love all, Negroes are the victims of a "double fall" from which there is no reprieve and in which there is no hope.

It follows that the racist understands himself and his race as the "white hope" for all mankind, in contrast with the Christian understanding of Jesus Christ as the one who loved all humankind fully, and God well, whereby he provides the way and hope for the oneness of man and God. Since all men reject this faith of Jesus Christ for other less demanding and inclusive faiths, the way is open for the faith in race and the "racist consciousness." Given the loyalty to race there emerges an anti-Negro consciousness in which the Negro appears as a "contrast conception" or "counter-conception" so sharp that Lewis Copeland, in an article entitled, "The Negro as a Contrast Conception," considers it "somewhat analogous to that between God and the devil in popular religion." [4] In a word, the racist's self-understanding is dependent upon understanding the Negro as the "opposite race" and/or "the race in opposition." The counter-racist way of identification is the Black Muslim articulation of "the truth about the white man." There is a significant difference between these common ways of knowing. White racists combine political power with racial hatred, and in the absence of power Black Muslims must settle for eschatological visions of the future.

Lewis Copeland suggests, "The essence of the racial contrast appears to be a moral antithesis which tends to be projected through all social relations," [5] an insight which Kelsey considers important in racism as a faith. There is a "moral antithesis" in God as "white" and the devil as "black," in the contrasts of adoring white women and deprecating black women, in the assertion of the Negro as the enemy of the white man "against which all whites must unite," and in the positing of the Negro as alien to the entire "public," not to mention the "private" domain of whites. This "moral compulsion" against the Negro not only makes political action necessary but stereotypes indispensable, bringing into being a system of self-fulfilling prophecy and the characteristic racist consciousness known as prejudice.

Inherent in this racist self-knowledge through knowledge of out races is the weakness of "insecurity and uncertainty" that paradoxically accompanies claims to racial superiority, requiring segregation to meet the threat of groups which should in theory be subordinated by nature rather than political action.

[4] Quoted in *Ibid.*, p. 37.
[5] Quoted in *Ibid.*, p. 39.

At this juncture Kelsey says to the Christian racist (perhaps to the non-Christian racist too) that there is no self-understanding or understanding of other groups in racism because it is based upon ultimate loyalty to nature. The Christian knows nature to be the gift of God to man for man to subdue, control, and direct for his good purposes. Self-knowledge and knowledge of others only results from prior knowledge of God since man's human being is derived from the Creator. Since "man must know God before he can know himself," there can be no knowledge of "himself out of himself, . . . man can understand himself only when he becomes true man, only when he is renewed in Christ." [6]

So, to be rid of his "insecurity and uncertainty," which is the aim of self-understanding, racist man is called upon to objectively scrutinize his faith in nature and to forsake this ideology, not for "the analysis of nature as required by authentic science," but for the certainty and security of the Christian understanding of man. By accepting the Christian way of knowing one discovers knowledge of oneself and other selves is possible only in inter-personal relationships or communion. Kelsey is saying, with recognition of the Negro as necessary for "knowledge of oneself," awareness of the Negro as a human being with "a claim upon me" cannot but follow. It is only a step beyond this to claiming the Negro as "my brother man," and as a "covenant partner, whom God has given to me." Nothing less than this personal relationship can overcome the racist classification of people as things, "unknown and invisible" members of useless out races without "claims upon members of in-races."

Kelsey believes an essential failure beyond self-understanding and understanding of others is the racist misunderstanding of "person and community." He distinguishes between the "natural-istic-racist philosophers," who claim man's existence is due to nature, and Christian racists, who do not make this explicit statement "when they are thinking and speaking abstractly." It is only when, for example, Negroes as a people are up for discussion that the racist Christian makes references to "blood," "nature," and "mongrelization," as opposed to the Christian doc-

[6] *Ibid.,* p. 57.

trine that man "owes his existence to God." If not in the abstract, there is no difference between racists in the concrete—"racism is complete self-deification." In rooting personality in nature, racism runs counter to the essentiality of Christ for authentic human "being-in-relation," the "truly human," as Kelsey interprets the matter. Man the independent-dependent symbiosis cannot find wholeness of being through the racist faith because nature is its ground of being and nature is itself a created element:

> Man is truly man and truly person only if he responds in obedient love to the divine call. He is so created that he has no true life except in God. He is an "independent-dependent" being who can only be himself in free response to the call of God in every detail of his life.[7]

Racism does not know man as "existence-in-love," who can only be himself "in the community of love" which honors each person as a distinct individual: "The Christian view of man is at once a radical individualism and a radical universalism."[8] If the key to being a person is "existence-in-love" and there exists "genuine community" only in the "community of love,"

> the radical universalism of Christian faith means that love knows no boundaries of geography, nation, race, or class.[9]

Consequently, racism obstructs human fulfillment by absolutizing racial barriers instead of allowing "existence and the freedom of the spirit" to be led by the "promptings of grace" beyond artificial restrictions into creative human interaction.

In his *Revolt Against Civilization*, the American racist Lothrop Stoddard states that nature determines human groups unequal. This biological argument is continued in *Black Monday* for white supremacy aggregations by Judge Tom P. Brady, who holds that the Negro's socio-politico-economic level is on a par with "the caterpillar and the cockroach." Christian racists add

[7] *Ibid.*, p. 76.
[8] *Ibid.*, p. 77.
[9] *Ibid.*

to the biological statements of Negro inferiority the claim that God has made the Negro defective in his humanity and therefore "caste systems" follow the order of nature and God. Paralleling these contentions, Kelsey discloses the affirmation of Christian faith in the equality of man as "the action and purpose of God." The biblical basis for human unity is a matter of faith, not of "empirical evidence," which is corroborated by contemporary science. Yet within this affirmation the Christian holds to individuality, unlikeness, and inequality which are in dire conflict with "racist particularism" that allows for inequality among human groups only, and not between individuals. Differences within the Christian community lead to the awareness of interdependence and the "Christian idea of communion," the answer to life together which racists would do well to heed.

The depth of racism is seen by Professor Kelsey in its logic of genocide, though it is countered by Christian humanism and the "insatiable need" of "sinful man" to be dominant over other men. Segregation is the most feasible response in a Christian civilization which allows racism to flourish along with the disposition to soften brutalities. Racists spend most of their energy in ensuring "permanent separation" of the races through espousal of superordination and subordination doctrines which effectively keep Negroes in their "place," without the handicap of physical separation interrupting the need to exercise dominance. Although the Church is "the one historic institution" which understands itself as living by the Spirit, the Church is subordinate to the "god of race" for many American Christians "when race relations are involved." [10] The authentic society of integrated persons and groups demanded by the Christian faith does not "exist anywhere on a large scale." This fact Kelsey contends does not "dismiss such a society as a human and Christian requirement." [11] An integrated society "is never fully realized," but it can be in "process of realization" where people are open to the transcendence of the Holy Spirit and unite in that center of meaning and value of which race is a part.

[10] *Ibid.*, p. 111.
[11] *Ibid.*, p. 115.

The final word of Kelsey to racists and racism is the possibility of being renewed even within a racist society. Thus, the individual racist can know release from "the special bondages and false perspectives imposed and inculcated by the racist faith." [12] A racist society may be inevitable but the racist may be converted to the new life of love and thereby gain a new lease on life through a new "self-affirmation," the acceptance of oneself as a divine gift through "self-surrender" and dedication of life to God. "The pride of racism is overcome by faith," hereby the racist loses his old "arrogance, independence, and self-sufficiency." He gains a thirst for righteousness through the experience of "the transforming power of grace." The racist cannot only become a renewed man in a racist society, he can become a "new man" with the knowledge that "security and fulfillment within himself" is impossible. The answer to racism is the answer to all human sin, the overcoming of self-centeredness through organizing life "from beyond the center of the self."

We have not concentrated on the scientific resources drawn upon so widely and skillfully by Professor Kelsey to logically demonstrate the errors of racism. His careful theological reflections have been passed over as well. Our intention has been to put in capsule what Kelsey means by racism as a faith in contrast with Christianity as a faith. Because this is a pioneering work in the field of Christianity and racism, we have sought to discover the relevance of traditional Christian faith in contemporary expression for Negro-white relations under the general rubric of racism.

The most general and obvious thing to be said about Mr. Kelsey is that he is a well-trained ethicist, a committed Christian, and a typical ecclesiastical rationalist who is like most white theologians in his unawareness that it is too late in the struggle to be engaged in highly theoretical gymnastics. Perhaps the work will win points with a few Christians of the author's extremely pious temperament, but the writer ignores the secular age in which he teaches. This is an age in which men do not take seriously theological jargon since it does not speak to their need

[12] *Ibid.*, p. 175.

for reason entwined with pragmatism. Basically, the work it seems to me is a sophisticated evangelical document aimed at converting the racists presupposed to be steeped in the fundamentals of Christianity. But even its evangelicalism will hardly make impact upon these Christian idolaters, framed as it is in scholarly terminology. Except for the Black Muslims for whom it has to be another piece of Christian ignorance, the book has nothing to say to the Negro who is both a victim of racism and a powerless racist. It is similar to Kyle Haselden's *The Racial Problem in Christian Perspective* in being addressed largely to whites, providing the Negro with no useful direction. In response to the complexity of Negro-white relations, Mr. Kelsey gives us the complexity of the Christian faith. He is a modern intellectual with the "moral stamina" to live with a great issue rather than attempt to resolve it by shallow approaches which dismiss the complexity of experience, but he has not plumbed this complexity.

The fundamental weakness in Kelsey's presentation is his addiction to rigid and unimaginative rationalism. This leads him to take racism and racists in America too seriously, since both racists and the doctrine of racism are not of great importance now. Kelsey misses the real issue of Negro-white tensions and color prejudice which are indeed on the increase. In their place he has chosen to focus on the questions of race and racism which have been effectively answered by science, social science, politics, and economics, if not directly by the Christian faith. "The Christian understanding of man" has been, perhaps, effective in the cause against racist and racism even though indirectly but what does it matter how the Christian understanding is expressed, especially after the war has been won with many battles—difference that makes no difference is no difference.

For example, Mr. Kelsey declares in his first chapter that doctrinaire racism in the United States is a modern justification for political-economic exploits and has evolved into an independent and "complete system of meaning, value, and loyalty." His intent in exposing and critically analyzing this dimension of America appears to be more than mere academic curiosity. He sees it as a real and sufficiently potent force to warrant his thorough criticism. But when one looks at the situation in America today and asks how many conscious, doctrinaire racists there are and how much influence white supremacy groups have even in the South, it is clearly insignificant, dwindling to little or no respectability with increasing rapidity. The combined forces of technology, television, social science, the courts, civil rights, and the voting power of the Negro have created an ethos in which doctrinaire racism is no longer tenable as a conscious force. Moreover, if there were a large remnant of "faithful" racists they would be, by Kelsey's own admission, unmoved by an appeal to what is termed liberal-rational interpretations of Christianity. Racists and Christian fundamentalists hold in common simple affirmations that are clear, dogmatic, and experiential. Racism appeals to a simple minority and insofar as it is tenacious the only effective way to deal with this fringe group is to ignore it or counter it with a force more powerful than exercises in logic, science, and rational Christianity.

A further indication that Mr. Kelsey is wasting his acute powers, as well as documenting how late in the game rational and institutional Christianity enters the sphere of Negro-white tensions, is his emphasis upon segregation as the central dynamic of racists in a Christian society. He brilliantly illuminates segregation as an ameliorative pattern and psychological crutch supporting man's need to dominate. But the clarification of a past issue hardly serves as a deterrent.

Not only is racism a conscious faith for a few and segregation an impotent political basis, but the interpretation of racism as a faith is a red herring. Now, Professor Kelsey has made an unmistakable advance over non-theological rationalists oriented in the social sciences in that he sees racism as a matter of belief and idolatrous worship. He contends that racism is not a religion but a faith *competing* with Christianity. To make his case, Kelsey points out that James Sellars' *The South and Christian Ethics* terms segregation a religion but Kelsey is "asserting that segregation is a facet of the larger faith of racism." [13] By faith Kelsey

[13] *Ibid.*, p. 34.

means a conscious, rational, doctrinal system of belief, including apologetics. It cannot be denied that systematic racism has and continues to exist. But the racist devotees of such a faith have been in the past and are increasingly so in the present an emotive minority. Even more significant is the fact that faith as a rational or quasi-rational systematics must by necessity be a conscious, or at the very least an unconscious, system. Kelsey might concede that conscious exponents of racism are few, but his point would be that this fertile minority provides the life line for a vast number of unconscious racists in America. It is these unconscious racists who would never make public their beliefs even under duress, instead they unwittingly express them in private or overtly under duress. It is these otherwise intelligent Americans whose unconscious racism becomes conscious conflict with Negroes that Kelsey seeks to disengage from racism. If the issue between Negroes and whites were on the conscious level it could be dealt with effectively as has been done in our society. Even if the issue were on the unconscious level, given the fact of crediting most Americans with being rational and responding to reason, the thrust of Kelsey's book is to reach the unconscious and bring it to the light of day where it can be rejected because it is illogical, unscientific, and anti-Christian. Unfortunately, the issue is far more complex than Kelsey perceives. Negro-white hatred is not so rational as a conscious faith. It is not so unavailable as unconscious mental powers. Kelsey is right in pointing out that racism and racists are a modern phenomenon, since the eighteenth and nineteenth centuries. The point he misses is that color prejudice emerged among European traders and conquerors in the fifteenth century. Thus, the issue is not as he supposes, either racism as a faith or racists as devotees. Kelsey is helpful in adding the religious dimension to rational explanations of racism, but he misses the depth of its complexity by terming it a faith which is a very modern problem, a product of the age of science.

We will clarify the weakness of rational-scientists and rational-Christianity as mistaking racism for color prejudice. The heart of the matter is that antipathy toward Negroes is an irrational, demonic, and preconscious religion. That which is unconscious can be brought to the level of consciousness by external expertise. This is the case even with racism and racists who are products of an age of science. But can reason alone effect, to say nothing of eliminate, that which is not only preconscious but a religion as well?

Because Kelsey is a rationalist he ignores the mysterious workings of the irrational, and subordinates religion to faith when the larger phenomenon of religion is expressed through faith only in part, and that on the conscious-unconscious level. What Kelsey has to say about racism, racists, and faith is acceptable, given his premises. His error is in the false premise that the conflict between Negroes and whites is a matter of reason and faith, rather than religion and preconsciousness. The answers he provides from his Christian understanding to racism may be indisputable for racists who are Christians, but what do they have to say to many non-Christian racists? Presumably, his use of social science and theology is to provide a perspective superior to either one alone and therefore an appeal to other than Christians. Fundamentally a rationalist, Kelsey believes that in explaining a belief logically and showing forth its ultimate evil those who hold to racism consciously (and unconsciously) will see it for what it is and turn to a better faith which Kelsey urges upon them.

Thus, he states that a racist who is a Christian finds himself in an ambiguous relation of giving loyalty to God and the god of race. Those who "have racism in their hearts" may not previously have faced up to what is required of a true racist—"the exclusion of out-races from existence," not merely from "jobs, neighborhoods, clubs, schools, or churches." This approach might be effective if these responses throughout the United States were really based upon racist faith. But they are presently and persistently inherent in the culture as religion which is not a matter of reason but historical responses that were a part of the cultural memory several centuries prior to the advent of racist racism. Negroes have been so economically valuable since their discovery by white Europeans that the thought of their elimination has never formed in the preconsciousness of whites, though it has occasionally been both a conscious and unconscious element in the minds of a few, both Negro and white, for brief periods of time.

In his definition of white racists and the Black Muslim racists Kelsey borders on setting up straw men. It is obvious when one accepts his typologies that failures of racism are parallel in both groups. But the value of the Black Muslim racism for Negroes is of far more significance for Negroes than white racism is for whites. In fact, white racism is a bulwark against the advancement of white Americans as the leaders of the world who have so much to give other nations and so many gains to be made in space. But the Black Muslim thesis has the potential of bringing the Negro into awareness of himself with pride whereby he can make a contribution as a people and ascertain the rights and goods which are his due. Hitherto, Negroes have been a colonial people and "the colonized man is an envious man," who dreams of one day repaying violence for violence and setting himself up in the place of his master:

> The violence with which the supremacy of white values is affirmed and the aggressiveness which has permeated the victory of these values over the ways of life and thought of the native mean that, in revenge, the native laughs in mockery when western values are mentioned in front of him. In the colonial context the settler only ends his work of breaking in the native when the latter admits loudly and intelligibly the supremacy of the white man's values. In the period of decolonization, the colonized masses mock at these very values, insult them, and vomit them up.[14]

When it comes to the Black Muslims, Kelsey has not seriously considered what the French psychoanalyst Frantz Fanon calls "the problem of truth," that in every age and among all people is "the property of the national cause."[15] The cause is not economic substructure and superstructure, "the cause is the consequence; you are rich because you are white, you are white

---

[14] Frantz Fanon, *The Wretched of the Earth* (New York: Grove Press, Inc., 1963), p. 35.

[15] *Ibid.*, p. 40.

because you are rich." [16] The point which the Black Muslims
wish to drive home, so evident today in the sphere of housing,
is not given its full due by Kelsey for these good reasons:

> The intellectual who for his part has followed the colonialist
> with regard to the universal abstract will fight in order that the
> settler and native may live together in peace in a new world.
> But the thing he does not see, precisely because he is permeated
> by colonialism and all its ways of thinking is that the [white]
> settler, from the moment that the colonial context disappears,
> has no longer any interest in remaining or in co-existing.[17]

By attacking deep problems between Negroes and whites on
the level of rational or antirational racism, Kelsey does not speak
to the seething hatred of Negroes by whites which leads to
Negroes hating whites. There is deeply implanted in the mind of
Kelsey the "narcissistic dialogue" of white bourgeois intellectuals
which states that "the essential qualities remain eternal in spite
of all the blunders men may make: the essential qualities of
the West, of course." [18]

These essential qualities receive their clearest expression in
Kelsey's interpretation of Christian religion and the Church.
Rather than interpreting the Christian faith and the Church
imaginatively so as to provide a hope for Negroes and a way to
bring whites under the judgment of this hope, Kelsey implants
white presuppositions that are foreign to the Bible. Thus his
work, from the perspective of sensitive Negroes and most of all
Black Muslims, means that the Church "is the white people's
Church, the foreigner's Church. She does not call the native to
God's way but to the ways of the white man, of the master, of
the oppressor. And as we know, in this matter many are called
but few chosen." [19]

Moreover, what value can secular, pragmatic, technological
man, Christian or no, place upon this orthodoxy: "Man must
know God before he can know himself"? What possible meaning

[16] *Ibid.*
[17] *Ibid.*, p. 36.
[18] *Ibid.*, p. 37.
[19] *Ibid.*, p. 34.

has this statement: "Man can understand himself only when he becomes true man, only when he is renewed in Christ"? It would be one thing if Kelsey interpreted these statements in such a way as to meet the condition of contemporary man, especially men caught up in Negro-white hatred—but he sets them forth baldly within a context where he is seeking to be effectively convincing. Given the title of Kelsey's book and his stated purpose in writing, one either has to conclude that Christianity is irrelevant to color prejudice or Mr. Kelsey's interpretation of Christianity fails to disclose its power:

> The center and meaning of man's life lie beyond himself. The meaning and worth of man's life do not reside in him but "in the One who stands 'over against' him, in Christ, the Primal Image, in the Word of God." Man is created in, for, and by love. His very life is an answer. It is responsible existence. He is so created that he must actively receive God's Word to be human.[20]

The truth is, Kelsey is most relevant when he is least theological: "The essence of human community is the union of persons in love. There is no genuine community except the community of love." These words can have relevance for Christian and non-Christian prejudiced people, unlike the claim that "true meaning and reality belong to Christ alone."

It is simply meaningless to claim radical individualism and radical universalism for Christianity and also claim that racists can be converted in a racist society. The uniqueness and inequality of each individual does not mean there can be wholeness or salvation for an individual regardless of the society. We are all engaged in this human enterprise together without our choosing to be born. And though we have the choice of determining our responses within the limits of our human nature and cultural particularity, we cannot achieve wholeness as individuals unless and until all men are so blessed. If men are created equal and die equal there is no sense of responsibility for my neighbor as myself, the meaning of love, where living unequally "between

[20] Kelsey, p. 76.

the times" is held out as a qualitative "leap in being" for some. To be sure, Kelsey wishes to say that faith in Jesus Christ is the way to overcome "the pride of racism." If it were only the case that fallen, sinful man lived by faith. No, Kelsey is too rational, too faith-oriented to speak a word of judgment and hope to Negroes or whites caught up in this society of color antagonism.

He is aware of the liberals in our society who engage in helping the Negro. But these liberals help the Negro as an abstract, universal man and "annihilate him as a" Negro. The liberal white, like the racist white, "fails to encounter" the Negro as a person and the liberal "fears all forms of collective consciousness, including the awakening" of the "Negro consciousness." To prevent the "Negro consciousness" from awakening, the liberal insists that "individuals really exist in an isolated state," there is no "Negro consciousness." Through this intellectual approach the rationalist-scientific-liberal destroys Negroness. To exist as a man, an American, the Negro can never exist as a "Negro." Kelsey does not himself find meaning in "Negroness," but rather in the universal Christian man: "For the new life, Christ is the captain. He is 'the way, and the truth, and the life'; and His kingdom is the transcendent goal of enduring hope."

This is Christian rationalism at its height. It is born of optimism which only the elite can share without seeking human avenues of power with which to be matched with present realities. In his final words, Kelsey is as much an escapist as he insists Black Muslims are of necessity. We must at least attempt to discover a more relevant, meaningful, and purposeful human response to color prejudice than rational scientists and rational Christianity provide the Negro.

CHAPTER III
RATIONAL MORALISTS AND THE
SCIENTIFICALLY ENGINEERED SOCIETY

WE HAVE EXAMINED the Negro-white conflict in America as seen by Christian and non-Christian rationalists, who explain this conflict by rooting it in racist dogmas and psychological-psychoanalytical terms which suggest solutions that are diffuse and therefore untenable. This failure to meet the issue is not due simply to the scholar's approach, so invaluable for providing alternative ways of perceiving Negro-white problems. Their answers do respond to the questions asked, but they have not asked the right questions.

Another approach to our fundamental social problem is taken by rational moralists who are not so concerned with the historical problem but want to understand the present situation with a view to bringing about changes. For the most part, these action- and program-oriented moralists are more realistic than rational scientists and rational Christians. Yet for the most part they too misunderstand the problem in its depth. In their optimism for the prospects of blacks in the future, rational moralists tend to ignore the necessity of black prospects through Negro self-awareness, as well as indigenous programs promulgated through indigenous institutions. While it is clear that the greatest weaknesses of our society are thrust upon the Negro, it is a question as to whether black prospects are dependent upon blacks' creating a new economic and value system through their frustrations, which would bring about a hoped-for change in a society "based on acquisitiveness, peace-through-terror, and the shallowness of inner imagination which is revealed by the trends of television programs which have the highest rating" to the Negro's quest for entrance into the society.[1] This may well be a bonus of the Negro drive, or possibly the future task of Negroes and whites together when both have been "deghettoized." But for the present the objectives of the Negro should be more narrowly focused upon a society in which there are prospects for black social acceptance. If this objective becomes dominant in the moral fiber of America other changes will be meaningful, if not there will just be changes.

We will now examine some of the most discerning programs pragmatic moral rationalists have promoted—with a special view to determining the meaning and significance of the role assigned to a heightening "Negro consciousness," his religious strength, and political power for initiating desired changes beyond reacting to changes.

The watershed of studies of the Negro and America is Gunnar Myrdal's *An American Dilemma,* written during World War II. This sociological and psychological study continues to influence the present and its concluding observations and estimations merit extensive consideration.

Myrdal's main observations that the low status of Negroes is due to "what is in white people's minds" and their view of what reality is, or ought to be, vis-à-vis the Negro, changes with the changes in Negro and white "people's beliefs and valuations."[2] From this social-psychological point of view changes were directly tied to World War II events, from which was expected "a redefinition of the Negro's status in America." This anticipated outcome was dependent upon actions "to be taken by whites and Negroes." Myrdal did not predict the "nature of this structural change in American society," though he did estimate "the most probable developments" which we are concerned to reconsider.

Myrdal rightly understood the decreasing impact and presence of the South's "Jim Crow apparatus" and with its demise

[1] Nat Hentoff, *The New Equality* (New York: Viking Press, 1964), p. 238.

[2] Gunnar Myrdal, *An American Dilemma* (New York: Harper and Row, rev. ed., 1962), p. 998.

the increase in "separation of the two groups in the South." But because he is a white liberal or rational moralist embued with "the faith that institutions can be improved and strengthened and that people are good enough to live a happier life," [3] he did not perceive the implications of the "growing mental isolation between whites and Negroes" in the South for America as a whole:

> Behind this potentially most dangerous development was not only the exclusionist policy of the whites, but also the sullen dissatisfaction and bitter race pride of the Negroes themselves. They were "withdrawing" themselves as a reaction to the segregation and discrimination enforced by whites.[4]

Myrdal was prevented from highlighting the "exclusionist policy of the whites" as the achievement of the North which the South is just beginning to imitate because Myrdal considered the social, judicial, political, economic, and educational problems as the major problems to be challenged. Moreover, though he knew the white Northerner is "most inclined to give the Negro equality in public relations and least inclined to do so in private relations," Myrdal was fundamentally persuaded that the "American Creed" and Constitution took priority in the rational North which could not "leave out the South or humor too much its irrationality." [5] This high compliment to the North was partly based on the questionable view that there

> the Creed was strong enough long before the War [World War II] to secure for the Negro practically unabridged civil equality in all his relations with public authority, whether it was in voting, before the courts, in the school system, or as a relief recipient.[6]

Even beyond these public areas, in "those non-public spheres" such as employment, the white Northerner was correctly estimated as "becoming prepared, as a citizen" to give the Negro "his just opportunity." Myrdal did not hide the distance the

[3] *Ibid.*, p. 1024.
[4] *Ibid.*, p. 999.
[5] *Ibid.*, p. 1015.
[6] *Ibid.*, p. 1010.

Northern white "preserves between his political and private opinion," pointing out that the Negro is "discriminated against ruthlessly in private relations, as when looking for a job or seeking a home to live in," for,

> as a private individual, he is less prepared to feel that he himself is the man to give the Negro a better chance: in his own occupation, trade union, office or workshop, in his own residential neighborhood or in his church. The social paradox in the North is exactly this, that almost everybody is against discrimination in general but, at the same time, almost everybody practices discrimination in his own personal affairs.[7]

Beyond these "personal discriminations which creates the color bar in the North," Myrdal saw more influential forces at work upon which his "faith" in "rationalism and moralism" fed and was fed. "The North moves toward equality" was a conclusion which Myrdal formed in no small measure as a result of his close association throughout the study with white liberals of the North who shared and reinforced his perspective. In addition to the liberal white minority and the Northern acceptance of the American Creed was the Northerners' inclination "to give the Negro equality in public relations." Thus Northern "public acceptance" of the Negro was the turning point in favor of the North over the South—that plus the Northern power. Since the North had the right spirit and the necessary machinery to practice "public equality," it needed only motivation and leadership. The motivation was supplied by the "war emergency." As a result of the war efforts, the Negro was given a new image through

> sympathetic publicity by newspapers, periodicals, and the radio, and by administrators and public personalities of all kinds,

and a new opportunity through "concentration of responsibility" in planned, regulated, nationally legislated and administered labor union policies affecting the "crucial economic spheres." The leadership, motivated by the war emergency, was supplied by government policies in planning and directing agencies to provide economic opportunities for Negroes and in making this a national

[7] *Ibid.*

issue bringing private enterprise into line as well. These are the reasons leading Myrdal to "foresee that the trend of unionization, social legislation, and national planning will tend to break down economic discrimination, the only type of discrimination which is both important and strong in the North." [8]

Subsequently, the personal discriminations of "the ordinary white Northerner" in the economic realm would be without basis and therefore effectively eliminated. The ordinary white opportunism, ignorance, and unconcernedness could be combatted both by "education" and the gradual discernment through publicity and policies what they are "doing to the Negro" and its consequences for "the democratic Creed." Because "private relations are increasingly becoming public relations, the white Northerner will be willing to give the Negro equality." [9]

Since the South "is itself a minority and a national problem" in economic as well as racial problems, its weakness and lack of unity against "a redefinition of the Negro's status" may in the short run bring increased tension and violence, but in the long haul even conservative white Southerners, Myrdal felt, "can be won over to equalitarian reforms in line with the American Creed":

We have become convinced in the course of this inquiry that the North is getting prepared for a fundamental redefinition of the Negro's status in America. The North will accept it if the change is pushed by courageous leadership. And the North has much more power than the South.[10]

With the possible exception of "labor relations," Myrdal's estimation of trends has been largely verified, particularly in the economic sphere.

Where Myrdal is confusing and misleading, if not misled, is not only in cloaking a rational moralist position in deceptive sociology-psychology, but also in the areas of "Negro equality" and "social equality." His central theme—that the North is the

[8] *Ibid.*, p. 1011.
[9] *Ibid.*
[10] *Ibid.*, p. 1010.

center of power and its only important form of discrimination is economic, which he estimated would be broken—led logically if not boldly or directly to the conclusion, so carefully, cautiously phrased: "Other types of discrimination will tend to decrease according to the law of cumulative causation." By "other types of discrimination" he presumably meant "social equality" in housing and marriage, not "Negro equality," which apparently related to the "public relations" and the "non-public relations" of employment:

> Unlike the white Northerner, who is most inclined to give the Negro equality in public relations and least inclined to do so in private relations, the white Southerner does not differentiate between public and private relations—the former as well as the latter have significance for prestige and social equality. More-over, he is traditionally and consistently opposed to Negro equal-ity for its own sake, which the Northerner is not.[11]

The first sentence of the above quotation is plausible, especially in view of the key final phrase. However, it is difficult to deter-mine if by "Negro equality" he refers to an early context in which "Southern liberals" were applauded in their determination that the "separate, but equal" doctrine be "followed out in its 'equality' aspect as well as in its 'separateness' aspect," or if it is to be equated with "social equality" in the same sentence, or if it is the same as "Negro equality" in the second sentence.[12] If, in the first sentence, "Negro equality" is to be understood as "public relations," so that white Southerner is distinguished from the white Northerner in unwillingness to grant "the Negro equal treatment by public authority," the point is well taken. But if, in the first sentence, "Negro equality" is to be understood as both "public relations" and "private" relations or "social equal-ity," and equated with "Negro equality" in the second sentence, then the distinction between the Northerner and Southerner can-not be made. Most distressing is Myrdal's stress upon the caste system while virtually ignoring deprivation, which leads not only

[11] *Ibid.*, p. 1011.
[12] *Ibid.*, p. 999.

to overstressing dominances of whites but even more a "Negro equality" viewed in contrast with white equality. In either case, the facts are that Northerners and Southerners are "traditionally and consistently opposed" to "social equality" with the Negro and therefore to "social equality." There is no white or Negro equality or "social equality."

If this point is not clear in Myrdal it is because he over-emphasized the value of the "public relations" and deemphasized the "private relations." As a consequence, greater emphasis was placed on the "deeper split" in the "moral personality" of the white Southerner than in that of the white Northerner. This position is understandable in the objective or "public relations" difference between the North and South twenty years ago. But Myrdal's estimation that the North would progress from "public relations" to "private relations" and "social equality" for the Negro miscalculated the North. Stephen Rose points up the present situation:

> Some observers maintain that, until now, the civil rights movement has been confined to the South. The aims of this movement have been largely in the area of eliminating the more brazen and obvious instances of segregation. To put it bluntly, the Negro in the South is only now beginning to experience the frustrations that the Northern Negro has known for years.

> Actually most of the protests could be classified as expressions of momentary anger, desperation, or frustration rather than cohesive, strategic steps in a positive movement. Indeed, most protests have been ineffective: they have not gained their stated goals.[13]

It is not expected that Myrdal would perfectly analyze the trends in every area, though he was superb. What went awry in the "public relations" estimation of the North was the over-optimism about Northerners' roots in the American Creed, reinforced by public policies, without taking cognizance of Northern whites' lack of experience with a large majority of Negroes in some

[13] Stephen Rose, "The Chicago Protests," *Christianity and Crisis,* July 26, 1965, Vol. XXV, No. 13, p. 163.

communities and the majority of Negroes in the North. Myrdal
was aware of this development and, for the reasons indicated,
underestimated both it and the Northerner:

> In the North the sudden influx of Southern Negroes during the
> Great Migration caused a temporary rise in social discrimina-
> tion. Since, in spite of this, there was much less of it in the
> North than in the South, the migration meant a decrease of social
> segregation and discrimination for the Negro people as a whole.
> It also seemed that, despite the sharp temporary rise on account
> of the migration, the trend in the North, too, was toward de-
> creasing race prejudice.[14]

Perhaps the fact that white Southerners "expressed a belief that
the Negro migration to the North would give the North more of
a share in the trouble of having Negroes as neighbors and that
then the North would understand the racial philosophy of the
South better" was not taken seriously, particularly since a
"deeper split" in the "moral personality" of the Southerner than
the Northerner was espoused. The present reversal may also be
temporary, but there is less reason to hold to the moral dichotomy.

What in effect has occurred in twenty years is that the South
has begun to "understand the racial philosophy" of the North
better. Myrdal was unerring in this estimation: "The North has
much more power than the South." This is not only the case
economically and politically, but in the deftness of dealing with
Negroes as well. It is the Northern pattern of ghettos which the
South is now setting up, an altogether recent Southern development but one which the North has always practiced with success.

If the reversal in the "public relations" of the North is
"temporary" and the ghettoizing of the Negro in the North is
preferable to the conditions of the South, it is unmistakably clear
that no "social equality" progress has been made and its like-
lihood is in doubt, to say the least. It is now clear that "social
equality" will not be conferred upon the Negro—only his initiative will bring it into being.

Myrdal miscalculated the difference between the North and

---

[14] Myrdal, *An American Dilemma*, p. 999.

the South. Not that he was unaware of the marginal difference in response to the Negro, but he chose to believe the Northern superiority in World War II would match a resolve to go beyond the economic discrimination when presented with the same opportunity to be engaged in "social equality" with the Negro, partly because his knowledge of Americans' low level of "respect for law and order and the administration of laws" was over-weighted by the view that they "could not afford to compromise the American Creed." Myrdal took the position that the caste system was dead because it is intellectually unrespectable; its beliefs are no longer nourished by academic authority. Since the inferiority of the Negro and prejudice are "irrational," and therefore indefensible, there is only "a considerable time lag between what is thought in the higher and in the lower social classes":

> People want to be rational, and they want to feel that they are good and righteous. They want to have the society they live in, and their behavior in this society, explained and justified to their conscience. And now their theory is being torn to pieces; its expression is becoming recognized as a mark of ignorance.

What Myrdal did not see is that the ghetto segregation of the North is not based on a social theory of philosophy as in the South. It is based upon practice rather than principle. Consequently, the denial of "social equality" is every bit as firm in the North as in the South—and far less guilt ridden. The North accepts the inevitable Negro as a human being and proceeds to keep him separate by social arrangements which are as effective and far less objectionable than legal means. This is the pattern the South is now beginning to follow. Both regions have had the same objective as regards "social equality," but as in every other area of life the North has been much wiser. Here there is no question of a "deeper split" in the "moral personality" of the Northerner and Southerner. What the North has taught the South is that "the white man can humiliate the Negro" by thwarting his ambition and keeping him ghettoized without starving, beating, killing, or "making the Negro's subjugation legal and approved by society." A change may have occurred in the beliefs

of Southerners, but Northerners and Southerners have been un-
changing in their values.

Ample evidence is available to refute Myrdal's estimation of
"Negro equality" and "social equality." Myrdal's *valuation* that
"the North is getting prepared for a fundamental redefinition of
the Negro's status" (which was rooted in his *belief* that economic
discrimination is "the only type of discrimination which is both
important and strong in the North") is now refuted by the
emerging confrontation in the North where progress in the last
twenty years has been rearward in comparison with the South.
On balance, the rational white Northerner is a figment of
Myrdal's romantic "rationalism and moralism" or the creation of
his "greater trust in the improvability of man"— afar more significant, even positive, dimension of man in general and the Northerner in particular than Myrdal discerns. In his closing "personal
note," Myrdal stated that he, with the "impetuous but temporary
intimacy of the stranger" retained throughout the study this
perspective of Southerners and Northerners:

> Behind all outward dissimilarities, behind their contradictory
> valuations, rationalizations, vested interests, group allegiances
> and animosities, behind the fears and defense constructions, be-
> hind the role they play in life and the mask they wear, people
> are all much alike on a fundamental level. And they are all good
> people. They want to be rational and just. They all plead to
> their conscience that they meant well when things went wrong.[15]

Myrdal is an intellectual, scholar, activist, in search of the
"practical formulas" for the "never-ending reconstruction of
society." With his tenets and conclusions highlighted, it is of
value to see the "practical formulas" espoused.

Whites have all the power, Negroes are only 10 per cent of
the population—this is the presuppositional dichotomy under-
girding Myrdal's formulas for overcoming the "American dilemma."

Myrdal's instrument for redefining the Negro status is social
engineering:

[15] *Ibid.*, p. 1023.

Many things that for a long period have been predominantly a matter of individual adjustment will become more and more determined by political decision and public regulation. We are entering an era where fact-finding and scientific theories of casual relations will be seen as instrumental in planning controlled social change.

The social sciences in America are equipped to meet the demands of the post-war world. In social engineering they will retain the old American faith in human beings which is all the time becoming fortified by research as the trend continues toward environmentalism in the search for social causation. In a sense, the social engineering of the coming epoch will be nothing but the drawing of practical conclusions from the teaching of social science that "human nature" is changeable and that human deficiencies and unhappiness are, in large degree, preventable.[16]

In a word, the changes in the "American dilemma" will be the result of activist whites structurally re-forming the society through social engineering instruments of social science.

Contrasted with this dynamically activist white dominance is the Negro, whom Myrdal relegates to a comparatively passive role in the "gradual realization of the American Creed." Drawing upon the good will, good sense, and the opportunity of whites to undo virtually alone what they alone did in placing the Negro in deprived and disadvantaged circumstances, Myrdal gives an ironic twist to paternalism and turns it upside down without changing or giving direction to the role of the Negro. At the conclusion the Negro is still dependent upon whites and is to have faith; for awareness of violations of the Creed and stricken consciences, with rational social engineering on the part of white Northerners and Southerners—good people all—will bring justice.

It is not that Myrdal sees the Negro as apathetic; he does not. He only sees him as a powerless political victim whose responsibility is limited to reaction:

"Negro defense organizations," "Negro advisors in the federal administration," improved education permeated by democratic-egalitarian values spurring the rising Negro protest, Negro self-

[16] *Ibid.*

consciousness for "defense and offense" replacing accommodation-patience-submissiveness, increasing strength of Negro press and national organizations and leaders, the Negro's acceptance of America and moral power of requesting only to be accepted, bitterness of Negro means both preparation to fight if attacked and unwillingness to cheerfully accept second class citizenship, negative power of Negro to withdraw from participation in national events such as war, the litigation preparedness of the N.A.A.C.P.

These largely negative effects of the Negro are the extent of his contribution, as Myrdal concluded:

> The Negroes are a minority, and they are poor and suppressed, but they have the advantage that they can fight wholeheartedly. The whites have all the power, but they are split in their moral personality. Their better selves are with the insurgents. The Negroes do not need any other allies.[17]

This concluding statement is not only a perfect illustration of white liberal *beliefs* and *valuations* in its assumption that the Negro's deprivation leads to unified impact upon split white consciences, but an apt commentary upon Negro protest movements of the present which have hitherto concentrated upon confronting the "better selves" of white power without equal emphasis upon developing Negro power.

At best, Myrdal hints at the potential power of the Negro, particularly in a passing reference to A. Philip Randolph's threatened Negro march on Washington. He does not connect this threat and its effective change in governmental policies with the power potential of the Negro, for "the whites have all the power." If power is the convergence of the control of force with advantages, Negroes have real power too. Myrdal's myopia at this point is that of the white and Negro liberals associated with him whose deference for social engineering ignored the real power in the white and Negro communities with which their intellectual gifts were neither attuned or supportive. Of course Myrdal stated that he could not foresee "the exact nature of this structural

[17] *Ibid.*, p. 1004.

change in American society." He took the position that "the outcome will depend upon the decisions and actions yet to be taken
by whites and Negroes." But as we have seen, on the basis of
the trends and changes taking place in World War II he discerned
the gamut of possibilities for whites, estimating "the most probable developments." He did not do the same for the Negro. This
liberal trend of opting for engineering over power was natural
for social scientists and it has markedly affected Negro-white
structural relations for the past twenty years. But these changes
have not aided the Negro masses so much as the Negro middle
class; they have not dealt with the fundamental issues of "social
equality." In the 1940's, social scientists labored under the delusion that power—particularly political power—was a force amenable to the rational influences of hardnosed economics alone, in
contradiction to which the irrational influences within politics
and religion were considered obsolete.

An elitist, Myrdal labeled lower classes "static and recep-
tive," security-oriented, and culturally fragmented to the point of
no leadership; consequently, they lack cooperation and sacrifice
for a common objective. Since the lower classes are "inarticulate
and powerless" in America, and "do not speak for themselves" but
only listen, the Negro, being the low man on the lowest end of the
class totem pole, was naturally relegated to the oblivion of inertia.
The Negro represented irresponsibility for Myrdal when compared with the privileged few, or what he termed the white "Pull-
man class," which has "a long line of American ancestry" and a
"disproportionate amount of the nation's brains and courage. Its
members have been willing and prepared to take the leadership
made so easy for them by the inertia of the masses." [18] Thus, the
problem of the Negro is largely a question of economics and the
answer lies in the individual leadership of the select white "Pull-
man class" to improve the economic condition of the Negro, on
the mistaken assumption that were all Negroes to earn no less
than $10,000 a year, tomorrow they would be out of the ghetto.
Seemingly, black prospects are most bleak.

This message of economics Myrdal continued to set forth as

[18] *Ibid.*, p. 715.

late as 1962, in the heart of his *Challenge to Affluence*. Even the Negro protests which indicate the need for political action beyond economic upgrading and shows the imperative role of the Negro churches and masses leaves Myrdal unchallenged:

> Even if this movement has been directed upon what can be broadly described as civil rights, it undoubtedly has its undertone and part of its momentum in the great poverty and high unemployment rate among Negroes.[19]

Myrdal's classic study of the Negro, which bypassed the function of power and the role of Negro churches and masses in deghettoizing beyond depovertizing this minority for an enlightened "white man's burden" emphasis, is drawn upon in *Minorities and the American Promise* by Stewart and Mildred Cole. Their main concern is the "conflict of principle and practice" in America and centers on the acceptance of and means to a dynamic balance between minority ethnic group diversity and cultural unity. The function of the Negro in achievement of democratic intergroup and interpersonal "social maturity within the cultural framework of American democracy" is nowhere to be found in this remarkable work, which deals thoroughly with every dimension of prejudice, discrimination, and segregation. Singularly addressed to whites by white liberals, this work is a detailed sociological-psychological strategic outline of how to be responsible:

> Two broad approaches to the situation are available: Americans can change their behavior as individual persons; and they can initiate changes in the structure of society, which in turn will modify the activities, attitudes, values, and personality patterns of its members. Neither approach without the other is adequate; both, working together, can greatly improve human relations.[20]

The detailed outline set forth throughout the book includes a treatment of every area but political power.

[19] Gunnar Myrdal, *Challenge to Affluence* (New York: Pantheon Books, 1962), p. 162.

[20] Stewart C. Cole and Mildred Wiese Cole, *Minorities and the American Promise: The Conflict of Principle and Practice* (New York: Harper & Brothers, 1954), p. 72.

As a study in character building, informed by intellectual activists, it gives no real direction to the Negro, but refers to him only in threatening or informative passages which briefly intend to prod middle class whites to action:

> Minorities resent unneighborly treatment, and are demanding fair play, including the rights of first class citizenship. They are raising their community sights to sense the fuller opportunities, liberties, and equalities that a democracy guarantees to its people; hence an increase in the number and intensity of intergroup conflicts.

> The Negroes have become markedly aggressive in an endeavor to slough off the servile folkways and customs that handicap them in a white-dominated society.[21]

> The initiative of minorities in building better human relations is noteworthy. Negroes are becoming socially articulate through the programs of the National Association for the Advancement of Colored People and the National Urban League.[22]

> Minority peoples also face obligation in their social roles. Specific responsibilities rest on every group. If Negroes, for example, want more jobs and freer job-upgrading opportunities, they must learn the American way of becoming acceptable.[23]

> Negroes . . . are assuming increasing responsibility for enriching their own economic and social lot, and are thereby participating more freely in an American way of life that is unifying and strong.[24]

This is the extent of understanding and supporting black prospects, so insignificant when compared with the extensive treatment of white prospects for democratic equality.

The National Urban League is an agency of social workers devoted to advancing the economic well-being of Negroes. It is thriving with a six million dollar budget and 700 workers, which is said to be more than all other Negro groups combined can

---

[21] *Ibid.*, p. 75.
[22] *Ibid.*, p. 89.
[23] *Ibid.*, p. 169.
[24] *Ibid.*, p. 249.

boast. The key to its success is more than its middle class orientation and economic orientation in the pattern of Myrdal (which,
incidentally, is the reason it has earned the reputation of being
the most conservative programmatic Negro organization), a
reputation which has no mean effect upon its ability to gain
high level and national support from leading industrialists
with financial backing. The key to its success is its dynamic
leader, Whitney M. Young, who has literally transformed this
organization into what is undoubtedly the most professional
of Negro institutions. Mr. Young's most singular writing is
To Be Equal, "a domestic Marshall Plan" for equal opportunity. An assessment of the role of the Negro as a power group
in this book discloses black prospects in an unusual way.

Mr. Young is a perceptive, competent, and resourceful administrator, who knows precisely what he intends the Urban
League to be and how to gain this objective. He is the social
worker in the civil rights field, and this school of thoughtful
analysis informs his basic presupposition that the Negro provides
an opportunity and not a problem for America. Although he accepts Myrdal's basic position that economic upgrading is the
fundamental starting and ending point "to be equal," and the
Coles' interpersonal dynamics as the approach, Young is equally
descriptive and prescriptive. He fastens upon law, employment,
education, housing, and health as the areas of basic concern which
he analyzes carefully and then systematically provides a strategy.
In each of these areas he is guided by the principle and experience
that the gap between white and black America is increasing so
fast that nothing short of a special effort for *the next decade* will
place the Negro on a competitive, equal basis:

> This is a situation which clearly calls for emergency action
> on a broad scale in urban communities across the land. Fact-
> finding committees, pilot projects, tokenism and halfhearted,
> one-dimensional, small scale efforts will not suffice. This nation
> and the world need a demonstration that we can bridge the
> social, economic, and educational gap that separates American
> Negroes from their fellow citizens.[25]

[25] Whitney M. Young, *To Be Equal* (New York: McGraw-Hill, 1964), p. 25.

I ought to make it clear that I do not believe in extraordinary measures to help more Negroes progress and become self-supporting simply because they are Negro. I believe we must receive assistance until we can make use of equal opportunities now opening to us because we are Americans, and no Americans ought to be deprived or disenfranchised economically, politically, or socially.[26]

Thus our call for an immediate, dramatic, and tangible domestic Marshall Plan is aimed at closing the intolerable economic, social, and educational gap that separates the vast majority of us Negro citizens from other Americans. Unless this is done, the results of the current heroic efforts in the civil rights movement will be only an illusion, and the struggle will continue, with perhaps tragic consequences.[27]

The effectiveness of the plan set forth cannot be described here, but a large measure of it is reflected in the Equal Opportunity Act. The civil rights movement functions as a motivating force or springboard for action on the part of whites both in and out of power structures:

Integration is an opportunity for white citizens to show to the whole world their maturity and their security. It is time for them consciously to proclaim the creative possibilities in that diversity from which they have unconsciously benefited.[28]

Thus, the book follows the pattern of the Coles and Myrdal in instructing whites rather than Negroes and goes beyond them in providing detailed blueprints for community action with a national, state, and local strategy. That the role of the Negro as a necessary power "to be equal" is given nowhere near "equal" consideration reflects itself in an admonishment to churches:

The church's responsibility does not and cannot end with acceptance of Negroes as communicants. Negro children must be tutored and provided with educational material and extra help so that they will be prepared for the opportunity to be equal.

[26] *Ibid.*, p. 27.
[27] *Ibid.*, pp. 27–28.
[28] *Ibid.*, p. 251.

Ministers must stand up and say no to injustice in their communities and in their own institutions. And they can start with
the church-run hospitals, with the dollars they spend for building and expansion, with the actions of the church as employer,
purchaser, contractor, investor, landlord, and administrator of
funds.[29]

Mr. Young often refers to the need for social equality but
does not deal in detail with its fundamentally sexual dimension,
leaving the reader to surmise that social equality for him is a
derivative of legal, educational, housing, employment, health and
welfare developments which are all wrapped up as an economic
package. A domestic Marshall Plan based on economics obviously
is insufficient and to the same extent the meaning of "to be equal"
is nullified. Mr. Young promises to deal with this substantive
issue in the future; for tactical reasons it does not fit into his
careful planning now. This is understandable, but it is in direct
conflict with the emphasis of his total program to "bridge the
social, economic, and educational gap."

In addition to the other non-social descriptive and prescriptive programs, Young includes citizenship responsibility as point
ten of his Marshall Plan which focuses upon the Negro:

Negro citizens must exert themselves energetically in constructive efforts to carry their full share of responsibilities and to participate in a meaningful way in every phase of community life.
It is not enough to man the machinery of protest. Equally important today and twice as important tomorrow is participation
in the responsibilities and opportunities of full citizenship in our
democracy. This means Negroes moving not only onto the picket
lines but also into PTA meetings; moving not only into lunch
counters but also into libraries; moving into both community
facilities and committee rooms, into both public accommodations
and public hearings; and, finally, moving onto the commissions
and boards to exercise their rights and insure their fair share.[30]

Although this directive is addressed to Negroes, its tone and application can only be intended for middle class Negroes. Lower

[29] *Ibid.*
[30] *Ibid.,* p. 31.

class Negroes—the masses—are given no guidance or means to self-help, yet they are the most in need of help and a way to help themselves. In Young's splendid scheme the morass of the masses finds no more solid ground on which to affirm their being than in Myrdal's work. This is a glaring omission by one who unquestionably knows and appreciates the civil rights struggle:

> The educationally privileged middle class Negro will share the horrors and hardships of his more handicapped working class brother as long as racism exists in our society.[31]

Aware of the alienation, suspicion, and increasing gulf between Negro classes, Young knows of no way in which the masses can be collaborators in the extermination of racism and seems to assume they can only receive and not give.

According to Young, it is the responsibility of middle class citizens to provide leadership. There are four levels on which Negro leadership now functions to enrich black prospects: a) the successful educators, businessmen, or professionals who serve as liaisons, symbolic models, or communicators of the movement; b) the direct actionists; c) the social engineers; and, d) the Negro heroes or role models of achievement. Young argues strongly for a diversified approach in Negro leadership and sees the Urban League's role to be the third level.

> The strategists, planners, and researchers, sophisticated in the nuances of social change, knowledgeable about the social sciences and economics, aware of community resources and skilled in mobilizing and organizing the community to take advantage of these resources. These are the people who can participate in policy-making and implementation, who read and understand the fine print, not only of a civil rights law, but also of laws covering retraining, public welfare, health, youth employment, vocational education, urban renewal, educational policy, minimum wages, and fiscal policies. They are trained in these fields, and they have chosen to work as paid full-time professionals in race relations or to serve without pay as volunteers.[32]

---

[31] *Ibid.*, p. 221.

[32] *Ibid.*, pp. 220–221.

In calling for cooperation among these groups it is clear that Young sees the way of the future as that of the third level of leadership "best represented by the Urban League."

While Young affirms

> today it isn't a case of the Urban League or the NAACP or CORE; it's the Urban League

and he is convinced that

> five years from now the Negroes' adversaries won't need the sit-ins and laws and restrictions that segregate.

Tomorrow the Urban League will hold sway, for

> at that point the conventional methods of protest will be useless. No legal action, no sit-ins, no picketing will help, because nobody will be stopping us on the basis that we are Negroes.[33]

The progressive optimism Young exudes reflects not only the obvious success of the organization he administers but his view of human nature. There is little awareness of white resistance, no less the threat of Negro masses as against the privileged few. It is difficult to determine how the total integration sought can be obtained, even with complete acceptance of Young's strategy, without work being done by the masses and on the private, intimate levels of social living. A clue is found in his equation of mass movements with "the conventional methods of protest." Young does not appreciate the role of power, the need for political action on the part of the Negro, and a community commitment which gives direction to the third level role of the Urban League, rather than being pulled up and pointed in the right direction by social workers. In assuming the proletariat has done all it could or be expected to do, Young has not perceived his failure to provide the masses of Negro citizens with what he deemed of high priority:

> a choice as to the most practical and effective methods for achieving full freedom and equal opportunity with all other American citizens.[34]

[33] *Ibid.*, p. 224.
[34] *Ibid.*, p. 225.

What Young has done is to present a brilliant defense of the Urban League and a formidable positive program from a Negro leadership point of view, but for whites and not for Negroes—with the exception of third level types of the future. This is a helpful extension of Myrdal's thesis, but it overlooks the depth of the ghetto, the Northern reversals, and the subtle ways of exclusion—it is a necessary but not sufficient approach "for achieving full freedom and equal opportunity," leaving out as it does the whole realm of political power of the masses. Young is correct in seeing the limited possibilities for Negroes in the professions and in business as an economic matter. But the lack of opportunity for Negroes in business is also a social dilemma, since business is based upon personal and private associations which are far less crucial in those professions in which Negroes most generally serve whites (e.g., education, social work, federal agencies).

Perhaps Young's failure to perceive what real freedom and equality demands centers around his analogy of the labor movement in the thirties to the Negro movement in the sixties. This does provide what is for him the imperative economic parallel. The difficulty is that the labor movement was a compromise of the organized working force of America wherein they accepted a share of the economic pie in lieu of direct attack upon the capitalistic system through revolution. But the labor movement has not succeeded in increasing Negro participants in middle class America; it has failed in its singular objective to improve the underprivileged economically. If the Negro movement is what Young calls a "revolution," it is not merely an economic one to be compromised through the upgrading of middle class Negroes and widening this gap to keep pace with the gap between whites and Negroes. What labor failed to achieve for all working class peoples of America, the Negro movement wants to achieve for Negroes, the inclusion of all in the society.

Young would have been more on target if he had used the analogy of Irish Catholics or Eastern European Jews who immigrated and won their way in society through internal political cohesiveness centered in religious communities, and the pressure upon the larger society to change through legal-economic-moral-social power. By focusing upon the mass protests, labeling them acceptable but dated, and opting for the rationalist approach of social engineering, Young is limited by the economic emphasis of the past, which he deemed progressive, rather than the political action of the future, which is the new demand and breakthrough of the Negro. Both economics and politics must be engaged in simultaneously. It is the task of middle class strategists to be engaged in the economic developments, to be sure. What Young ignored is the role of the masses in political action, community democracy wherein they alone can become responsible beyond dependence, which is quite other than demonstrative social protest. Economic developments can be advanced without the lower class being involved in social engineering, but this will not be full freedom and equality without political involvement, which also needs a leadership vanguard which can only act with, not for, the masses.

The assumption that the masses can only react does not take into account the advance of the protest movements over the inertia of the past. Without this perspective there is no projection of what hard work and imagination could bring about in the nature of community politics in the new urban-secular setting, where political power increasingly is present in the Negro populace. Nothing less than concerted political action will make the special economic effort Young calls for meaningful, for even trained middle class engineers of society can lose their way in the mire of politics without the constant pressure from the community. Men are good but not so good as to live by sheer truth or knowledge without conflicting interests. Writing as though expertise functions apart from vested interests, Young ignores the masses, power, and religion. He places the black prospects in the hands of black technicians who will take charge with white armor. Other Negro organizations may cooperate by providing the opponents on the battleground for the knights of faith in shining new methods, but religion—specifically the masses in the churches—can be, at best, spectators basking in the light created by technicians confirming their right action with moral support.

Young's blindness to the significant future role of Negro

churches in the emergence of black prospects finds its vision limited by the history of these institutions, pointedly underscored by E. Franklin Frazier in his posthumous work, *The Negro Church in America*:

> The Negro church and Negro religion have cast a shadow over the entire intellectual life of Negroes and have been responsible for the so-called backwardness of American Negroes. Sometimes an ignorant preacher backed by the white community has been able to intimidate Negro scholars and subvert the true aim of an educational institution. It is only as a few Negro individuals have been able to escape from the stifling domination of the church that they have been able to develop intellectually and in the field of art. This development is only being achieved on a broader scale to the extent that Negroes are being integrated into the institutions of the American community and as the social organization of the Negro community, in which the church is the dominant element, crumbles as the "walls of segregation come tumbling down." [35]

This is a devastating indictment of Negro churches and at the same time the highest compliment to their real importance throughout the Negro community. What neither Young nor Frazier saw is the possibility of converting this influence and power to good and positive use. Both assume that the Negro churches' past record is its future. If the Negro church and Negro religion "have been responsible for the so-called backwardness of American Negroes," in the context of the urban-secular society and the accomplishments of the civil rights movement, it would seem that this is a force which will not cease and desist tomorrow and that it might be worked at to further the prospects of blacks.

Actually, Young, the social worker, and Frazier, the sociologist, are informed by a late 19th century antipathy to religion in general. Frazier believed "the Negro church continues to be a refuge, though increasingly less a refuge, in a hostile white world," and did not even hold forth the redemptive option of integrating Negroes and their religious institutions "into the institutions of

[35] E. Franklin Frazier, *The Negro Church in America* (New York: Schocken Books, 1964), p. 86.

the American community." [36] Frazier hoped not only for the withering of Negro religious manifestations but of all religion as well.

Yet, while Frazier permitted the negative forces of Negro religion to dominate his thinking to the extent of refusing to perceive any value in Negro churches (which were for him the agency of "social control"), he documented the historical role of this institution:

> Organized religious life became the chief means by which a structured or organized social life came into existence among the Negro masses.[37]

> The leaders in creating a new community life were men who with their families worked land or began to buy land or worked as skilled artisans. It is important to observe that these pioneers in the creation of a communal life generally built a church as well as homes. Many of these pioneer leaders were preachers who gathered their communicants about them and became the leaders of the Negro communities. This fact tends to reveal the close relationship between the newly structured life of the Negro and his church organizations.[38]

> These societies were organized to meet the crises of life—sickness and death; consequently, they were known as "sickness and burial" societies. The important fact for our study is that these benevolent societies grew out of the Negro church and were inspired by the spirit of Christian charity.[39]

> As a result of the elimination of Negroes from the political life of the American community, the Negro church became the arena of their political activities. The church was the main area of social life in which Negroes could aspire to become leaders of men.[40]

> The masses of Negroes may increasingly criticize the church and their ministers, but they cannot escape from their heritage. They

[36] *Ibid.*, p. 81.
[37] *Ibid.*, p. 30.
[38] *Ibid.*, p. 33.
[39] *Ibid.*, p. 36.
[40] *Ibid.*, p. 43.

may develop a more secular outlook on life and complain that the church and the ministers are not sufficiently concerned with the problems of the Negro race, yet they find in their religious heritage an opportunity to satisfy their deepest emotional yearnings.[41]

There is real ambiguity in Frazier: in seeing the contributions of Negro churches he ignores them as indicators of future possibilities. He sees hope in integration for the middle class but none for the lower class, since the masses cannot shake off religion and superstition as does the rising middle class:

The religious behavior and outlook of the middle class Negroes is a reflection of their ambiguous position as Negroes rise to middle class status and become increasingly integrated into the American community. To the extent that they are becoming really assimilated into American society, they are being beset by the religious dilemmas and doubts of the white middle class Americans. On the other hand, for the masses of Negroes, the Negro church continues to be a refuge. . . .[42]

This ambiguity which admits past but bars future contributions of Negro churches, which sees frustrations in the Negro middle class which cannot shake a religious heritage and is not accepted into the whole society fully while the masses retain allegiance to Negro institutions, really indicates a dogged refusal to accept past changes due to a new situation as indicative of possibilities for future changes due to the urban-secular pressures.

Frazier did not perceive the positive values of a secular society which forced Negro churches to be less rigid moralistically and more open to meeting the needs of Negro people, however inadequately and superficially. This change, which he called "secularization of Negro churches," was for him a denial of past religious life and an indication of its uselessness, rather than a sign of its possibilities:

By secularization we mean that the Negro churches lost their predominantly other-world outlook and began to focus attention

[41] *Ibid.*, p. 73.
[42] *Ibid.*, p. 42.

upon the Negro's condition in this world. The most obvious evidence of secularization has been that the churches have been forced to tolerate card playing and dancing and theater-going.[43]

He reported even more important changes describing the values of Negro churches,

their interest in the affairs of the community included recreational work and contributions to the world of a social welfare agency like the National Urban League or organizations fighting for civil rights like the National Association for the Advancement of Colored People.[44]

In a number of northern cities the pastors of large Negro churches have been influential in politics and have received important political appointments. . . . Reverend Powell has not only been a political leader of Negroes but he has also marched with them in the boycott of stores which refused to employ Negroes.[45]

These changes in the past indicate possibilities for the future of Negro-white relations in America—which depends on the Negro masses, and the church remains the center of their life.

Changes in the future were not foreseeable because of Frazier's bias against religion and churches as defense mechanisms:

The church is the most important of these institutions in which the masses of Negroes find a refuge within white society which treats them with condescension if not contempt.[46]

He was justified in the judgment that "the Negro church can no longer serve as a refuge as it did in the past" and right in this discernment:

The masses of Negroes continue, nevertheless, to attend the Negro churches and the Negro church as an institution continues to function as an important element in the organized social life of Negroes.[47]

[43] *Ibid.*, p. 51.
[44] *Ibid.*
[45] *Ibid.*
[46] *Ibid.*, p. 71.
[47] *Ibid.*

Since the church is "the most important cultural institution created by Negroes" and it is being undermined less rapidly than "the institutions which embody the secular interests of Negroes," it is logical to conclude that this institution of natural power ought not to be ignored but rather goaded into taking responsibility commensurate with its importance. This is particularly the case if Frazier is correct in viewing the church as a social institution. As these institutions are "drawn into the complex social organization of the American community" and given its documented forms of change to meet past situations, it would be more logical to conclude that Negro churches not only should but can be centers for concerted action with power, rather than the illogical conclusion reached by Frazier:

> A Negro sociologist proposed that the Negro church, being the largest organized unit of Negro life, incorporate some of the functions of the new forms of organized social life which are required in the city. It is apparent, however, that this proposal was impractical since the Negro church could not perform the functions of the new types of associations necessary to life in the city.[48]

Nothing is less apparent in the field of politics as Frazier has shown. In the field of social work it is not so much that the Negro church cannot perform this function but that it is not its function to perform—it should support the social welfare agencies like the National Urban League as Frazier pointed out it has done.

Social scientists of the social engineering variety know that there is an iceberg of underlying hatred and resentment in whites directed toward Negroes. If the middle class can repress their exclusion through escape in exceptional situations, the lower class masses cannot, and this is the crux of the matter. Thus, to confront the white middle class with conscience-relieving ideals and programs are doubtful approaches to the eradication of white hatred which takes the form of prejudice, discrimination, and segregation. The appeal to a healthy America of unity amidst diversity through equal opportunity in education, health, welfare,

[48] *Ibid.*, p. 72.

housing, employment—what Frazier termed the "so-called process of integration, which is only an initial stage in the assimilation
of Negroes into American society"—will hardly occur in the next
decade, as Young anticipates. These special efforts and appeal to
good will are helpful. But much more can be done to improve the
status of Negroes by building up substantial political pressure in
the Negro community to demand rights. The power structure may
relinquish minimal opportunities in a gradual process for conscience sake, it will provide the necessary inclusion only as power
is brought to bear. There is no greater potential power than in
the Negro people in urban communities, especially in the North,
and no greater means to this power than the churches. It is in
these organizations that the masses who are subject to police
brutality, economic, social, and political disadvantages find their
release. It is there they must find their life together in power.
White people will respond to such power, without which black
prospects will be visions of occasional success. Social scientists
and others who deem full freedom and equal opportunity imperative will have to face the historicity of the masses in churches
and forsake the old pattern of attempting to ignore or reverse the
direction of history for the sake of influencing it so that the right
kind of people will direct it. Otherwise the future will be resigned
and consigned to those who "have neither an intellectual heritage
nor a social philosophy except a crude opportunism which enables
them to get by in the white man's world."

Black prospects of the masses have been increased by social
scientists' advancement, by the force of litigation, conscience, civil
rights demonstrations, and subtle weapons of truth through appeal to democratic responsibility of the white power structure.
They have been limited by the unwillingness or inability to engage in political development among Negro masses which is admittedly more difficult and outside the particular interest and
competence of social engineers. Yet, the deprivation of the Negro
is so complex that clean lines of responsibility are inapplicable if
the objective is the inclusion of a whole people into the society
with the marks of color a positive rather than negative. The particular discipline or field of competence chosen by the individual

does not carry with it immunity from politics and therefore religion since the political power of the Negro is now locked in churches.

Benjamin E. Mays' *Seeking to Be Christian in Race Relations* is written for whites and while it is a positive response to religion, it does not evidence awareness of economics or politics and therefore what it means for Negroes "to be Christian in Race Relations":

> The basic issues of life are not political or economic. They are religious—God, man, ethics, and spiritual values. A belief in God and in man as revealed by Jesus is the most important issue facing the world today. If we could ever get the proper attitude toward God and man, we could easily settle our political, economic, and social questions. I am talking about a belief in God which expresses itself in action. The true Christian not only has faith that leads to action, but he has faith that ultimately the result of his action will be good.[49]

Obviously this is the kind of simplistic statement of religion and life which horrifies the social scientists. They would largely accept Daisuke Kitagawa's assertion in *The Pastor and the Race Issue* that "most sermons on race relations preached from the pulpits of Protestant churches are mainly *moral exhortations* to abide by the Supreme Court decision or by the law of the land." [50] Social scientists and engineers could find common ground with Kitagawa's observation: "The race crisis is fundamentally a problem of *intergroup* relations rather than *interpersonal* relations." While both Kitagawa and the social scientists would differ in their responses to religion,

> no attempt at a synthesis of theology and sociology is intended, however, but rather the start of some dialogue *between* theology and sociology,[51]

[49] Benjamin E. Mays, *Seeking to Be Christian in Race Relations* (New York: Friendship Press, 1957), p. 79.

[50] Daisuke Kitagawa, *The Pastor and the Race Issue* (New York: The Seabury Press, 1965), p. 57.

[51] *Ibid.*, p. 119.

they are one in instructing the white world to the exclusion of the Negro world:

> When we talk about the pastor and the church he represents, we should also think of them in relation to (a) government, both as a law-making and a law-enforcing agency; (b) public service agencies, governmental and voluntary, which are directly concerned with race problems; (c) various social action groups, racial and interracial, including professional human relations agencies; and (d) university and other research agencies such as those sponsored by foundations.[52]

Kitagawa's concentration on whites is based not only on awareness of the white power structure but a less critical view of Negroes than whites, and therefore an underestimation of the role Negroes have to play:

> Negroes are united by an aspiration for things yet to be achieved, while whites are united by a concern for things they have already achieved and now fear to lose. The Negro group tends to be future-oriented, while the white group, more or less, tends to be past-oriented.[53]

The obvious lack of unity among Negroes is in political concert, where the greatest need is (though there is unity in suffering). What is needed is not so much to comfort the afflicted dimension of the Negro as to afflict his taking comfort in the future. Insofar as there is recognition of Negro power and the need for it to be exerted, it has been located in the obvious but wrong places. Liston Pope helps to verify this in his *The Kingdom Beyond Caste* where the "principal organizational vehicles" of power in the Negro community

> are such agencies as the National Association for the Advancement of Colored People (to which many whites belong), the National Urban League, and many other such agencies. . . . Whatever segments of the white population may think about them, many of these organizations have proved that they can be extremely effective; the sincerity of their purposes and the

[52] *Ibid.*, p. 103.
[53] *Ibid.*, p. 85.

legitimacy of their methods are seldom called into question by objective observers.[54]

C. Eric Lincoln, in *My Face Is Black*, is perceptive of the gap between emphasis upon Negro leadership and the demands of the masses:

> Negro leadership will never be able to deliver at a rate satisfactory to those they are attempting to lead to freedom. The forces of resistance have been too firmly entrenched too long. If America finds herself in real trouble, it will not be because Negro leadership has failed, but because America herself has failed.[55]

A social scientist favorably disposed to religion and thoroughly knowledgeable about Negro disinheritance, Lincoln nevertheless addresses whites in the armor of "mood ebony":

> We may sit on our hands and hope that the problem will go away. We may, if we choose, continue to dole out little bits of democracy like bribes to a peevish, insistent child. . . . But we will pay a horrible and unnecessary price, and we will be lucky if it need not be paid in blood.[56]

Neither economic nor political guidelines are spoken of as the way of the Negro to make the most of his potential power. The substitute for offensive power is offensive anger; Negro churches are ignored as a source of unified strength in daily engagements beyond protests. Lincoln's final word is dated and not enough:

> But the point to be established here is that the Negro in America, who has received less consideration and more abuse from the hands of the American white man than any other people anywhere in the world, has stood steadfastly behind him (and, when permitted, beside him), with a degree of patience and loyalty that is unique in the annals of time. Let the white man recognize this now, before it is too late, and learn to love mercy and do justly.[57]

[54] Liston Pope, *The Kingdom Beyond Caste* (New York: Friendship Press, 1957), pp. 101–2.

[55] C. Erich Lincoln, *My Face Is Black* (Boston: Beacon Press, 1964), p. 129.

[56] *Ibid.*, p. 132.

[57] *Ibid.*

It is already too late for the white man to simply "recognize" and "learn to love mercy and do justly" without the force of power that is less subtle than truth. And clearly, the Negro masses cannot afford to wait for this event; the future has no bearing upon their present suffering. If bloodshed must come it ought to be after the Negro has exerted his power through political change so that failure will be truly representative and not just white but white and black. Then America would deserve the verdict: "America herself has failed." That the only possibility for America lies in the conflicting and coordinating power of whites and blacks may not be open to Lincoln since he has firsthand knowledge of Floyd Hunter's analysis of Atlanta decision makers and making: "None of the leaders in the Negro community may operate in the same echelons of power as the top leaders in the total community." [58]

There is no southern city in America where the split between a very large and prosperous Negro middle class and very large and deprived Negro lower class is so impressive as Atlanta, though New Orleans comes close. The dependence on leadership is really a confirmation of the lack of power which is due to the lack of organization and hard work necessary to make the Negro community cohesive and bring forth a leader who speaks out of political power for the community, rather than a leader who speaks out of the more tentative spirit of protest. Daniel C. Thompson concludes, in *The Negro Leadership Class*, that in New Orleans

> insofar as the formulation or execution of policies and practices governing the civic, political, economic, educational, professional, and cultural life of the community is concerned, Negroes are powerless.[59]

The reason for New Orleans Negro leadership's being nowhere near the top power group is that

[58] Floyd Hunter, *Community Power Structure: A Study of Decision Makers* (Chapel Hill: University of North Carolina Press, 1953), pp. 138–39.

[59] Daniel C. Thompson, *The Negro Leadership Class* (Englewood Cliffs: Prentice-Hall, 1963), p. 165.

whites who occupy the top power positions in New Orleans are pledged, or assumed to be pledged, to the preservation of a biracial social system that, according to its inherent nature, relegates all Negroes to an inferior social status. This means that Negroes who seek to achieve racial equality are automatically resisted by white men of power.[60]

Thompson has defined the situation in every community, North and South, and revealed the indispensability of a singular power structure in each Negro community. A social scientist responsive to the interdependence of religion, economics and politics, Thompson perceives the answer not in the development of a power group representing the entire Negro community but through the "leadership class." The "leadership class" takes the form of the Coordinating Council of Greater New Orleans made up of the representatives of segmented Negro life,

> all major religious denominations, civic organizations, political factions, professional societies, educational agencies, and social clubs in the Negro community are represented.[61]

The leadership *class* is necessary because there is no unity and strength in the Negro community of New Orleans to develop and support a leader. This *class* of leaders is based upon class, not power, and each leader maintains an independence based on the status of his organization. For the most part, the Council is far more representative of the middle class than of the lower class and therefore tends to be more of a plutocracy than a democracy. Its failure is not in its intention to get things done for the Negro community via negotiation rather than power, nor is its failure in the endeavor to present a solid leadership front as leverage to move the white power structure. Its failure is rather in representing class groups rather than the whole Negro community, and in being pseudo-political. This may have brought "greater unity than has been experienced at any previous time" among "approximately one hundred Negro leaders," as a result of the New

[60] *Ibid.*
[61] *Ibid.,* p. 171.

Orleans school crisis of 1960, but it did not result in the unity anticipated in the mayoralty elections of 1962 and 1964. In short, its failure is its purpose:

> The expressed purpose of this organization is to coordinate the resources and talents of the various types of Negro leaders in the solution of common problems. That this could be done was unequivocally demonstrated in a short voter-registration drive just prior to the 1962 mayoralty election. This effort was based upon what amounts to a new approach to political behavior. Thus, whereas political parties are active locally in terms of geographic areas, wards, and precincts, the Council conducted its voter-registration drive upon the assumption that concentrating on organizations would be more effective than concentration on the traditional neighborhood. Each member organization, therefore, was asked to assume responsibility for seeing to it that every one of its own members become registered voters.[62]

Such an organization is the beginning and not—as set forth here—the end. To be sure, Negroes in New Orleans, as in every Negro community, have been beset by "three typical patterns of race relations leadership: segregationist—Uncle Tom; moderate —racial diplomat; and liberal—race man." This lack of a dynamic and united leadership is due to exploitation and divisiveness through self-interests within the Negro community and the clever capitalization upon this by the white community. But such lack of unity is not the fault of the white power structure. Unlike many rural areas of the South, Negroes in New Orleans had the power of the ballot prior to the 1965 voting bill. Thompson, a graduate of a theological school and professor of sociology, is in possession of the "resources and talents" to effectively coordinate the Negro community through the churches, but has preferred the short circuit of class leadership to which he belongs and in which he has pioneered. Thus he avoids the admittedly difficult work of coordinating the masses. Within the white community there is a white power structure which gives the community direction; it will include and be responsive to the Negro community

[62] *Ibid.*, p. 170.

when it exhibits its *power* rather than *protest* structure. Until then there will be concessions of a "biracial social system," but Negroes will not be "near the top power group" and there will be no equal social status.

There is a great deal of conversation these days about "the Negro revolution in America," nowhere more popularly illustrated than in the book of this title by William Brink and Louis Harris. According to these authors this "revolution" means "freedom now" or the ascertainment of "Negro rights." Briefly, this means an economic "revolution," for though it includes the "*right* to integrate," Negroes "neither expect nor especially want full integration with whites now." In the "six major areas of discrimination" (jobs, education, housing, voting, public facilities, social life) the priority is equal economic treatment through higher pay, more abundant jobs, better housing:

> Every day, television reminds the Negro of the whites' comfortable way of life—suburban houses with modern kitchens, shiny new cars and dishwashers, power mowers and neatly trimmed lawns. Most Negroes would like a greater measure of these things they see whites enjoying every day of their lives. They "want in." And this goes to the core of the Negro dilemma. . . .

> To share in the wealth, quite obviously the Negroes need jobs that pay them an adequate living. To qualify for such jobs the Negroes need education. To get a good education they must live in neighborhoods where the schools are good. And to do that they have to have the money to pay for decent housing. This vicious circle has long existed and shows no real signs of being broken yet.[63]

If this is the force "breaking the vicious circle," or what is meant by the "Negro revolution," it is no "revolution." To "want in" economically is legitimate, necessary, and right, but the most militant and visionary are not concerned with sharing the fruits of this most abundant society:

[63] William Brink and Louis Harris, *The Negro Revolution in America* (New York: Simon and Schuster, 1964), p. 155.

A small but significant number of Negroes, particularly in the leadership group, feel differently and do not emphasize materialistic goals. They are apparently alienated from middle class American society for deeper reasons than inability to share in the wealth. One leader expressed this feeling when he said in the survey that the Negro's biggest need was for "an honest facing up to the distorted values and negative aspects present in the majority society." [64]

This indeed is "the core of the Negro dilemma." For the potential "revolution" of Negroes "to achieve their goal of full citizenship" is to accept or transform the "distorted values and negative aspects present in the majority society." These are neither the natural economic desires "to share in the wealth" nor its concomitant human inclination toward "materialistic goals," or the unrealistic desire to change immediately and radically the economic system rather than forcing it to swiftly use its capacity for all "to share in the wealth."

Rather than the unnecessary economic dilemma of materialistic goals or a new economic system, the "revolution," insofar as it is a "revolution," is social equality—the touchstone of economic and political equality. Brink and Harris distort this truth by calling it "a lot of mixing of the races," twist it by labeling it "a massive outpouring of Negroes from their ghettos into white suburbs, schools, restaurants, social organizations and churches." Part of this misstatement of the "revolution" is due to the concentration on what the authors call the "rank and file" Negroes, who by the admission of Brink and Harris do not "have any real idea of what it means to be a part of society." [65]

Brink and Harris think there is something revolutionary in envying "the advantages of white society" and conclude that "one of the clearest purposes of their revolution now is to share in those advantages." [66] Given this economic interpretation, they are right:

[64] *Ibid.*
[65] *Ibid.*, p. 23.
[66] *Ibid.*

The realization of these high hopes rests with whites and just how viable they will be in the face of the revolution's demands.[67]

Of equal and perhaps more importance are the hopes that rest with Negroes; this is the political concert which brings responsibility and self determination beyond economic materialism. Both economics and politics are indispensable forces to the real "revolution" which is social equality, for without the latter objective, economic and political gains will be but exercises in futility.

Harris and Brink miss the self-determinative black prospects in their concentration upon either national elections or the unlikeliness of "any all-Negro political party." In their concentration upon the "new leadership" which is often the minister in all-Negro protest and improvement organizations, they affirm that "the Negro church has done as much as or more than any other segment of Negro society for the Negro's cause." Yet they do not see connections between the potential of Negro ministers and churches doing more for the self-determination of Negroes and the fact that the "Negro church" of which they speak is the exception rather than the rule. These distinctions are evident in the contrasting statements of "Wyatt Tee Walker, the slim, bespectacled young Negro Baptist minister who is King's aide-de-camp in the Southern Christian Leadership Conference":

> Wyatt Walker of the SCLC has estimated that no more than 10 per cent of the Negro clergy have been active for civil rights, and he has said that, in the Birmingham marches of May 1963, only about 20 of the city's 250 Negro ministers participated.[68]

> In both the Negro and white community, the Negro church has often been made a joke, but the fact is that it's the most organized thing in the Negro's life. Whatever you want to do in the Negro community, whether it's selling Easter Seals or organizing a nonviolent campaign, you've got to do it through the Negro church, or it doesn't get done.

[67] *Ibid.*, p. 165.
[68] *Ibid.*, p. 108.

> The church today is central to the movement. If a Negro's going to have a meeting, where's he going to have it? Mostly he doesn't have a Masonic lodge, and he's not going to get the public schools. And the church is the primary means of communication, far ahead of the second best, which is the Negro barbershop and beauty parlor.
>
> There's no way to tell what would have happened to the Negro if he had not had the church. I'll say flatly that if there had been no Negro church, there would have been no civil rights movement today.[69]

It seems strange that Walker and King would leave such a powerful institution to set up another "to practice social gospel." Nevertheless, if the "Negro church" is only partially as central, effective, and indispensable to the Negro community as Walker declares, there is certainly no alternative to it for the political union so necessary for social equality beyond the economics of housing, jobs, education, and public facilities.

The authors knew the substantive issue, the response to which determines whether there is a "revolution" or not, but were too interested in the progress of the South toward the stagnancy of the North to deal with the bleak black prospects through the measure of "revolution":

> The priorities of Negroes are also clear: Equal rights *now*, especially in jobs and education. Housing restrictions, they feel, should be lifted, although most Negroes expect that they will still live in dominantly Negro neighborhoods for some time to come.
>
> When they were asked about six major areas of discrimination [employment, education, housing, social life, public facilities, voting rights], a majority stated that they felt they would be better off five years from now [1963] in all but one area. The exception was voting rights; nearly half of the rank and file Negroes thought that things would be the same as now, and 81 per cent of the leaders agreed. However, a further breakdown revealed that most of those who expect no change were from the North and felt that they already had full voting rights.[70]

[69] *Ibid.*, p. 101.

[70] *Ibid.*, p. 164.

What Harris and Brink suppress in their desire to be optimistic and prove progress in America (in fact there is no real progress in the essential area of social equality) is boldly and baldly highlighted by the University of Wisconsin sociology professor Karl E. Taeuber, whose *Scientific American* article was quoted by Ben A. Franklin. Mr. Taeuber suggests the truth which most social scientists and social engineers pass over: segregation in the major cities of America is not due to economic poverty, poor housing, lack of education or inadequate social welfare:

> Even if Negroes gained full economic equality in the distant future, their residential segregation from whites would be considerable.[71]

The civil rights movement has been largely spent on altering the patterns of the South, which is far less important than altering the patterns of America's nerve center, the urban North. In this area housing is the issue to which attention has to be given, beyond cultural deprivation, education, and poverty disadvantages. If there is a "revolution" it is about assimilation and it is in the Northern nerve center of America, for "outright discrimination"

> is the principle cause of Negro residential segregation, and there is no basis for anticipating major changes in the segregated character of American cities until patterns of housing discrimination are altered.[72]

There is no workable program presently that will bring this about. This is due to the absence on the part of the Negro of a political center which is aware of and demands full participation in the society, instead of accepting economic upgrading with an attitude of keeping separate—the attitude which reinforces disadvantages:

What is needed is radical social change, but radical change is a

[71] Ben A. Franklin, "Urban Lag Found in Desegregation," *New York Times,* August 8, 1965.
[72] *Ibid.*

threat to many people and there are a lot of pressures operating now against it.[73]

Not the least among them is the Negro himself, so that in optimistically calling for improvements in essentials or even

talking about a way out of the urban segregation trap in 10 years, there is no evidence of a workable program now that will do it.[74]

It cannot be done without the Negro's taking the initiative. It is true, as Brink and Harris have stated and others have found awesome, Southern

Negroes have shown time and again that they are prepared to demonstrate, picket, boycott, or go to jail in order to achieve their goal of full citizenship.[75]

But the same dedication is not found in the fundamental area "of living in a mixed neighborhood *as a social experience*— particularly for their children."

The kind of program the Negro needs cannot be expected from so able an administrator as Secretary Robert C. Weaver, who keenly analyzes the problems of urbanization without providing radical solutions in his *The Urban Complex*. The best program and strategy to date has been articulated by Bayard Rustin in his preface to a national political program: "From Protest to Politics: The Future of the Civil Rights Movement." He begins where all advancement of black prospects must begin:

We must recognize that in desegregating public accommodations, we affected institutions which are relatively peripheral both to the American socio-economic order and to the fundamental conditions of life of the Negro people.[76]

Rustin declares the economic dimension essential but sees it in interdependence with the political dimension, calling for a

[73] *Ibid.*

[74] *Ibid.*

[75] Brink and Harris, *op. cit.*, p. 154.

[76] Bayard Rustin, "From Protest to Politics: The Future of the Civil Rights Movement," *Commentary*, Vol. 39, No. 2, February 1965, p. 25.

strategy "for the building of community institutions or power bases." The reason for this shift "from protest to politics" is further clarified in this statement:

> The very decade which has witnessed the decline of legal Jim Crow has also seen the rise of de facto segregation in our most fundamental socio-economic institutions.[77]

At issue is not "civil rights" but "social and economic conditions," destroying the myth which states that "the removal of artificial racial barriers should result in the automatic integration of the Negro into all aspects of American life."[78] Rustin scores against white moderates like Eric Hoffer who call for a self-help program on the part of Negroes in this dynamically unlimited technological society:

> They ignore (or perhaps see all too well) the potentialities inherent in linking Negro demands to broader pressures for radical revision of existing policies."[79]

And he scores equally against the "no-win tendency in the civil rights movement":

> I fail to see how the movement can be victorious in the absence of radical programs for full employment, abolition of slums, the reconstruction of our educational system, new definitions of work and leisure.[80]

This position has merit because of its "revolutionary" thrust:

> The term revolutionary, as I am using it, does not connote violence; it refers to the qualitative transformation of fundamental institutions, more or less rapidly, to the point where the social and economic structure which they comprised can no longer be said to be the same.[81]

Rustin is convincing in declaring that it is impossible "to frighten white people into doing the right thing." However, his

[77] *Ibid.*, p. 26.
[78] *Ibid.*
[79] *Ibid.*, p. 27.
[80] *Ibid.*, p. 28.
[81] *Ibid.*

fundamentally economic orientation fashions even social institutions into economic ones and deemphasizes the institutionalizing white hatred which is not equivalent with "social, political, and economic institutions." Rustin clearly sees that Whitney Young's "special effort" is middle class oriented; for the desperately poor " 'Preferential Treatment' cannot help them." He does *not* see that his own suggested outline "of economic reforms which are most immediately related to the plight of the Negro community" will not deghettoize the Negro, however much it may geographically relocate him. He speaks of "evolving from a protest movement into a full-fledged *social movement*" which to him seems to mean economic reconstruction.

Though the plight of the Negro is such that structural economic changes without social "deprejudicing" (which places whites on the defense through a Negro offense) are not enough, Rustin clearly spells out the first step—political action. Speaking within the framework of existing political democracy in America, neither the civil rights movement

> nor the country's twenty million black people can win political power alone. We need allies. The future of the Negro struggle depends on whether the contradictions of this society can be resolved by a coalition of progressive forces which becomes the *effective* political majority in the United States. I speak of the coalition which staged the March on Washington, passed the Civil Rights Act, and laid the basis for the Johnson landslide— Negroes, trade unionists, liberals, and religious groups.[82]

Where does this political power to meet the needs of the Negro lie? In the increased "swing vote" of the urban Negro, which has to be strategically employed:

> If there is anything positive in the spread of the ghetto, it is the potential political power base thus created, and to realize this potential is one of the most challenging and urgent tasks before the civil rights movement. If the movement can wrest leadership of the ghetto vote from the machines, it will have acquired an

[82] *Ibid.*, p. 29.

organized constituency such as other major groups in our society now have.[83]

Rustin did not intend to "delineate a total program," but his emphasis upon economics and political power at presidential elections leaves much to be said and done in local communities day in and day out. For while the socio-economic structures can be changed through influencing Washington, the psychological effectiveness of the ghetto cannot be eliminated without breaking down the social barriers in each local community, or restructuring private communities along with the socio-economic ones. This demand must be that of the Negro about a "social movement" of social integration; "the limit to what Negroes can do" has not been reached. As Rustin suggests, the right questions, calling for involvement in "the reorganization of American political life," have yet to be asked; they alone lead to proposing alternatives to

public works and training, for national economic planning, for federal aid to education, for attractive public housing—all this on a sufficiently massive scale to make a difference.[84]

As Rustin stated in another article:

The civil rights movement is one of the few forces in American society today capable of acting as an effective social catalyst.[85]

The movement must make its own political revolution [italics mine].[86]

Mr. Rustin does not go so far as Michael Harrington's statement in *The Accidental Century* in which Harrington declares America needs a new pattern of ideas and ideals or socialism because it is neither the function nor intention of Big Business to meet the revolutionary demands of technology—improving the economic condition of the masses. But Rustin is on the same wavelength.

[83] *Ibid.*

[84] *Ibid.*, p. 31.

[85] Bayard Rustin and Thomas Kahn, "Johnson So Far: Civil Rights," *Commentary*, Vol. 39, No. 6, June 1965, p. 46.

[86] *Ibid.*, p. 45.

It is undoubtedly the case that America needs a new ideology to meet the unprecedented problems and possibilities of automation and cybernetics. Presently, whatever progress is made in these areas the Negro will be benefited the last and the least. However, though the Negro's meaningful integration is dependent upon the total well being of the society, he has the additional problem of being accepted into the society as a social equal, the starting base of whites, irrespective of the extent America approximates greatness. Above and beyond economics is the group problem, toward the elimination of which the Negro has a revolutionary contribution to make. Negroes cannot ignore rethinking of economic planning, production, and leisure, but as Rustin himself puts it: "We cannot claim to have answers to all the complex problems of modern society." For if there is any truth in Donald N. Michael's projection, in *The Next Generation,* that the economic treadmill foretells the Negro as running further behind even as he runs faster and harder and gains more, the unification of Negroes in political power must entail a primary thrust toward social equality without which the vicious economic circle cannot be broken. To wait for equal economic opportunity to begin the drive for social equality is to opt for better second class citizenship, as the history of the civil rights movement to this point has shown. The economic reconstruction of society is not assured, and even if it were the Negro-white group problem would not be changed. Whites of the "noble savage worship" will not cease and desist from what has become among sophisticates (like Tom Wolfe in his *The Kandy-Kolored Tangerine-Flake Streamline Baby* histrionics) the height of reverse condescension as revealed in Jack Kerouac's *On the Road:*

> At lilac evening, I walked with every muscle aching among the lights of 27th and Welton in the Denver colored section, wishing I were a Negro, feeling that the best the white world afforded was not enough ecstasy for me, not enough life, joy, kicks, darkness, music, not enough night.[87]

[87] Jack Kerouac, *On the Road.* (New York: The Viking Press, Inc., 1958), p. 180.

Mr. Harrington realizes the need for more than the new ethic beyond the present ethics of scarcity, more than a new ideology—a new religion, which for Harrington is fundamentally economics:

> The exaltation of man is not a blasphemy against religion, it is religion's only hope. Rootless city people trapped in a sterile, routine, yet perplexing, world will lack both the motive of hunger and that of freedom. They will thus exist in between any need for God. Atheistic humanism has much the same problem as religion.[88]

Harrington is as emancipated as any liberal can be from what Kenneth B. Clark calls

> the prevalent beliefs that the predicament of the masses of Negroes reflects their inherent racial inferiority; that the poor are to blame for the squalor and despair of the slums; that the victims of social injustice are somehow subhuman persons who cause and perpetuate their own difficulties; that the more responsible and superior people of the society not only have the obligation for the "irresponsibles" but must be vigilant to see that all of the power of government is used to protect them and their children from them; and that any contrary or compassionate interpretation of the plight of the poor or the rejected is merely the sentimental and naive expression of impractical do-gooders or "bleeding hearts." [89]

But Harrington is of the Paul Goodman and A. J. Muste school, calling for a change first in the values of the society (e.g., acquisitiveness, peace-through-terror, television mentality) in preparation for an integrated society without poverty, thus ignoring an alternative highlighted by Nat Hentoff in *The New Equality*:

> There is, however, a prospect that if, through socially oriented planning, the economy of abundance which is possible with

[88] Michael Harrington, *The Accidental Century.* (New York: The Macmillan Company, 1965), p. 174.

[89] Kenneth B. Clark, *Dark Ghetto: Dilemmas of Social Power.* (New York: Harper & Row, 1965), p. 75.

automation can be extended to all, the resultant change in the distribution and definition of work could alter our values. . . .

Professor Theobald recognizes that "the guarantee of an income only provides freedom from want, freedom from complete conformity to the prevailing views of society. An Economic Security Plan can only give a man the means to be free; it will not ensure that he will use those means. The discovery of the proper uses of freedom is the fundamental task of the remainder of the twentieth century.[90]

Hentoff sees political action as the only way out of the ghetto for most Negroes, paralleling the mode and model of Bayard Rustin.

Without doubt the most far-reaching and informative perception of and contribution to black prospects comes from the experience and pen of Kenneth B. Clark. Dr. Clark holds a balanced view of economics, politics, and religion in the struggle for socio-politico-religio-educational equality. His uniqueness is the discernment of the social dynamics of the ghetto, which is not a theory to expound, or place from which to escape, but a condition which confronts America:

Chronic and remediable social injustices corrode and damage the human personality, thereby robbing it of its effectiveness, of its creativity, if not its actual humanity.[91]

The most important psychological deprivation is the historic role of the white male of having available "white and Negro women" and restricting meaningful competition with Negro males. Resulting in large measure from the civil rights movement,

the emerging, more affirmative sexual pride among Negro males may have as one of its consequences an increasing trend toward more open competition between white and Negro males for both white and Negro females. One of the further consequences would probably be an intensification of hostility of white males toward interracial couples and toward the white female participants, reflecting the desire on the part of the white male to

[90] Nat Hentoff, *op. cit.,* pp. 238–39.
[91] Clark, *op. cit.,* p. 63.

preserve his own competitive advantage. One would expect him then to employ his economic and political power—without suspecting the fundamental basis of his antagonism—to maintain the inferior status of the Negro male for as long as possible.[92]

Professor Clark appreciates and supports the call for economic upgrading, but clarifies the social dilemmas which are not equitable with poverty:

> White America is basically a middle class society; the middle class sets the mores and the manners to which the upper class must, when it wishes influence, seek to conform, at least in appearances, and which the lower class struggles to attain or defensively rejects. But dark America, of the rural and of the urban Negro, has been automatically assigned to be a lower class society; the lower class sets the mores and manners to which, if the Negro upper class wishes influence, it must appeal; and from which the Negro middle class struggles to escape. As long as this chasm between white and dark America is allowed to exist, racial tensions and conflicts, hatred and fear will spread. The poor are always alienated from normal society, and when the poor are Negro, as they increasingly are in American cities, a double trauma exists—rejection on the basis of class and race is a danger to the stability of society as a whole. Even though Negroes are in a minority in America—approximately one-tenth of the population—a minority that is sick with despair can poison the wellsprings from which the majority, too, must drink.[93]

To bring about the necessary transformation, Clark turns to the necessity of power, that force required to bring about socio-economic and political changes. The social change "required to determine and translate goals into a desired social reality" lies dormant in the ghetto's social institutions: "If Negroes are to use their new-found energy most effectively, it will be necessary for them to learn the ways of power and to avoid the delusion of pseudopower." [94] Among these institutions Clark includes

[92] *Ibid.*, p. 69.
[93] *Ibid.*, p. 21.
[94] *Ibid.*, p. 155.

political machines, the press, social welfare, and the churches. His acute analysis that the ineffective exercise of urban ghetto power has been due to the lack of experience and sophistication resulting from the leaders' failure to focus "their energies on civil rights or matters of general public concern" leads to a positive appreciation of the role of the masses and the possibilities within their churches:

> The potential power of the Negro church lies in the fact that it does attract large numbers of the masses of Negroes.[95]

While Clark does not hesitate to specify all the weaknesses of the Negro churches, neither does he concentrate solely upon Negro leadership and the tendency to spend "energies on building and maintaining the institution itself." He sees and encourages the potential not just of religious leaders and professional civil rights workers but of each local minister and the Negro institutional church itself working on community problems, although he does not carry this insight to its logical conclusion of religious institutions as community political power bases. Simultaneously "the most pervasive social institution in the Negro ghetto" and yet noninstrumental in the wider use of power,

> the church as an institution has not yet found the formula for effecting change without alienating its strongest supporters. If any reconciliation or resolution of this conflict is possible it would seem to depend on the ability of church leadership to state clearly and unequivocally the terms for such resolution which are consistent with the basic moral and theological positions of the church and thereby to assume the risk that the practical controllers of power within the church will accept, comply with, and use their power to reinforce this position, rather than rejecting it as in many Southern and Northern churches. But even if, in response to this challenge, the lay leaders of the church oppose its stand for justice, the moral strength of the church would have been affirmed and the issue between the demands and the direction of practical economic and political power on the one hand and moral and spiritual

[95] *Ibid.*, p. 175.

power on the other hand would be clarified. The façade of power which the church now presents would be removed, and the church would be forced to develop a genuine prophetic role.[96]

Insofar as the churches in the Negro community are its primary social institutions and they are to a large degree independent, they possess the essential resources for genuine power. Their limitations in financial resources and "organizational stability for a long-range conflict" does demand for success, as Clark suggests, the pattern of Powell and King gaining the necessary mass following and organizational skills outside the bounds of the local churches "by strength of personality and articulateness or by sound and sincere leadership." As the Reverend Leon Sullivan of Philadelphia discovered his church to be the "springboard to help him win over a wider community support" for an economic boycott and gained the cooperation of his ministerial colleagues, there is every reason to believe such cohesiveness in each community could be created as a permanent political base and perhaps form a national coalition with civil rights organizations.

In *The Fire Next Time*, James Baldwin underscores the emerging awareness in Negroes that

> one can give nothing whatever without giving oneself—that is to say, risking oneself.[97]

In the case of Negro-white group relations this inability of whites to give themselves is reflected in the fact that dealing with "hard problems" has not included this dimension of risk; at best there have been "concessions made in order to stay on top." Since "the sloppy and fatuous nature of American good will can never be relied upon" for the necessary transformation, the only "real change in the Negro's situation" can come about through substantial

> changes in the American political and social structure. And it is clear that white Americans are not simply unwilling to effect

[96] *Ibid.*, pp. 178–79.
[97] James Baldwin, *The Fire Next Time* (New York: Dial Press, 1963), p. 100.

these changes; they are, in the main, so slothful have they become, unable even to envision them.[98]

This being so, the black prospects are dependent upon gaining what whites have—power. The source of this lies in the fact of being black which, paradoxically, "is a political reality." The objective of 'this black power or "political reality" is not to imitate "the white man's public or private life," nor is the objective to become another ethnic political bloc *qua* political bloc, or even to simply gain economic equality. The objective of this black power is unique, the indispensable way to awareness of our common black and white Americanness and therefore need of each other. This communion has a price:

> The price of the liberation of the white people is the liberation of the blacks—the total liberation, in the cities, in the towns, before the law, and in the mind. Why, for example—especially knowing the family as I do—I should *want* to marry your sister is a great mystery to me. But your sister and I have every right to marry if we wish to, and no one has the right to stop us. If she cannot raise me to her level, perhaps I can raise her to mine.[99]

To change the fate of white over black everything now, we must assume, is in our hands; therefore, the Negro cannot ask whites to give themselves but he must make them give themselves as he gives himself by doing all in his

> power to change that fate, and at no matter what risk—eviction, imprisonment, torture, death.

Baldwin does answer the question of how this impossible possibility is to be accomplished by Negroes. He asks the key question without answering it: "How can the American Negro past be used?" The past of the American Negro has largely the church as the center, and in the present the masses still make their pilgrimages there. If to the past social function of the Negro church there can be added a present political function, it will

[98] *Ibid.*, p. 99.
[99] *Ibid.*, p. 111.

bear witness to what human history in general and American Negro history in particular exemplifies—"Nothing less than the perpetual achievement of the impossible."

There is an increasing consciousness among "the relatively conscious whites" of their "duty now," which must be forged with the equal consciousness of "the relatively conscious blacks" to "now dare everything"

to end the racial nightmare, and achieve our country, and change the history of the world.

The daring of the Negro must be based in political reality. Fortunately, Martin Luther King, Jr. is aware that the spectacular achievements in the South, for which he cannot be given too much credit, only threaten its patterning of the ghetto North. King's turning of his popular person and movement to the North shows increasing signs of political acuteness. Unlike the less sophisticated South, there is no obvious power structure in the North composed of a select and known group of whites who make the decisions for the community. The complexity of decision making in the urban North is as much entangled by bureaucratic overlapping as by political self-interests. This complex system is not the least reason for the lack of unity and leadership among Negroes. It may be that King can bring the necessary unity and leadership needed if his political involvements become more than moral calls for Negro bloc voting infused with an ounce of political realism to a pound of political idealism. In *Why We Can't Wait*, King concludes:

American politics needs nothing so much as an injection of the idealism, self-sacrifice and sense of public service which is the hallmark of our movement.[100]

If King can combine the "persistence, aggressiveness, and discipline" of the movement with the necessary skills, indigenousness, experience, and responsibility of political power structures and generate the energy of "the million Americans who marched

[100] Martin Luther King, Jr., *Why We Can't Wait* (New York: Signet Books, 1963), p. 151.

in 1963" directly within "the electoral process," there will be power enough. But such an accomplishment will be less easy than a march, requiring as it does commitment to a lifetime of day-to-day, full-time involvement. The hope lies with professional politicians who are elected by a political machine controlled by an informed electorate; not, as King thinks, the talented few Negroes of "unimpeachable character" who have made their reputation as leaders via every route but the political one:

> Such men as Judge William Hastie, Ralph Bunche, Benjamin May, A. Philip Randolph, to name a few, have remained aloof from the political scene. In the coming period, they and many others must move out into political life as candidates and infuse it with their humanity, their honesty, and their vision.[101]

If the way of liberating whites and blacks is through the "Negro potential for political power," free from the "corruption and manipulation by political bosses," King can make no better contribution than through the natural centers of power in Negro churches, which can become effective political machines as well as social centers. This will require the hard, steady, and imaginative capabilities of a King in each community. Perhaps even Martin Luther King, Jr. can no longer remain "aloof from the political scene" and must as a national candidate "move out into political life."

Thomas F. Pettigrew points out that up to the present, "protest is a reform movement and not a revolution" because the aim of the protest is "to change norms" rather than to overturn basic values.[102] Health, employment, business, income, housing, voting, and education are the present emphases of the "reform movement" which demands "all, here, now"—by which is meant economic gains within the present system. Perhaps the complex socio-economic structures would require significant changes in values were these demands to be met. But there are other criteria than economic values in a revolution. It is suggested

[101] *Ibid.*

[102] Thomas F. Pettigrew, *A Profile of the Negro American* (Princeton: Van Nostrand, 1964), p. 192.

here that the basic value of white-dominated America is a preference for whites which is perpetuated in large part because of the
assumption in the "reform movement" that economic and social
equality are two different forces which can be gained separately.
The strategy has been to begin with economic gains. Even the
political emphases of late center upon economic demands. But
the gulf between whites and Negroes is that whites begin with
social equality and may or may not gain economic security, while
Negroes may or may not gain economic security but never social
equality. To be depovertized is not to be deghettoized. If the
Negro community becomes conscious of white as the basic value
of this society (reinforced through subordinate beliefs in democracy and the free enterprise system, which cannot be changed
by Negroes' being upgraded in the present form or any new
form of beliefs), a cohesiveness of ghetto victims might be possible to break the vicious circle of white dominance which is
only objectified in economic deprivation. It is not inevitable that
economic reformulation or reconstruction—whatever pattern economic equality for the Negro takes—will lead to revolution. If
the Negro uses his power for social equality and demands the
end of singular white power he may not succeed, but a revolution
will be in deed. In any case, short of daring everything for the
sake of black and white communion, Negro opportunities will
continue to be dependent upon whites.

If we are correct in our assumptions, it is incumbent upon
us to present alternative ways of viewing the issue, between
Negroes and whites, the sources of a Negro self-image, the root
of his strength, and direction in which he must move to win
respect and gain acceptance. It is upon this task that we shall
set about in the remainder of the book.

PART TWO
WHITE FOLK RELIGION

CHAPTER IV
IRRATIONAL COLOR PREJUDICE:
AMERICA'S PRECONSCIOUS WHITE FOLK RELIGION

WE HAVE CONTENDED that color prejudice or hatred of Negroes by whites is not adequately explained by the rational-scientific theories of racism and psychoanalytical analyses of prejudice. The basis for our dissenting judgment is the fact that racism is a relatively modern phenomenon of the eighteenth and nineteenth centuries. With the publication of Darwin's *Origin of Species* there arose the first documented classification of human beings with scientific verification. There followed upon this scientific development, in the 1850's, Count de Gobineau's pseudoscientific and racist *Essay on the Inequality of Human Races*. This classic racist tract resulted in the tradition of racism which fastened upon class conflicts among Europeans at first, with the intent of proving Aryan superior nobility, then became a matter of nationalism. With the aid of Social Darwinism and Herbert Spencer, doctrinaire racists provided a theory to support the long practised treatment of Negro slaves as sub-humans. However widespread the racist theory of white superiority and black inferiority may have been, it did not affect the centuries-old practice of relegating the Negro to less than human status. At best it sustained through rational argument a pragmatic response spread widely throughout northern European cultures engaged in slave trading. Thus, to dislodge the rational racist theory through proving it to be antiscientific only affects conscious or unconscious levels. The subterranean depths of this Negro antipathy is not thereby affected, nor its tenaciousness released.

What the rational scientists fail to fully understand is that for many color prejudice is central to their lives, evoking a cultural deposit more deeply embedded than rational theories. Yet when the religious dimension of color prejudice is perceived by a Christian rationalist such as Professor George Kelsey, he sees it as a rational faith which he then attempts to alter with a superior rational Christianity. This procedure—countering one rational faith with another—doesn't work because it misses the central irrational dimension of both the racist and Christian faiths. Rational science and rational Christianity respond only to the manifest surface expressions rather than latent and hidden propensities of irrational racist religion.

If one begins with the reality of Negro-white injustice and seeks to bring about necessary changes by direct social action, without aiding the Negro to see his self-identity, his destiny, his imperative role in the reformation of the society, the activity will be seen but it is no more effective than the misguided theories in eradicating the abiding issue.

It is our contention that the dominant whites' color prejudice against Negroes is rooted in irrationalism that should be seen as the preconscious religion of the white folk. By irrational we mean a persistent, pervasive, and effective force which is neither unreasonable nor in conflict with reason but one which governs human intercourse on a more elementary level than reason. It is other than rather than opposed to or in conflict with reason. This elemental force of the irrational is given expression in religion. By religion we mean neither a rational faith nor a theological system of beliefs in relation to the Christian God, but a cluster of accepted practices stemming from the culture and expressing an ultimate concern. Unlike repressed desires which are inaccessible to self-consciousness, the preconscious means those desires and associated ideas of which the individual psyche is unaware but which are accessible to self-consciousness. By white folk we mean the northern European Protestants who colonized this continent and determined its basic attitudes and behavioral characteristics.

In the first chapter we have shown ethnocentrism to be a universal inclination of human groups to take pride in their primary and secondary groups seeing them as qualitatively preferable to other human aggregations, an attitude which tends to be modified in time by interaction with different peoples. Belief in cultural, political, and religious superiority, when accompanied by the means of power to dominate, has been a cruel and inhuman force for subjugating and dividing conquered groups. Still, even these divisive forces have been healed through intimate contacts over varied periods of time, often by means of intermarriage. However, as an instrument for cleavages between human groups racism is without parallel in human history because of its latent tendencies toward annihilation of the out group and its attempts at permanent segregation by means of coercive laws, tacit agreements, or subtle discriminatory actions. The claim of racism of support in nature, science, and the Bible makes this will to superiority immutable. Because its basis—purity of blood—arose in the age of rationalism and science and feeds upon these universally accepted methods (distortedly to be sure), racism has become the most flagrant antirational and antiscientific spirit in the modern world. No other movement has proven to be its equal in embarrassing rational western society. In cultures outside the West there may well exist antagonisms toward other groups even to the extent of refusal to be intimately associated with them, but nowhere but in the West are human divisions based upon scientific theories of racial inequality. In the most rational culture in mankind's history the height of selfish egotism and unreasoning fear of cohabitation leads to inexhaustible diatribes against miscegenation.

Having suggested certain basic approaches, we turn now to color prejudice—the hatred of and contempt for American Negroes by American whites, which we are now intent upon revealing as a distinctive western value preference, of enormous influence in the United States.

From the seventh century A.D., Mohammedans engaged in enslaving Africans to enhance the life of economic luxury among the wealthy. Through these centuries the religion of Moslems, so steeped in brotherhood, prevented their ever engaging in color prejudices. It was not different with southern European traders, who in the fifteenth century first began to deal in the African slave trade. Under the dominance of the Roman Catholic Church, missionaries to the heathens embarked with Spanish and Portuguese traders for the purpose of converting the Africans. The virtual absence of color prejudice among these early European slave traders was due to the will of the Roman Catholic Church. It is true that color prejudice emerged even among southern Europeans as they colonized Latin America, though it never became a religion with them, brutality did not become a prescribed way of treatment, laws were created for the well-being of the slaves, intermarriage was not seen as intolerable and often proved to be a viable option.

There followed after the hegemony of Roman Catholic countries in the slave trade its usurpation by northern European whites. In sixteenth century Europe a number of factors converged which led to an "elective affinity" between Protestant-Puritanism, capitalism, slave trading, and color prejudice which we perceive as unique without claiming that of necessity Protestantism and capitalism gave rise to color prejudice. The sixteenth century is marked by the Protestant Reformation in which the Netherlands, Germany, France, Scotland, and England were most affected in the break from Roman Catholic traditionalism in religion, political government, and economic enterprise. The most advanced economic territories of the Holy Roman Empire joined in both the religious and economic Reformation, in Calvin's ethic of asceticism by which hard work leads to the earning of money not to be spent in high living but to be used for capital investment in an emerging industrial economy. With the capitalistic acquisitiveness and the extension of a free economic enterprise there developed a ruthlessness for individual gain justified by a religious "calling" to escape the fear of damnation and to exhibit marks of being one of the "elect." In the place of Roman Catholic other-worldly asceticism, Calvinism promoted hyperactivity in this world and a rationally controlled moral life which gave a sense of security, confidence, superiority, and intolerance.

This religious independence, methodical hard work, competitive individualism, and the rewards of capitalism reinforced the spirit of individual salvation: thus the concern of each man for himself, living by his own moral codes, accountable only to God and his conscience. All of these forces meant that the slave trader and his contemporaries were singularly interested in profits. Given his religious-capitalistic values, he could not but be intolerant of people who were so obviously damned as to be slaves. There was no question in his mind that the slaves represented an inexorably God-forsaken lot. Since slaves did not possess self-assertiveness or the drive for acquisition they were considered of no worth in and for themselves but became real capital goods for the slave traders' market. With little risk, except venture on the high seas and the initial capital outlay, slaves became the perfect prototype of bourgeois capitalism—no capital outgo for wages and enormous dividends from their labor. For the free Protestant entrepreneur, spirited by capitalism, the slaves had to be damned for their great glory. After all, "God helps those who help themselves" was basic to the ethos. There was no question about who was helping whom. Capitalists of Europe dominated by Calvinism could not understand people caught in this condition of slavery on other grounds than for their use. No white Protestant could imagine being enslaved, striving as he was for worldly goods as a means of overcoming the fear of damnation. Thus it was not reason, ethics, theory, or theology which caused Protestant exploiters to immediately connect colored skin with sub-humanity—it was the most practical response imaginable by the most practical men history has known. To be European was to be white and a master, to be an African was to be colored and the slave of the white European master—nothing could be more obvious than the utter depravity of the slaves. It was simply assumed from the beginning that colored people were destined (damned) to be slaves and slaves were destined (damned) to be colored people without religious inheritance. Since there was no hope for these creatures they could be owned and put to whatever use their masters desired—preferably immediate and large capital gain—without any regard for their treatment as human beings except that which was necessary to ensure their profitableness.

This is the beginning and meaning of color prejudice as

preconscious preference of whites for whites. There is inherent
in this purely practical attitudinal-behavioral response an irrational element of individualistic desire not to be damned or
thought of as having the marks of damnation, the urge to show
the fruits of being one of the elect so inseparable from glorifying
God through good works and the hope of salvation. One clear
way of giving psychological, if not theological, evidence of being
"elected" was to be economically successful. The ownership of
slaves clearly met this need for visible economic success. Above
all, there was bound up in this practical pursuit a deep religious
commitment. It was not a religion of devotion to God. It was a
religion of making money, of profit-making or capitalism. The
spirit of capitalism had to be the religion or ultimate concern,
in time if not at first, because the spirit of Calvinism made no
promises of election, salvation, on the basis of merit. Regardless
of the intensity of super-worldly activity and gain Calvinism
demanded of all, there were only a few to be chosen and the
choice lay in the inscrutable will of God—which naturally led
from a concern to gain wealth for the glory of God to the gaining
of wealth for self-gratification and public demonstration of "election." The irrational pull toward the holy which the Protestant
Calvinist deeply felt was prevented from realization by the Calvinist doctrine of predestination and double damnation. But the
forces unleashed by Calvinism were so strong that they could not
be repressed and found their fulfillment in substituting for the
presence of the holy a distorted religion of spirited capitalism.

Far more important and lasting than Calvin's religion in the
culture of industrial Europe was the religion of Calvinism.
Persons who were not Calvinists found in capitalism their ultimate concern. Therefore, whether a follower of Calvin's religion
or not, the captain of the slave ship like the capitalists on the
homeland devoutly practiced his religion of Calvinism. To view
African slaves as sub-human was part of the same response of
color prejudice—turning these creatures into capital goods satisfied the irrational drive and became the means for the realization
of the ultimate concern, capitalism, the religion of North European white folk. For the sake of this religion no sacrifice was

too great, including human beings. Even Christians placed a higher value on capitalism than Christianity, for in any conflict between the two, as in slavery, capitalism won out. Slavery ended when it was no longer a necessity or profitable for the industrial society, not because the Christian faith took precedence over capitalism. At bottom, color prejudice is a deeply religious problem and most of all an irrational religious problem, precisely because of its "elective affinity" with the Protestant white folk religion of capitalism-Calvinism.

The full meaning and power of this "elective affinity" can only be understood in America, where European beginnings in Calvinism-Puritanism-capitalism-slavery-color prejudice gained their fullest expression. The religious symbiosis of color prejudice began with the sixteenth century slave traders, who found the assumptions of irrational depravity unchallenged by the Church at home and spurred by capitalism formed in the preconsciousness of European Calvinists. Heirs of this religion, Puritan settlers, dominated the American colonies for two hundred years prior to the rise of doctrinaire racism in eighteenth century Europe.

The American Puritan Church did not challenge slavery or color prejudice. Puritans held in common this preconscious white folk religion of whiteness as essential. White preference for whites was a claim of the Puritan preconsciousness prior to that of the conscious doctrines of Calvin in any conflict of the two. This preconscious religion of the white folk held Calvinism to be the highest expression of divinity and world asceticism, and capitalism to be the best proof of Calvinistic virtues. They saw Puritanism as the white man's religion, and America as a Protestant-Calvinist Christian nation responsible for the extension of western Christendom and particularly the Puritan cultural-social-religious-political-economic ethos.

The abiding virtues of the "Plymouth gentlemen" and the conservative Puritan colonists of the Massachusetts Bay were their strong sense of justice and order, ethics and theology, embedded in the covenants for select whites. This Puritan tradition eventually permeated the nation and rose to the fore in times of crisis, such as the belated, bright, and numerically limited aboli-

tionist movement. Noble ideals were clear and definite, but the
spirit of British Puritanism was an intellectual aristocracy dominated by the John Endicotts and the Sir William Berkeleys who
developed the oppressive pattern of the establishment. Thus, the
unmistakable covenanted theological ethics did not include religious liberty and voluntarism for the Roger Williamses and
William Penns. The underlying spirit of British Puritanism is
described by Max Lerner as intense, inverted, crotchety. It was
not judicious or humanist.[1]

This spirit is unmistakable in the colonial state churches
where indentured servants and poor whites were segregated by
class status to the back pews or standing room in the rear. The
freedom Puritans sought and maintained was strictly for themselves and their way of life. This way of life was confessional
orthodoxy "maintained by suppressing nonconformity and per-
secuting heresy."[2] Not only was the true religion of the covenants
the cultivation of orthodoxy for a minority; this small body in-
stituted for their purposes the European Christendom patterns of
cult and culture, religion and politics, church and state to Christianize the world society.

To civilize the colonies required a mission to the Indians.
The few converts were uprooted, re-formed and reordered—only
the European political order was recognized.[3] In Littell's words,
the religion of Puritan white folk insisted from its inception in
New England to its development on the Great Plains that

> converts of the missions should adopt the food, housing, clothing,
> social patterns, property ownership, and cultural values of white
> western civilization.[4]

White Puritan folk religion was firmly entrenched by driving out
the Indians who refused to be civilized or religionized. The failure

---

[1] Max Lerner, *America as a Civilization* (New York: Simon and Schuster,
Vol. I, 1961), p. 20.

[2] Franklin H. Littell, *From State Church to Pluralism: A Protestant Interpretation of Religion in America* (New York: Anchor Books, 1962), p. 160.

[3] *Ibid.*, p. 24.

[4] *Ibid.*

of this mission to the Indians was not only due to Indian independence but equally due to the whites' vision being limited by European Christendom and its colonies, or, more to our point,

> to the general inability of white American Christians to distinguish between their tribal mores and culture and the essential matters of faith.[5]

Aside from these basic peculiarities of the Puritan attitudes, American white folk religion is not understandable apart from the background of slavery in previous human cultures.

It would be difficult to discover in human history a culture without a religious dynamic, or, until relatively recently, one without a slave labor base. It is sufficient to recall that all the great empires of antiquity were built with slave labor. This was no less true of empires from which came the Hebrews and the religion of Judaism. Slave labor from this early time is well documented and the people of Israel themselves were "chosen" while in bondage to Egypt. Their passage from slavery to freedom was within an ancient environment which accepted slavery: their former status as bondmen was not a disadvantage in the development of the Israelite nation. In the pattern of the surrounding empires and monarchies, the Israelite monarchies used slaves who were Hebrews, as well as slaves who were captured or purchased foreigners. There was legislation in Israel protecting Hebrew slaves bought for six-year terms, specifically in the Holiness Codes, whereby these slaves were to be redeemed in the Year of Jubilee through negotiations by relatives or by outright release by their owner. It is clear that the theocracy of Israel did not include the same kind of religio-ethical legislation for non-Israelite slaves; they remained indefinitely in the status of bondmen. While no stigma was attached to a slave who became a free man, slavery was a divisive force even in this theocracy. The clearest example is that of the role slaves played in Solomon's public works at Jerusalem.

This once acceptable but now deplorable prevalence of slavery in the ancient world, inextricably bound up with religious

[5] *Ibid.*, p. 7.

practices, became a custom of the "chosen people" of Old Testament times and continued in New Testament times under the aegis of the "enlightened" Graeco-Roman culture. Throughout the Old Testament and New Testament periods, slavery had no connection with race. Although Jesus Christ's clear intention, without making a reference to slavery, was to unite both "bond" and "free" without respect for race in his Kingdom, the New Testament writers reflected the history of Israel and the dominant Graeco-Roman culture in making no direct attack upon the institution of slavery.

The Christian Church in the West suppressed slavery when it unified governmental and ecclesiastical realms in what is generally known as Christendom.

Slavery remained largely repressed in the West until the sixteenth century, the period of the Roman Catholic-Protestant split, rising nationalism, and colonization from European bases. Roman Catholic colonizers, specifically Spaniards and Frenchmen, were not only steeped in the universalism of Roman Catholic teachings, but were aware of and had been in contact with dark-skinned peoples. Thus, the Spanish and French not only imposed their religion and culture on the Indians in the Americas, but intimately associated with them. Intermarriage with their slaves imported from Africa was not the exception for the Spanish-speaking people. Fundamental to the Spanish colonizers was the understanding of extending the empire and the Church, not of fleeing from either or beginning *de novo*.

The colonizers on our eastern shores were influenced neither by the universal Catholic teachings nor by people of different "races." Certainly, they did not come to these shores for the purpose of extending an empire, but to develop their Puritan Christendom. Among these colonizers were many Englishmen who desired to purify the Church of England which had broken with Roman Catholicism—even more, they were the Congregationalists who were enemies of the state.

Heretofore largely isolated from people of other "races," these English Puritans set out to establish a colony in which they could put into practice their religious and civil rights. They were

also concerned with gain in an economic venture. Believing themselves to be the "new Israel," the "chosen people," they established
a theocracy. But their theocracy differed from that of the "chosen
people" of Israel, whose democratic tendencies were perceived in
"all the people" deciding on national problems in an assembly or
congregation of "all the inhabitants." In ancient Israel the political
authority had rested with the whole people, not a selected few.

Further, Puritans differed from the Israelites in making no
provisions in legislation or religious practices to include concern
and protection for African slaves or Indians. Their theocracy was
highly selective and exclusive even of other Englishmen, and the
"new Israel" simply excluded provisions for the people of other
"races." While the Puritans were able to carry out the European
tradition of white indentured servitude and incorporate the indentured within the body of white outcasts, their narrow-minded personal preoccupation and preference for whites resulted in their
inability to associate with or care for the Africans.

Consequently, the "new Israel" differed from the "old Israel"
not in its acceptance of slavery, but in limiting slavery to Africans
and linking slavery and being African to human inferiority, decadence, depravity, and degradation. For the first time in the establishment of a body politic, slavery became equated with a particular "race" and was tied to being black, with no provision for
release from bondage. Most of all, the kind of intermingling with
people of all different "races" which was characteristic of ancient
Israel and later of Spanish colonizers was treated by Puritans as
anathema.

The exclusiveness of the Puritans even among other Englishmen of white skin is understandable against their background of
politico-socio-religio-economic radicalism. What is difficult to
comprehend is why the Puritans alone developed an ineradicable
anti-blackness. It is necessary, if not sufficient, to point out that
these Englishmen were possessed by a sense of being God's special
people, who took seriously the Calvinistic teachings of predestination so contrary to the beliefs of early Israel, so anti-Catholic
in spirit. To this must be added the ultimate concern of capitalism
and the isolation which had prevented their experiencing in their

history different cultures and "races." "Chosen"—and therefore intolerant—their hope was to break down every barrier which threatened their "calling" to be pure and undefiled.

The Puritans, then, were possessed by a rigidly inflexible religiously based opposition to evil, which was any person or thing foreign to the Puritan mind-set. Given these interrelating forces, it is not difficult to see how the Puritan preoccupation with purity would reject outright even impurity of skin color. While social deviation was here associated not with "race" but with slavery, once the Puritan preoccupation with religious exclusiveness and isolation fastened on this threat of blackness to its purity, it was unshakeable. The interesting term used to designate the slaves and their descendants was, curiously enough, not African, but Negro, directly from Spanish, where "Negro" equals black.

In English black is connected with morbidity and white with virtue. The same semantic significance may be found in other cultural groups, but it is difficult to find another which has made so much of this difference, tied it to one human group and supported it in religio-social covenants. Puritan double mindedness fostered the love of general ideals and principles, the hatred of a specific "race" and culture. To the Puritans Africans were nothing—but why did they and their descendants make so much of nothing?

It is possible to relate the sinister connotations of black and the righteous connotations of white to a preconsciousness fed by the English language. Black is associated with evil: devil, darkness, blackguard, blackball, blacklist, disease, despair, blackout, blackhearted, "the outlook is black," death. White is associated with purity: wedding gowns, angels, clean, white hope, "that is mighty white of you," truth. However, there are positive associations with black: black beauty; and negative associations with white: bloodless or white with rage, pale white. Technically, black is the absence of color, white the presence of color. Although these polarities are discernible in many languages, the question still persists as to why they involve value judgments—"white race," "black race."

The depths of disadvantage which Anglo-Puritans attributed to Negroes and which subsequently resulted in their position can find meaning, finally, only in what we might call an "elective affinity" between *black mystique* and *white mystique,* and the religion of Calvinism. The "new Israel" was fascinated by its special mission not only as the "chosen people," but as one whose very religious understanding demanded no deviation from pride in uniformity. The Hebrew "chosen people" had found themselves a minority in a strange land and therefore had proceeded to adapt to the socio-cultural ways of the dominant Middle East in order to live an exemplary life which would allow them to contribute their unique understanding of God to all mankind. The Puritans, on the other hand, were unable to associate with or adopt from the Indian and African "races," demanding capitulation of both to their culture and religion. As a result, the Indians resisted to the point of extermination or decimation. The Africans remained as the confirming symbol and reinforcement of the Puritan rightness and righteousness. Africans were equally "chosen" as the example *par excellence* of God's special calling to the Puritans. Africans became symbols of the *black mystique* so necessary for the *white mystique.* It is not that the destruction of the African culture and debasement of the Negro was for the Puritan mind-set a psychological crutch or negative base upon which to stand as an assurance of superiority. To the Anglo-Puritans the Negro was no threat. The Negro was rather a presence over and against which the virtues of Puritanism could be hammered out into the shape preconceived. Negroes were human resources "chosen" for the purposes of Puritan re-making, the surest sign of present evil and the test of righteousness. To accept the Negro would be to accept evil. The Negro could only be allowed that much positiveness to affirm the progressive faithfulness of the Puritans—thus, slavery was eventually condemned—but not enough to permit his disappearance as a sign of the Kingdom's arrival and the loss of special work for the Puritans to do—thus, the Negro could never be accepted as equal.

This is the *black mystique,* the absolute necessity of the absolute presence of the devil to be conquered, isolated, whereby the *white mystique* might rule forever in righteousness. The pervasive influence of the Puritan mind-set—the need for the Negro as the devil and personification of evil—was increased with the breakup of the Puritan establishment and was carried out to extremes in the South and West. In the South there was the greatest deviation from Puritan purity. There they were tempted by the devil and enticed into intimate relations with him, quite opposite from that of the Puritan unwillingness to freely associate with the Negro even in his own bailiwick of pitch blackness. Perhaps no clearer example is present than that of the Puritan dimension reflected in the Mormons' lack of full acceptance of the Negro as a brother who cannot expect participation at all levels. Mormons are the most Calvinistic and least Christian body in America, in theory as well as practice.

If there is any question about whether the authoritarian, aristocratic establishment of America's white folk religion and culture superseded the diminished but ever-present strains of religious liberty and equal justice in the founding of the nation, the experience of the Negro dispels it. For while the original form of white folk religion meant the elimination of the unuseful Indians, its continuation in the Creed of what Lerner calls the "American metaphysic of promise" and the "metaphysic of Christianity" resulted in the destruction of the useful African and his transformation into the depressed Negro. The attempt to civilize the Negro compartmentally with separate standards within the Protestant "metaphysic"—promise and Christianity—gave rise first to the establishment by Negroes of their own churches and finally the civil protest.

White folk religion, involving the tyranny of the minority, "Puritan statecraft," and capitalism, is the myth of America as the land of the free and the home of the brave, no less than as a Christian nation, but only for the established few. The interaction of Puritan-Anglican disestablishment and revivalism (mass evangelism, home missions, orthodoxy, voluntary membership) in the old colonies took the form of "Christianizing" the majority of common people. These earliest revivals had as their target the whole man and the whole society; the appeal was enthusiasm and emotionalism, rejected by the intellectual elite. Here we have an example of what E. Digby Baltzell calls "the conflict between the divisive forces of caste" which seek to maintain a white Anglo-Saxon Protestant (WASP) "monopoly of upper class institutions,"

> and the cohesive forces of aristocracy which ideally call for gradually evolving upper class institutions that constantly assimilate new men of talent and power, regardless of ethnic or racial origins.[6]

Abraham Lincoln perceived the logic of this "nativism and racialism":

> Our progress in degeneracy appears to me to be pretty rapid. As a nation, we begin by declaring "all men are created equal." We now practically read it "all men are created equal, except Negroes." When the Know-Nothings get control, it will read "all men are created equal, except Negroes, and foreigners, and Catholics." [7]

Despite the noble attempt to redeem the common man in New England, the earliest revivalists provided no sustained effort on behalf of the Negro, and certainly not with the thought of full equality or full freedom.

White folk religion did not die with the disestablishment and the New England revivals. Those who fled westward to the frontiers were no more devoted to the principles of Christian liberty and the brotherhood of all Christians than were their oppressors. They sought their own brand of liberty and set up the outposts of Puritan statecraft. They were even more intolerant of nonconformity and legislated for a white Protestant morality:

> What H. L. Mencken resented and repudiated in "Keokuk, Iowa," was the same stark righteousness and unflagging industry, aesthetic barrenness and latent intolerance which earlier critics had found so unattractive in New England Christendom.[8]

That white folk religion is endemic to America is incontrovertible. Unlike the biblical faith, which was left on the ideal plane, white

---

[6] E. Digby Baltzell, *The Protestant Establishment: Aristocracy and Caste in America* (New York: Random House, 1964), p. 24.

[7] Quoted in Baltzell, *op. cit.*, p. 25.

[8] Littell, *op. cit.*, p. 61.

folk religion became the practice which all but obscured the brotherhood of man emphasis in the Bible. This practice or detailed application of irrational color prejudice is what I mean by America's preconscious white folk religion.

The obtuseness of white folk religion, what is termed "culture religion," is of primary importance precisely because Littell's distinction cannot be sustained:

> Discrimination against American Negroes in the churches and in society at large are two different issues, and require different solutions, although both are products of cultural norms rather than the Christian faith or democratic tradition.[9]

The entire society is shot through with this preconscious Calvinism, the white Church cannot dislodge it from its midst without eliminating it from the society.

Puritan white folk religion—hypocrisy—began with what Alexis de Tocqueville called intelligent, well ordered, moral men of Europe "known for their talents and their acquirements," who sought in the new world a place "where they could live according to their own principles." These principles led on the one hand to the Congregational covenant, interpreted by Perry Miller to be a "theory of society" constituted "out of the consent of the governed" and the "pre-stated terms of God's eternal law of justice and subordination," [10] articulated in John Winthrop's "model of Christian charity":

> By the first of these laws [nature and grace], man, as he was enabled so, withal [is] commanded to love his neighbor as himself; upon this ground stand all the precepts of the moral law, which concerns our dealing with men. To apply this to the works of mercy, this law requires two things: first, that every man afford his help to another in every want or distress; secondly, that he perform this out of the same affection which makes him careful of his own good according to that our savior (Matt. 7. 12): "Whatsoever ye would that men should do to you." [11]

[9] *Ibid.*, p. 133.

[10] Perry Miller, *The American Puritans* (New York: Anchor Books, 1956), p. 78.

[11] *Ibid.*, p. 80.

In this portion of what Miller authoritatively designates "the fundamental document for comprehending the Puritan mind," the legalistic-ethical-theological covenant applied only to the recognized "fellow members of Christ." For on the other hand, those who compacted under the two rules of justice and mercy, "whereby we are to walk, one towards another," found no difficulty with their Indian "neighbors" although the Indians threatened their determination "to live according to their own principles." To be sure, the Puritans did not, like the Spaniards, pursue "the Indians with blood hounds, like wild beasts," nor provide the survivors of their massacres the pleasure of mixing with these conquerors. The Puritan ethical attachment "to the formalities of law" would permit only the "brotherly assistance" of the Indians "to a grave." *White folk religion* is subtly set forth in all its irony by de Tocqueville:

> The Spaniards were unable to exterminate the Indian race by those unparalleled atrocities which brand them with indelible shame, nor did they even succeed in wholly depriving it of its rights; but the Americans of the United States have accomplished this twofold purpose with singular felicity; tranquilly, legally, philanthropically, without shedding blood, and without violating a single great principle of morality in the eyes of the world. It is impossible to destroy men with more respect for the laws of humanity.[12]

Insofar as the brotherhood emphasis of the Bible has been tempered by puritanical white folk religion, it has contaminated the entire society and culture. Unable to tame the Indians, Puritan principles effected their physical expulsion, a pattern which continued on the frontier to the West and South. While not exterminating the Negro, either, he was kept in limited numbers and at a distance.

There was a peculiar trait in the colonizing Englishmen of abhorring both violence and people of different races. The principle of freedom was cherished, but not the practice of equality.

[12] Alexis de Tocqueville, *Democracy in America* (New York: Schocken Books, Henry Reeve (tr.), 1964), Vol. I, p. 423.

European Spaniards and Frenchmen viciously abused Indians and Negroes but intimately mixed with them in love and marriage. European Englishmen rigidly restrained their involvement with Negroes to legal and proper formal situations without informal or social relationships. The covenanted modes of equal justice, mercy, and love were reserved by Englishmen for selected Englishmen and Europeans. Obviously, Negroes were no threat to the Puritans, nor from the beginning can it be maintained Puritans were white supremacists in any racist sense—only in a religious sense. What issued in white folk religion, taking precedence over principles inextricably bound in theological and political covenants, grace, and nature, were the more fundamental presuppositions of economic gain—"pride of origin" and "personal pride." De Tocqueville capsulizes the British Puritan spirit, which is the most powerful influence that Englishmen have stamped upon the social and cultural life of America: "The white citizen of the United States is proud of his race, and proud of himself." [13] This can be translated as white folk religion, more salient than creeds or the Creed in which it is not stated and need not be; it is preconscious.

If this conclusion is correct it means that the Puritan mainstream religion of theologico-ethical-social covenants was rooted in the creation of the one god—capital—not in the universality of the Creator. Thus, the Calvinistic orientation of predestination was reinforced at least as regards the Negro. It became the priority of being white, English, and European. Against this background of pride, the emerging floodtide of white folk religion makes understandable its logical fulfillment on the American frontier, West and South. At bottom, the gods of capital and clan gave ultimate sanction and meaning to a religion *for* whites and *against* Indians and Negroes.

Those white frontier settlers not fortunate enough to be gentlemen, educated, and bearers of past accomplishments, formed the majority who were excluded from socio-religious compacts through which the colonies were managed. The less favored majority was powerless, without official membership in the congrega-

[13] *Ibid.*, p. 446.

tions or representation in the civil government. The majority of frontier Englishmen learned the ways of power control from the aristocratic elite and their inclination toward "pride of origin" was reinforced by the same behavior patterns.

Max Lerner states the thesis that America represents three centuries of dynamic revolution, New England being its source and support. This thesis is borne out in the case of the oppressed Protestant majority which fled the aristocratic hegemony of the East. The Puritan exclusiveness and establishment was so inherent that the oppressed sought not so much freedom in principle as freedom to live according to their own dictates, in much the same way as their oppressors. As with the Puritan oligarchy in the East, their successors in the West continued the pattern of establishing churches which dominated the cultural, moral, and educational life of the frontier.

Instead of the vehement theological-ethical covenants of the sophisticated elite, frontier white Protestantism concentrated on the moral deviations of the common individual. "Emotionalism" and "enthusiasm" were the tools of revivalism, substituted for covenants. Rather than perceiving frontiersmen as the majority of those who were not included in New England Christendom, the churches operated from the "myth of America as a 'Christian nation'" which it was their business to reinstitute. There was "no intention of abandoning the civilizing function of Christianity, of giving up the dream of America as a Christian nation." [14]

This white mission of civilizing continued the spirit of the Puritans in finalizing the work they had begun on the Indians. The way became that of removals and reservations, augmented by

the Puritan assurance of an inner rightness of purpose, plus the 100 per-centism of the Yankee spirit of "go" and "get," plus the land hunger of the pioneer and the profit hunger of the land speculator, plus the dynamism of the "west-ward course of empire" and the doctrine of America's "Manifest Destiny." [15]

[14] Littell, *op. cit.*, p. 59.
[15] Lerner, Vol. I, p. 13.

With the Indians out of sight, if not out of mind, Protestants maintained their churches as the courts of justice, passing judgment on drunkenness, fornication, easy living, business dishonesty, and disorderly walking. Without doubt, Littell's observation that the churches rendered a valuable service is accurate.

However, the values of revivalism and mainstream religion became dissipated in the equation of genuine religion with moral crusades. Moral crusades were the breeding grounds for intolerance and conformity, even more oppressive than their forerunners. In this soil white religion flowered as Protestant nativism and moralism and its seeds were sown over the land. White folk religion sought through the power structures of government and churches, and even through clandestine movements, to maintain the good old white Protestant society. As a result, white folk religion is basically anti-Negro.

This colonial and frontier tribalism is most ominous today in the negative response to the Negro Protestants who on the basis of principled biblical religion would appear to have an advantage over other so-called non-nativist groups. Will Herberg's sociological analysis of white Protestantism as the great "transmuting pot" shaping the form and content of Roman Catholics and Jews contends that in this "pot" the characteristic American "ethnic and cultural integration" takes place:

> The principle by which men identify themselves and are identified, locate themselves, and are located, in the social whole is neither "race" (except for Negroes and those of Oriental origin) nor ethnic-immigrant background (except for recent arrivals) but religious community.[16]

If America is religiously based and determined in the present as in the past, that religion is not faith nor the principles of biblical religion but the strength of white folk religion—what Herberg calls "the American Way of life" or "American religion"—among both "religionists" and "secularists" which rules the Negro an exception. White folk religion is a part of the warp and woof of

[16] Will Herberg, *Protestant, Catholic, Jew.* (New York: Doubleday, 1953), p. 50.

America, and it is on the increase in spite of the fact that the principles of biblical religion and democracy are also rising. Baltzell makes this clear in the present organized efforts "to retain social power within a castelike social stratum," to the disdain of the liberal democratic and authoritarian aristocratic equilibrium. Nothing could be clearer than the "liberal democratic" dismissal as harmless of the white America which has not perceived the Negro as an acceptable individual, as well as his protection of past privileges and prestige in a degenerate caste system. Moreover, the "gentlemenly racism and nativism" of a "closed WASP upper class," white folk religion is unique in its origin and continuation:

> The Negroes in America are, of course, faced with equally important, and far more acute, problems, but their total situation —and the test of our moral conscience posed by it—is for the moment quite different from that of the Jews, and far too complex to be dealt with here.[17]

Like most white liberals, Oscar Handlin's silent assumption is that Negroes are like all other minorities and share the same fate and possibilities. The elite individual exceptions and general progress he sees ignore the crucial differences which distinguish the Negro-white relationship from that of any other minority experience.[18]

Kenneth K. Bailey does not connect the hegemony of English Puritanism and its reestablishment in the South as the singular factor making race relations

> the one problem which most unsettled—and indeed—imperiled —the southern churches.[19]

Bailey sets forth the cause in socio-economic terms, which are here perceived as the symptoms of the more pervasive white folk religion. He does perceive "the determination to keep the South

[17] Baltzell, op. cit., p. x.

[18] Oscar Handlin, Fire-Bell in the Night: The Crisis in Civil Rights (Boston: Little, Brown and Company, 1964).

[19] Kenneth K. Bailey, Southern White Protestantism in the Twentieth Century (New York: Harper and Row, 1964), p. 136.

a white man's country" in his approval of Ulrich B. Phillips's conclusion that such determination "is the cardinal test of a Southerner and the central theme of Southern history." [20]

White folk religion, the priority of the white mystique, is like a malignant tumor American Protestants have always harbored with the aid of the irrational preconscious religion of Calvinism. This tumor is not to be identified with the cancerous condition of the cultural invasion of non-biblical religion which spreads or is arrested in different generations depending upon the regenerative powers of genuine religion in any given epoch. There are a host of critics within the churches concerned to renew biblical religion by calling it away from the present "religion of democracy," the attitude of "religion in general," "maturing national religion," "overemphasis on man's chummy relation to God," "temptation to elevate an attitude toward religion to religious ultimacy,"—from "faith as a sure-fire device to get what we want" which reassures us about "the essential rightness of everything American":

> In this kind of religion there is no sense of transcendence, no sense of the nothingness of man and his works before a holy God; in this kind of religion the values of life, and life itself, are not submitted to Almighty God to judge, to shatter, and to reconstruct; on the contrary, life, and the values of life, are given an ultimate sanction by being identified with the divine. In this kind of religion it is not man who serves God, but God who is mobilized and made to serve man and his purposes— whether these purposes be economic, property, free enterprise, social reform, democracy, happiness, security, or "peace of mind." [21]

White folk religion is an entirely different phenomenon from the failure of white Protestants to realize their biblical faith in daily practice among whites. There is a biblical standard which is known and brought to bear upon these deviations. There are implicit possibilities for renewal and the straightening out of en-

[20] *Ibid.*, p. 160.
[21] Herberg, *op. cit.*, p. 285.

tanglements, a continuous process facing each generation. Even if it were possible, as it is not, to straighten out biblical religion by the unsnarling of non-biblical religion in a given generation, this would occur among whites only without any bearing upon the elimination of Negroes from their sphere of concern.

White Christians and white congregations can be and are being challenged through the constant reopening of clogged channels which permit only a trickle of biblical religion to flow into its subsidiary streams. These subsidiary streams—suburban-urban, rural, or regionally-oriented culture congregations—may ignore or defy biblical religion but they cannot long endure without being affected by its outreach in the form of seminary graduates, lay movements, ecumenical endeavors, and theological journals. All of these are informed by new demands in the new age, and it is they who are the forces for renewal of white congregations.

The malignancy of white folk religion as it is disseminated means that in addition to the indispensable efforts of renewal within white congregations there is required a reordering, a reformation, a restructuring of the most radical (root) nature if the values of biblical religion are not to be denied whites or reserved for whites alone. The renewal of society is constantly necessary because life is always a tension between good and evil —there can be no evil without good and no good without evil in human society. The principle of renewal is a realistic one which alone is not deluded by the false hope of eliminating evil and perpetuating good. Rather, the escalating possibilities of good and evil following the meeting of them on one stage of life calls for a new form of response to good and resisting evil in each succeeding stage. The objective of the present is to equalize the opportunities for obtaining the good and overcoming the evil. The Negro does not have this equal opportunity either in the churches of whites or in other institutions which dominate this culture-society, nor will he gain it through their renewal.

Eradicating white folk religion is far less possible than the renewal of white institutions which deviate from the biblical-democratic mainstream. Indeed, it is not necessary, for the history of America has shown that whites can defy their verbal commitments in relation to their white god and white brothers. Neverthe-less, the eradication of white folk religion is indispensable because it is the undeniable demand of this new historical era which can no longer be disregarded. It is a far more formidable demand than the constant necessity of renewing and restructuring. The King-dom of God will not thereby come in, good and evil will remain in tension, but men will face an old human problem here re-pressed and this release will provide more energy to meet the new human problems that call forth the concerted resources of all human beings which cannot be met by a caste-like establish-ment of white minorities.

The elimination of white folk religion will be most difficult for whites since it is a fundamental tenet of their preconscious-ness. Only if Negroes will do battle to the death with white folk religion can it be eliminated. The loss of racial pride, which now comes from Godliness, will mean the confrontation of biblical religion with just human defiance, and a real gain in human re-sponsibility. There is an increasing number of whites who are ready to go beyond the acceptance of the few exceptional Negroes. Paralleling this drive to overcome white folk religion is the in-creasing resistance among Negroes to the responsibilities of real humanness. Whites' preference for whites, less articulated in the present but just as real as in the past, is yet to be matched by blacks' preference for blacks, which will be fully articulated in the future if it is to be a dynamic force for the oneness with all Americans. The advantage of the Negro is that he is both an African and a European in blood and culture, an undeniable real-ity which conflicts with the rising attempt of whites and Negroes to make of him a pure entity rather than the hybrid he is. To live in both worlds at once is the Negro's responsibility, a de-manding and exciting one which it is hoped *The Politics of God* will both illuminate and support.

CHAPTER V
PRECONSCIOUS WHITE FOLK ETHICS

CONTEMPORARY THEOLOGIANS have described religion as an ultimate concern which may be a preference for a god or gods instead
of God. This we have seen to be the case with irrational color
prejudice, the preconscious religion of Calvinism, and preference
for whites. Because so many contemporary Christian ethicists
have declared much of our culture to be concern with gods rather
than God, we naturally look to them to provide even stronger
leadership than their secular rational scientist and rational moralist counterparts. But in a different way and for different reasons
they, too, harbor western values and hold them in higher esteem
than the biblical tradition.

Theologians with an ethical bent have been influential within
the confines of ecclesiastical circles vis-à-vis the culture-religion
of whites. Their impact has been primarily in the sphere of social
action, rather than social change. Social action among Protestant
ethicists is clearest historically in response to the privatism and
individualism of that form of revivalism which turned from interest in changing society to problems of personal morals while the
"Social Gospel" is the rubric under which public issues took
precedence over the subjectivism and individualism that centered
upon tobacco, alcohol, dancing, and light living. The "Social
Gospel" is a century old movement which has sought through the
norm of the Kingdom of God to "Christianize" America's economics, politics and culture by spotlighting the issues of labor,
business, "race relations," war and peace. With exceptions of
various points in this century, the "Social Gospel" movement has

largely served as a rallying point of new thinking and acting among churchmen, but with little effect in changing the society. The "Social Gospel" corrected Protestant moralism in

> the posture of churches which speak to and for the whole population in the same tone of voice which they direct to their own membership, . . . the attitude of religious bodies which have come to think of themselves as the religious voice of a society.[1]

But it did not correct the assumption of a Christian ethic which was knowable and realizable for the society as a whole, nor its base in white folk religion. The tension between the Kingdom of God and the ethics of white folk religion was hardly perceived, and where perceived was a minor note.

The most vehement critic of Protestant moralism and the Social Gospel, Reinhold Niebuhr, who has had more impact upon American politics than any other Protestant ethicist, rejected the previous emphasis upon "Christianizing" America, replacing it with a concern for justice. The potential for challenging white folk religion was latent in Niebuhr, but white folk religion and its ethics were not challenged by this great prophet. Presently, Niebuhr's ethical perspective looms large for those who seek either to go beyond his espousal of Neo-orthodoxy or to counter it. In any case, the fundamental problem of questioning the presuppositions of whites in America, the beginning for any real impact upon congregations in particular and the society in general, has not been the work of many Christian ethicists.

Most Christian ethicists affirm that there are many ethical possibilities besides Christian ethics, or a single norm within Christian ethics, in our pluralistic society. Thus, it would appear obvious and natural for Christian ethicists to deal substantively with the human issue of Negro-white divisions. There are many points of view which can be carried forth with equal worth as regards economics, politics, war, and peace, without being in violation of the Kingdom of God. Differences will and ought to exist with regard to patterns of socio-economic, cultural be-

[1] Littell, *op. cit.,* pp. 97, 163.

havior. In the sphere of utility, it is difficult to perceive what unique offering Christians have, or for that matter, any real change they can or ought to bring about. The Kingdom of God does not presuppose Christian economics, Christian politics, Christian technology. The Kingdom of God *does* presuppose the acceptance and equality of all human groups by each human group within each and every socio-cultural pattern. The division of Negroes and whites in America is a direct contradiction of the Kingdom of God. It is, moreover, the only problem of group living to which the Christian bodies can make a contribution to the society at large through precept and example.

Nevertheless, the preconscious white folk religion remains because it has not been consciously dealt with, because it has not been eliminated from the preconscious stream of religion teachers and preachers, administrators and laymen.

Clearly, it is difficult to distinguish between the scholar and layman who is engaged in the teaching and practice of Christian ethics. Professor Paul Ramsey has reminded us that "every Christian is to some degree a Christian ethicist," responsible for the living, transmission, interpretation, and direction of the Christian life.[2] Insofar as the academic Christian ethicist is here singled out for criticism, it is due to his commitment as a professional to teaching and practicing Christian living. It is this professional group which has been insensitive to the freedom and equality themes of the Kingdom of God, the unitive themes which demand social change beyond "social action." It is a matter of record that the source of American dynamism by which the Anglo-Saxons dominated the society on the strength of white folk religion is the same source of Anglo-Puritan ethics—the North, specifically the Northeast. Here, too, white folk religion continues to avoid the substantive issue so imperative for social change in harmony with the Kingdom of God. The South has always been and continues to be a reaction to the dynamic spirit of the North, both in things spiritual and material.

The substantive issue, that of the brotherhood of man in-

[2] Paul Ramsey, *Christian Ethics and the Sit-in* (New York: Association Press, 1961), p. xvi.

extricably one with the Kingdom of God in America, must involve the complete acceptance of the Negro group. In the past and present, spokesmen for Christian ethics have taught, in all-white institutions whose exceptions proved the rule, a white folk religion which at best permitted concentration upon the single Negro as an example. There are many ethicists who can claim the acceptance of a Negro as an individual in every primary, voluntary, or private association, possibly excepting the family. With individual Negroes there has been healthy social intercourse without the general inferiority-superiority exclusiveness. But the acceptance of an individual Negro is not the substantive issue which faces Christian ethics. It is the deghettoizing of *all* Negroes and freeing them from this spiritual-psychological-physical status deprivation that is the issue. Yet, Christian ethicists generally have not been ruled by the Kingdom of God theme. Nor can they be free for the Kingdom of God until white folk religion is disintegrated, which cannot be accomplished apart from the concomitant deghettoizing of all Negroes. This accomplishment is not alone the peculiar province of law, business, labor, politics, economics or the federal-national-local governments and all their equal opportunity achievements. For the heart of the American dynamic is religion. Thus the full acceptance of the Negro group is the concern of the ethicists, who have been more concerned to speak within a segregating-discriminating ethos than to run the risks involved in changing it; and it must be their concern even to the extent of losing a place in the kingdom of this world for atonement with the Kingdom of God. Indeed, because religion is so crucial in this society, profane and demonic as it may be, and because the exclusion of the Negro group is so acute a malaise in the churches *as* the society, the responsibility belongs especially to Christian ethics. Insofar as we have moved, or are in the process of moving, from a Protestant-dominated, through a pluralistically religious, to a secular-dominated society, Christian ethicists are in a position to facilitate the demise of the anti-Kingdom of God force, white folk religion.

Since Christian ethicists are involved in the *ethos* which takes precedence in white folk religion over the *mythos* (e.g., the

Kingdom of God theme in the living words of Jesus), they are not free for the *kairos* (e.g., that time of God's choosing when the conditions are right for human acceptance of humanity). Without spelling out the various manifestations, the essence of this *ethos* in Negro-white group relations can be abbreviated in nativism and racialism, so subtle among these white Christian thinkers.

Bearing in mind the presupposition of the writer that the North is the pacesetter for America in religion as elsewhere, the white folk religion of Christian ethical teachers may be generalized through two dominant motifs. One motif of white ethicists is that the problem of Negro-white relations has been solved for the Church and society, meaning that from a theological-theoretical perspective a consensus has been gained, leaving only the task of putting it into practice through the various agencies of society. This is the white liberal line which marvels at the unprecedented opportunities granted to a minority of the minority. This view borders on the ghetto element in white folk religion, gradualism through inserting into society a few Negroes at a time, and is blind to the substantive problem of deghettoizing all Negroes who are in bondage regardless of their earning power.

Another motif of white ethicists is that Negro-white problems are not settled but they have had their day in Christian ethics, which must now get on to something else. From a practical point of view the standpoint is that the direct action of students and laymen has been so extensive as to make teaching and preachments little more than sounding brass and tinkling cymbals in the hollow church chambers. What is ignored or misunderstood is the difference between social action and social change. With all of the social action in civil rights, there has not resulted the deghettoizing of the Negro, the central problem in the North which the South is just now learning.

These two misleading motifs are instructive as to the restlessness of quixotic ethicists who cannot wait to be on the frontier of other issues, as well as their failure to see that all other issues in which they can be effective are dependent upon effecting changes in Negro-white group relationships. The sparse participation of laymen in social action and the resistance of the majority is over-looked. The timidity and fear of Northern pastors and laymen are further implications of these motifs. Most of all, Christian ethi-cists are not the bearers of the prophetic movement in this era. Freedom, justice, and equality among human beings of different groups have been doled out to the Negro, while white ethicists turn to minute implications of ideal freedom and equality. Chris-tian ethicists are deeply involved in and responsible for the con-dition of this era, "when truth is without passion, and passion is without truth," a criticism Karl Marx made of his time.

When one seeks to discover the internal procedures and inter-ests of Christian ethicists which prevent their leadership in de-ghettoizing the Negro, and releasing themselves from white folk religion, the lack of a definition of Christian ethics looms as a barrier. Here one is forced to interpret ethics as the practice of and reflection upon human behavior from the perspective of the Christian tradition for the purposes of responsible personal in-volvement, transmitting the tradition, and clarifying the con-tinuing and contemporary issues, and developing guidelines or strategies to effect social change. The weakness of Christian ethics in America has been in the area of group conflicts. This weakness is embedded in the basic components of Christian ethics: theo-logical biblical reflection, philosophical models, and socio-eco-nomic political strategies. It is not difficult to see that the com-petitive academic pressure to develop a respectable discipline is exhausting, demanding energies which churn out theories that are expended in action without change. Christian ethicists should have much to contribute in leading us out of the black and white ghet-tos, but like so many Americans their love of knowledge and their awareness of the human sacrifices of others have not trans-formed their awareness into responsibility.

Mainstream Protestant theology distinguishes between the order of Creation, the order of nature, and the order of politics. The order of creation, in which the intention of God and man were one, has been radically severed in this aeon after the "Fall." Though the order of nature remains the same, as well as the inten-tion of God that man control it, there is no direct reestablishment of the original order of creation by man through his control over the order of nature. Thus, in the time between Creation and its fulfillment in the Kingdom, God is at work but his purposes are not carried forth "onward and upward" by His human creations. Progress in subduing and controlling nature is seen in Christian ethics to be confused with progress in attunement with the order of creation. The key word is *order*. In this aeon of "hardheartedness," as Jesus described the time after Creation and before the realized rule or Kingdom of God, complicity in sin (in which human interests take priority over and therefore are in conflict with the purpose of God) is inescapable. Therefore, in order to exist at all among conflicting human interests with little relation or attunement to the order of creation, the universality of sin makes necessary, though not sufficient, the order of politics.

The tradition of the Church as the repository of theology and its implications for society together with American Protestantism's historic ties to governmental authorities have aided the mainstream tendency toward conservatism. These factors—the concrete expressions of a white society for whites—are seen as needing restructuring along white premises. Failing to effect the economic changes once called for by the "Social Gospel" there has resulted the acceptance of order for whites that ruled out radical (root) changes in society with regard to the group contradictions among whites and Negroes. Even the liberal thread running throughout reveals a belief in the myth that white groups and Negro groups are not inevitable; the differences are to be overcome without conflict through the upgrading of individuals.

From the hypothesis that order is fundamental in a "fallen world," it is projected that the current order of Negro-white group disorder is preferable and necessary. It is but a step from this projection to that of this present order as the only order possible. Subsequently, it might be projected that the present order is to be conserved or cautiously modified, and that injustices are inevitable for groups as well as individuals, for otherwise there will be no order.

On the one hand, the present order is not viewed as less than the best order. The changes brought about through the courts are proof of the good intentions and possibilities. The more conservative of the conservatives take the view that the disorderly civil rights movement exemplified by Martin Luther King, Jr. is disruptive because it leads to widespread lawlessness, giving birth to student riots and other fringe actions, when the maintenance of law and order through support of the courts is as far as the Christian ethicists should go. It is assumed that Negroes are better off or will be when the laws shake down into the local communities, a liberal view which overlooks the American tendency to disregard law when it conflicts with white folk religion.

On the other hand, the goals of the present order are considered realized through the civil rights movement because it is within the bounds of the tradition. Were Christian ethicists to take the route of national boycotts or press for social change via hardnosed pursuits that alone can result in deghettoizing the Negro, this would be unacceptable.

On the whole, Christian ethicists do not support, let alone initiate, changes which would transform this order. Loyalty to this order, not to the order of creation or to the Kingdom of God, binds Christian ethicists. The doctrine that man is inescapably involved in sin becomes associated with the need for order and confused with the support of the current order. Negro-white group strains are seen as evidence of inescapable human entanglements, not of the opportunity for relieving an unnecessary burden from their sheer human-versus-human conflicts of interest. The conclusion is that all men are involved in sin, the Negro is a man and so is involved in sin, and since sin is sin and not to be graded, the suffering of the Negro is just another instance of sin. Implicit throughout this conservatism of liberal whites is a vision of the Negro as an individual, without awareness of the ghetto from which no Negro can escape. Therefore, the radical restructuring of order to eliminate the exceptional injustices to the whole Negro group is either not considered, or if it is, it is ruled out.

This white folk ethical predisposition to emphasize stability is further extended through philosophical models that support particular interpretations of white folk ethics. Theology and philosophy are mutually supportive of the white mystique. A typology of several significant philosophical models current in the dominant group illustrates the rationale for which deghettoizing is not a live option.

The typology of these models includes legalism (natural law ethics), organicism (teleological ethics), situationalism (pragmatic ethics), and mechanism (orthodox ethics). These philosophical models are not descriptive of any particular system of individual ethicists *in toto;* they are suggestive of the various models selected by various theological schools: Calvinists, Arminians, Anabaptists, and Lutherans.

In legalism or formalism, Aristotelian or Platonic, there is an underlying affirmation of classical idealism. The good can be known from past experience and realized through obedience to the predetermined law of reason, nature, duty, or God. These ideals tend toward theistic and natural law theories of Christian ethics and often betray a static model. Underlying formalism is an idealistic monism that exists and needs only to be perceived, rather than a dynamic process of increasing, infinite complexity. Those who are top dogs are apt to handle this perspective more easily than the underdog.

Situationalism tends toward radical individualism, radical pluralism, without any connection between what occurs in one section of the country or the world and another. It is situational —each situation is to be determined on its own merits. Its strength lies in pragmatism, thus action. Its weakness is the isolation of complex human persons and structures and their interaction. The problem of groupness rather than individuality for the Negro cannot thereby be fully conceived. Reformation theologies and the free churches often find support in this philosophical model.

Organicism emphasizes an emerging unity, an example of which is American Personalism, and is strong on the dynamic nature of man. It tends toward an indefinite, growing, and, therefore, unlimited view of what man is or will be prior to experience. Here the emphasis is upon evolutionary human developments. Its idealism tends to unity and shuns the real disunity of groups.

The fourth traditional model is mechanism, either absolute

determinism and prediction or the relative mechanism of inde-
terminancy and probability, whereby prediction is certain within
a margin of error. Mechanism is the expression of contemporary
evangelical conservatives, with extreme emphasis upon the individual, in total ignorance of complex socio-cultural forces.

With the exception of mechanism, these models have inherent
capacities for restructuring the present order to meet the present
needs of Negro-white groups. They are, however, so encrusted by
traditional interpretations of theology and philosophy that they
are not free to develop in this environment their creative possibilities. Thus, the following is too often the case:

> The moralist—philosopher or theologian—following in Plato's
> footsteps—without possessing Plato's boundless imagination—
> thinks it appropriate to impose upon life itself those checks and
> counterchecks by which an enlightened society protects itself
> against itself. He mistakes the necessary but superficial and
> unstable order of organized society for a metaphysical reality.
> He rarely questions the values of a given situation radically—
> he leaves that, unlike Plato, to the prophets. He is concerned
> with teaching men how to fit into the given civilization, how to
> accept, uphold and preserve it—often far beyond the time of its
> usefulness.[3]

Given a theological presupposition of a sinful world which
must be tolerated even without the insecurity of radical social
change, the strategy of Christian ethicists is already predetermined. Then, in addition to theological and philosophical ground-
ings, the academic Christian ethicist is usually an expert in a
discipline such as political science, sociology, law, or psychology.
Out of these triple perspectives a stance evolves. Since most social
sciences tend to be long on analysis and short on direct changes,
it is not surprising to discover that Christian ethicists have not
relieved the poverty of directions for fundamental alteration of
society by calling into question the white mystique.

Since Niebuhr's *Moral Man and Immoral Society,* no major
theological work has contributed to a constructive change in

[3] Werner and Lotte Pelz, *God Is No More* (Philadelphia: J. B. Lippincott
Co., 1964), p. 37.

Negro-white ghetto imprisonment. At best there have been moral reflections upon actions of the past by academicians. The non-violent protests suggested by Reinhold Niebuhr reflected the action of Gandhi and have been finely worked by Martin Luther King, Jr. But they were directed toward the South, which in fact takes its lead from the dynamic North, while adding demonic conclusions. The North has considerable basic work to do, and yet no strategy for the North has been set forth. The dearth of leadership among northern Christian ethicists in Negro-white group relations has resulted in a widespread status quo, which King is attempting to fill in Chicago. Even Reinhold Niebuhr took the position that Negro-white tensions were too tough to shape creatively, a position which has remained predominant among academic Christian ethicists.

The white social order, strengthened by theology, philosophy, and social science, has resulted in no real deghettoizing. Influential scholars have misunderstood, ignored, rejected, or misconceived the substantive issue of the Negro-white dichotomy.

Christian ethicists have not seriously questioned the present order and its irreparable detriment to white society and the Negro. In this racist society, Christian ethicists have been unable to accept the value and necessity of force. François La Rochefoucauld's (1613–80) secular doctrine of man is still with us and parallels at many points the Protestant doctrine of selfishness as the center of all human behavior. His suggestion for transmuting this human propensity is in direct conflict with the Protestant view of order: "Right and might rule the world; fight till right is ready." This suggestion of force is in fact more valuable as regards a realistic approach to Negro-white groups than the following Protestant perspective:

> The primacy of order to justice, and, as we have indicated, of tolerable justice to any order, can never be forgotten by the Christian who knows the basic conditions for the external possibility of any fellow humanity's being assured under God's governance of this central world.[4]

[4] Ramsey, *op. cit.*, p. 119.

Rochefoucauld recognized power as inevitable and justice as indispensable in human affairs, implying an emphasis added in Niebuhr's celebrated dictum:

> Man's capacity for justice makes democracy possible; but man's inclination to injustice makes democracy necessary.

Force is inevitable in democracy, not antithetical to it. But traditionally, force has been more accidental than planned.

It is imperative to go to Karl Marx for a positive view of force or power, missing from Protestant ethicists. Marx was perceptive of the role of force inherent in the historical process on the way to his version of the Kingdom of God—the classless society. However, Marx did not commit himself to the position of force as the only method for maintaining the truly human society. Marx put it this way: "Force is the midwife of every old society pregnant with a new one."

Emmanuel Mounier provides further light for the value of force so alien to Christian ethicists. It is difficult to ignore him when he reminds us that St. Thomas Aquinas understood magnanimity to be a component of force:

> A secret bond is thus affirmed which unites force to the splendor of the world and the generosity of the heart. It is more than Christian realism, it is Christian humanism in all its largeness as born of this matrix. Force is of its nature at once the solidity and the abundance of all reality. Tension of being, it is the stuff of space. Patience of waiting, it is the stuff of time. Triumphant over death, it is the servant of the eternal.[5]

Force or power is alien to white folk ethics when the issue of Negro-white group conflict is considered, though the use of governmental authority is not, since power has been for the white majority. Christian ethicists contribute less than is possible to the adjudication of ethnic tensions not only because of the disinclination toward force but also because of the tendency to perpetuate the stereotype of "race." Christian ethicists use the

---

[5] Emmanuel Mounier, *The Spoil of the Violent,* reprinted in *Cross Currents,* Vol. XI, Nos. 1–3, 1961, p. 48.

notion of "race relations" because it is popular and widely understood to signify Negro-white relations. "Race" automatically
means the Negro in America, an indication of his perverted status.
It is clear that Christian ethicists in the academic world hold a
sophisticated view of what many term "race relations." Perhaps
it would be better to talk in terms of reality and call it "race
tensions," since relations are limited at best. The minor point to
the contrary notwithstanding, many courses in ethics have a section on "race relations." The very term "race" means that
students are reinforced in their values even though the course
may unmask this conditioned reflex. Unfortunately, academic
Christian ethicists influential in denominations and congregations have yet to be alerted to or to alert the powers that be
to the fundamental disvalue of promoting "race relations Sunday," for this institution again obscures the group conflict by
focusing upon selected individuals.

The portent of "race" is a direct contradiction of biblical
and theological presuppositions of Protestantism. While the
social concept of "race," that is the idea of superior and inferior
"races," is no longer a live issue, implicit in the continuing use
of "race relations" is a biological concept of "race,"

that with any particular species there exist different populations
of the same species which are distinguished from one another
by the possession of certain distinctive hereditary traits.[6]

Professor Ashley Montagu has written that

when the theory of evolution was first announced it was received by the wife of the Canon of Worcester Cathedral with
the remark, "Descended from the apes! My dear, we will hope
it is not true. But if it is, let us pray that it may not become
generally known." [7]

This criticism may be viewed as inconsequential since ethical
thinkers aid the continued use even in Christian circles of tra-

[6] Ashley Montagu (ed.), *The Concept of Race* (New York: The Free Press
of Glencoe), 1964, p. xii.
[7] *Ibid.*, p. 1.

ditional "racial" terminology. It does serve further to document
the contention that Christian ethicists are not prepared to meet
this issue. Their general acceptance of the idea of "race" may
help to explain why Christian ethicists have yet to denounce
it, as Montague has done, as "unsound when applied to man";
the doctrine of man cannot bear the weight of "race" in its usual
sense of meaning "Negro." "Race" might best be replaced by
"Negro-white groups," which is direct and without hidden meaning. Christian thinkers have not begun to reflect upon this concept as more divisive than helpful; the conception of "race" is
"emotionally muddled," a "trigger word," which "takes for
granted what should be a matter for inquiry." The Christian
faith, specifically its doctrine of man, knows only the "human
race." Even the casual use of "race relations" by sophisticated
men declares, like the Canon's wife, "My dear, I always thought
that there was such a thing as race." "Race" has been reduced
to mean Negro, rather than ethnic groups which may be defined

> as one of a number of breeding populations, which populations
> together comprise the species Homo sapiens, and which individu-
> ally maintain their differences, physical or genetic and cultural,
> by means of isolating mechanisms such as geographic and social
> barriers.[8]

"Race relations"—here is evidence of the mystique of black and
white among Christian ethicists, who carelessly move from "race
relations," to "Negro churches," "Negro leaders," "Negro teachers," and "Negro institutions," as if they were the same as
"churches of Negroes," "leaders of Negroes," "teachers of Negroes," and "institutions of Negroes." No one doubts that "white
churches" is a contradiction in terms, yet few ethicists perceive
this when they use the expression "Negro churches."

A further indication that the theology and models of Christian ethicists have converged into a pattern providing precious
little direction for real change is the questionable banner of "liberal" which so many proudly accept. In this area of ethnic relations, is it not a contradiction vis-à-vis our unexamined pre-

[8] *Ibid.*, p. 25.

suppositions to accept the label of "liberal"? They would be more consistent to view their stance as "moderate." It cannot be taken for granted that Christian ethicists are "liberals." "Liberal" is understood to mean not only persons who are open to questioning their presuppositions, their models and inclinations, but persons who are as concerned with deeds as with thoughts, with lived experience through action to social change, as well as with the manipulation and articulation of ideas. The difference between the "liberal" and the "white liberal" is in the spheres of social action and social change in the present. Christian ethicists have in fact been true to their white folk religion tradition: it is clear that their careful deliberations about the right action have not issued in involvement with change, nor in leadership in action and change.

Negro-white separation is the major source of conflict infecting our entire society. Within the confines of conservationist theology and philosophy, Christian ethicists would be consistent with their concern for the present order were they to follow through from the thought processes of reflection and strategic planning to direct social change. It is difficult to determine how the accepted role of guiding human action—here specifically in ethnic tensions—can be more than "academic" apart from practical power, applying force to socio-economic-political advantages.

Were sufficient power to be supplied, would it be possible to discover or bring into being a pervasive positive advantage to whites that would compensate for the loss of white folk religion? Is the prevailing preconsciousness of a white society for whites too strong for reconversion? What is more important, is white security steeped in fear of the Negro? Are there concrete economic advantages that will take precedence over racial pride? Can not the discovery of other options to white dominance be central to Christian ethicists?

Paul Ramsey is helpful in pointing out that the sit-ins, boycotts, and other forms of protest spring from deep "Christian as well as human impulses." [9] Precisely! Legal procedures, equal

[9] Ramsey, *op. cit.*, p. x.

opportunities in housing, welfare, health, economics, politics, and employment *are* "Christian as well as human impulses." In these efforts the "impulses" of Reconstruction-I are being repeated. What is new is the Negro's challenging by "direct action the conscience of the white man." [10] There is less to be excited about in these efforts than is often assumed. Reconstruction-II may be successful, but the reading of John Hope Franklin's *From Slavery to Freedom* to Eli Ginzberg's *The Troublesome Presence* makes it clear that the question haunting us for generations demands to be widely articulated and met directly. The ghetto wounds are not healed when one is enfranchised, accommodated in public facilities, and able to earn commensurate with his ability. Even then the ghetto shadow continues to cast its ominous spectre over white America and limit its freedom.

With this reality in mind, is it tenable for Christian ethicists to continue the classical patterns of white folk ethics? It does not reflect America's unique dynamism. White folk ethics shy away from that amount of force, even bloodshed, necessary for restructuring the patterns of ethnic inequality.

Force is inevitable in this sphere of conflict, however it is tempered. Christian ethicists are not confronted with the conflict alone. They may have, though not alone, the necessary discernment and magnanimity. At the heart of Christian ethics is the refusal to take the life of another in any personal threat and the demand to take life where necessary to protect the life of a neighbor. If in ethnic tensions (the key to which is the voluntary and private realm) Christian ethicists have a new opportunity,

> then let the sail be bent to the main-mast, and let the ship of the Faith, issuing out from the harbor where it lies rotting and anchored, sail before the wind towards the furtherest star, indifferent to the darkness around it.[11]

Alexis de Tocqueville wrote of the United States in 1832 that "the most formidable of all the ills that threaten the future of the Union arises from the presence of a black population upon

[10] *Ibid.*
[11] Mounier, *op. cit.*

its territory." [12] It is still the case that the various European and Negro ethnic groups "are attached to each other without intermingling; and they are alike unable entirely to separate or to combine." [13] Indeed, it has been said that if ever America undergoes great revolutions they will be brought about by the presence of the black race on the soil of the United States. If we are in the beginning of a "great" transformation—and I think we are —it is not being aided or abetted by Christian ethicists who recoil from social change. The traditional deference to order results in the failure to see the transformation as a social and cultural transformation of white preconsciousness. Only social and cultural changes bring about political changes that bring about structural reforms.

Unless Christian ethicists wish to become involved in resistance to the change being demanded now, they will themselves have to undergo a transformation.

The first step toward a transformation within Christian ethics is to rethink the white tradition. Are its presuppositions of white folk religion helpful in this ethnic revolution? Do the doctrines of creation, nature, and community aid in destroying unjust Negro group exceptions of great magnitude? There is enough knowledge and experience upon which to act. This is not entirely a borderline situation where one acquires knowledge. The urban secular culture has provided guidelines for the extensive processes of transformation inevitable within white ethics and white society.

The first step toward a transformation is reflection upon the confining traditionalism that abhors radical breaks with the past —a breakthrough in the reactionary and dominant white Protestant theologies, theories, strategies, and inactivity in ethnic conflicts.

If the first step of radically questioning tradition is to move beyond updating and modifying the white Protestant stance, another move is imperative for a transformation within Christian ethics. This second step must be an existential encounter with what the Pelzes call the "words of Jesus." The revolutionary Jesus

[12] De Tocqueville, *op. cit.*, p. 424.
[13] *Ibid.*

has been hemmed in by theological systems. The non-radical emphasis of traditional Christology goes hand-in-glove with a theology of order, reinforcing the inclination toward stability and opposed to change. This tradition deemphasizes the transformative life of Jesus. The intricate systems of theology emphasized by the church in the past can only be continued in ethnic conflicts at its peril.

The presupposition and motivation of Christian ethics is the discernment of God's reconverting activity in each era of this aeon of "hardheartedness." It implies openness to the possibility for human behavior through perception of God's revelation for transformation in the living words of Jesus. Christian ethics in a restructuring era requires a style of thoughtful faith-in-action, the source of which is the transforming, renewing, restructuring, dynamic power of God revealed in Jesus' style of life. Jesus said: "Follow me. . . . I am the way, the truth and the life. . . . Ye shall know the truth and the truth shall make you free":

> The words of Jesus call us out of the order which man has so painfully imposed upon himself. They encourage us to take lightly the claims and duties of family, clan and state; to neglect and to by-pass the roads of authority and power; to free ourselves from religion, from our longing for the objective, the proof, the metaphysical and mystical security.[14]

Jesus' entire life was a freedom from the present order and for a better order.

If Christian ethics is to be engaged in the cultural transformation, it will require a prior internal revolution to recapture in its life the radical action in the transforming thoughts and deeds of Jesus. Without deference to the disorderly Jesus, traditional theologies crowd out his authority. If there is a uniqueness in Christian ethics, it is the transformative life style of Jesus.

If the internal transformation is pervasive, Christian ethicists may be free of white folk religion. If beyond simply appreciating the transformation, ethicists are to become guides within it, new

---

[14] Pelz, *op. cit.*, p. 99.

possibilities within the order call for imaginative workmen. Perhaps a different model from the classical ones would be useful for providing new possibilities of social change, if only in challenging the old models to reconsideration. A different model might aid ethicists increasingly to "do Christian ethics" as well as to "think Christian ethics." The white groups need to change in order to transform their white preconsciousness beyond guilt into responsibility, to bring forth the radical possibilities inherent within Christian ethics. A different model would need to draw upon the radical tradition of the Old Testament prophets and its fulfillment in the life of Jesus bypassed by contemporary white ethicists, as well as be embued with real humanism which understands the deep seated white preconsciousness and the complex socio-politico-economic structures.

It is difficult to conceive of a model of biblical-humanist dimensions to widen the white vision. It is possible that the classical roots and modern vision of Karl Marx's philosophical humanism complements the Old Testament spirit of Jesus. The dynamics of the early Marx's understanding of class consciousness would be helpful in correcting the white stigmatism, together with psychoanalytical understanding of Anglo-Saxon preconditioning and social structuring. Such a complex model would take seriously Jesus' transformative stance within the Kingdom of God, his abiding concern for the outcasts of the society and unbending labor for the oneness of humanity transcending the superficial aspects of group differences which tend to be disruptive. Along with Jesus' stance and Marx's philosophical humanism, depth psychoanalysis and sociological imagination would do well to add existential commitment to effect social change. It is doubtful whether the white group needs and Negro group demands can be understood or acted upon without first calling into question the presupposition of Caucasianism in Christian ethicists and ethics.

The New York Times and Oscar Handlin to the contrary, the Negro is not a new immigrant to be considered in the light of immigrants from European countries. He has been in this nation from its inception. It is true that the North, where Christian ethicists largely reside, now faces his urban presence for the first time because of the Negro's great numbers there, but he is not new to the North. Previously he could be ignored by white ethicists or made an exception to their guardianship of white folk religion. It is the Negro's demand for preferential treatment, the call for making up past injustices by deghettoizing the whole group that is new and threatening. It is claimed that preferential treatment is antidemocratic, antiChristian, and yet that the widening gap between the Negroes and whites is not.

Roman Catholic immigrants were able to move ahead in this once Protestant-controlled society because of the support of the church and the fact that these migrated Europeans were Caucasians. Their strength lay in political power and pressure, too. The Jews have moved ahead in this society because of their historical business acumen and love of learning. Both were supported in the present by the past. This is not the history of the Negro. In our secular society, if one is white and has political or financial power and knowledge, or knows the right people, he and his group can move ahead. Heretofore, by systematic design and not by accident, the Negro has been deprived of all of these criteria. White ethicists do not perceive their support of this tradition in their traditional emphases which perpetuate Negro disadvantage.

If the Negro is to be fully assimilated into our society, the present establishment of pluralism and small ethnic community organizations of secondary groups will have to be unmasked and undermined. The old social in-approach through control of power networks, conditions, and structures was the key to social equality in our society. This old pattern for escalating individuals and groups is being challenged by the underlying implications of the demands of the Negro. A radically new approach must be called forth.

Heretofore, Jews, Catholics, and Protestants balanced each other out through pluralism, retaining their sub-groups which served the purposes of identity and advancement. The Negro now intends that the system which has blocked him while advancing most other groups in society be abolished. It is *social discrimination* per se—the series of establishments based upon heritages and traditions in America today—that is being attacked by the Negro. The dissolution of established groups, not merely political representation or tokenism in other areas of life, shapes the cultural revolution. The oratory, bourgeois attitudes, and behavior notwithstanding, Negroes are not interested in their own schools, maintaining their own distinctive groups, maintaining their own distinctive employment agencies and housing communities. This is not due to lost pride or identity. It is due to the understanding there is nothing of value in separateness for whites or Negroes worth preserving. To preserve Negro institutions qua Negro institutions means to preserve segregated institutions, residences, and intimate associations. What every other social group in our society wishes to hold onto, the Negro wishes to demolish. The demand is not for mere opportunities, it is for equal economic, political, social and educational results. These results will require the abolishment of all establishments based upon being white and the insertion of the Negro into the total community, whereby group exclusiveness based on accidents of birth of any and every kind can be eliminated. Christian ethicists have yet to provide leadership on this frontier.

The Negro transformation means the establishment of a new order through disestablishment. It is opposed to defending the status quo as some would have us do on pretense of "a proper regard for order, for neighborhood, and for affinities that constitute this humanity of ours during this time between the times." [15] When basic rights are involved, is it really the case that "in the legal and social order a limit must be placed upon the means used to advance the cause of justice"? [16]

The ethnic revolution means that the Negro as he advances is not being assimilated into the old world but into a new world which the effect of his assimilation creates:

[15] Ramsey, *op. cit.*, p. 60.
[16] *Ibid.*, p. 65.

In that world there is only one American Community, and in that world heritage, ethnicity, religion . . . , are only incidental and accidental personal characteristics.[17]

Obviously, this need to push for new communities which will transform the past requires a whole new concept of human living. Where better than in the teachings of Jesus can there be found spiritual grounds for this new community to replace white folk religion? Where can one turn for understanding and support to challenge the possibilities latent within classical models of men except in Marxian philosophy, infused with existential sociological and psychoanalytical knowledge? If Christian ethicists are to guide they will need to be engaged in direct change, beyond direct action. Though this be a "fallen world," it does not follow that the white models which serve to discern and defend what has been need be perpetuated. The claim that "justice ought not to override entirely the question of law and order" is no aid to transformation.[18] For the transformation is not about disrespect for the rule of law. It is not merely "seeking legally to change the law and to find out what is the law." The transformation seeks to change the preconsciousness of whites and thereby the group behavior patterns which may be legal or illegal, but which in any case are the bases for white exclusiveness or exceptional inclusiveness. Were the transformation about laws, then one would only seek to change the law. But the transformation is about changing the voluntary spheres of life in our society which can be realized only through voluntary action. That is, the Negro will get his full due in this society as regards the law and legal procedures. But this will not be accomplished immediately nor will it bring about his full due.

In this transformative period, "what is dark and not unknown is the relationship between those who side with justice and their implication in the evils they oppose." Thus, the related problem to be faced and determined in this revolution is "our

[17] Nathan Glazer, "Negroes and Jews: The New Challenge of Pluralism," *Commentary,* Vol. 38, No. 6, December 1964, p. 45.

[18] Ramsey, p. 75.

own relationship to evil, its reflection of ourselves." Is it not too much to say that Christians "who do not suffer injustice have a vested interest in injustice"? Do Christians know how much of their institutional "savings bank interest is coming from investments in Harlem and Bedford-Stuyvesant real estate, those hovels from which super profits are made by jamming human beings together as no brute animals could be jammed without their dying"? [19]

Where does one begin to transform if one is an academic Christian ethicist? One begins by discovering the fear of radical change rooted in white folk religion. One begins by hearing afresh and heeding the revolutionary words of Jesus. One begins by probing and discharging white folk ethics. One begins with a new model that removes the blinders of white ideologies, ideals, privileges, and preferences. One begins with professional societies, departments, seminaries, academic administrations, and larger realms of influence to save white groups, whose healthfulness is directly tied to the condition of the Negro groups.

In the final analysis the coming transformation in ethnic relations is not a question of whether or not there will be a radical change in the establishments of American society; it is a question of whether Christian ethicists will precipitate its change.

Whether or not there is a transformation resulting from new ethnic confrontations can only be a question for those who perceive the present as a variation of the past. The changes in the areas of education, economics, and politics do not disclose the new situation. Far-reaching changes in these areas can aid but not exhaust the basic issues. At bottom, the Negro's demand is for full assimilation, which requires his *warm* welcome into the pool from which we select communicants in our intimate, private spheres of life. Is this possible apart from alterating beyond recognition these old social and family ties?

In this sphere, Christians have a clear imperative and opportunity. For the test of a society (if Jesus can be trusted) is who is included, and on what basis, in those refreshing intimacies

[19] Arthur Miller, "Our Guilt for the World's Evil," *New York Times Magazine,* January 3, 1965, pp. 10–11.

after working hours. The war on poverty, upgrading in jobs, new housing codes and public accommodations are symptoms of the disease. But it is in the social dimension that the cancerous tissue resides. Can it be removed without killing the organism? If Christians who are scientists fail to guide in removing the malignant social tumor, less skillful hands may do so.

If the new frontier in ethnic relations is the same old one, it is new insofar as it is yet to be faced. It has been with us for three and a half centuries. Who can doubt that Christian ethicists have something to contribute—a revolutionary ethic for an ethnic revolution. Admittedly, the traditional models and forms of behavior have been acceptable and functional for white Christian ethicists. Like all other people, they have at stake their sense of identity which is being threatened by the transformation. One can only hope that "we shall overcome," for in the final analysis the transformation is not a matter of merit, it is a matter of need, a question of scarcity which pervades all. Fortunately, Jesus' revolutionary words still have power, they are at work transforming models, laws, and institutions, even men— hopefully Christian ethicists.

If Jesus' "revolution" has real force and his call to "follow me" is heeded, Marx may be helpful on the way: "Force is the midwife of every old society pregnant with a new one." Then the question is, who will be a midwife for my Lord? So far Christian ethicists have been imbued with white folk religion like their secular counterparts and have not responded, "Here am I, Lord, send me." Consequently, white laymen, Christian and non-Christian, have not been challenged to root out white folk religion. It is a question: Can Christian ethicists be depended upon to bring real health to America through social change? The answer is no! Force is necessary! Their endeavors are absolutely necessary in a society based on white folk religion, but they are not sufficient. White folk ethics require Negro folks to be transformed.

PART THREE
GOD'S HUMANIZING AGENTS

CHAPTER VI
BLACK HOPE

THE HEART of New Testament religion is evangelism, the mind, message, and mission of which, as Will D. Campbell points out, is not created by churches or churchmen. This mainstream Christianity is the revelation of God to be proclaimed by the Church:

> We know that God so loved *the world*, with *all* its people, their sins and problems, that He became like one of us and dwelt among us and died that we might all be one people—His people. We know that God was in Christ reconciling the world to Himself and breaking down all barriers and walls of hostility which separate us from one another and from Him. We know that God, in establishing the Church, has enlisted us to proclaim that message of reconciliation. We know that we are called, not to build a Kingdom, but to bid men enter one already established, here and now, in which race is as irrelevant a category as redhead, baldhead, fat man, lean man. We also know that Jesus fed the hungry and healed the sick and bade his followers do the same.[1]

Mainstream religion's theme is *katallagete!*—"be reconciled!"

But instead of obedience to this kingdom demand established by God for every human group and person, mainstream religion has been superseded by established white folk religion, whose kingdom is a direct contradiction of the Kingdom of God.

This kingdom of and for whites is the ultimate concern of the dominant group in America. It is all the more demonic be-

[1] Will D. Campbell in *Katallagete*, Vol. I, No. 1, June 1965, p. 5.

cause its irrational pretension to mainstream Christianity perverts as it represses the demand of reconciliation. This racist heart is proliferated and compounded in what the critics of popular religion ("peace of mind cult") and church attendance call "culture religion." These critics see "racism and nativism" as characteristics of culture religion, failing thereby to distinguish between white folk religion and culture religion. Culture religion we will have with us always, at least until white folk religion is expunged from the preconscious and conscious minds of whites. It is this dastardly endeavor to storm the Kingdom of God and make it subsidiary to the kingdom of whites we have declared anathema, not only because it is the presupposition of the dominant white folk churches but because this (irrational) spiritual preconsciousness has spirited the entire social-cultural matrix of American life. In this respect, there has never been separation of church and state in America.

The only radical human challenge to white folk religion and its social-cultural establishment is the Negro. The element of reconciliation has been primary in the genuine religion of the Negro folk. They have joined it with the democratic creed. Both have been at the heart of the Negro folk; they have accepted the authentic declarations of these religious and secular creeds. Freedom and equality with and for all are for the Negro folk both an affirmation of mainstream religion and the creed of democracy as well as a protest against their repudiation in white folk religion. The heart of Negro folk religion is the heart of mainstream religion which, however, has been perverted by white preconsciousness. This perversion has repressed the heart of the religion and democracy, initiated by the "chosen people" and set forth in the Old Testament, which Jesus declared as established in the Kingdom of God—the preconsciousness of the Kingdom is *katallagete!* The Anglo-Puritans preconsciously declared biblical religion and democracy applicable to whites only and a minority of whites at that, forcing its willful and minority spirit upon the majority.

Freedom and equality with and for all—Negro folk religion —is the genius of the Negro folk. Developed not out of an elite breakthrough of its minority but the suffering of its majority, it parallels the genius of religion and democracy rooted in biblical faith. As a result of this suffering by a whole people for four centuries and placed in the perspective of the Bible, we contend here that the Negro cannot be understood or understand himself except as another "chosen people." By their stripes may all be healed. The Negro does not yet perceive himself as the "suffering servant," a man of sorrows acquainted with grief for a holy purpose. It is true that Christians claim themselves to be God's "new Israel," called to be his "suffering servant" people. But in the western world of whites this claim has been reduced to a mythical hope with precious little relationship to reality. The Jews' claim is based upon the experience of a people, not upon a rational promulgation of an ecclesiastical institution as with Christians. Whites can hardly claim to be "stricken, smitten," because they are whites or Christians. Negroes can only perceive themselves to be afflicted by God:

> But he was wounded for our transgressions, he was bruised for our iniquities; upon him was the chastisement that made us whole, and with his stripes we are healed. All we like sheep have gone astray; we have turned every one to his own way; and the Lord has laid on him the iniquity of us all.

> By oppression and judgment he was taken away; and as for his generation, who considered that he was cut off out of the land of the living, stricken for the transgression of my people? And they made his grave with the wicked and with a rich man in his death, although he had done no violence, and there was no deceit in his mouth. Yet it was the will of the Lord to bruise him; he has put him to grief; when he makes himself an offering for sin, he shall prolong his days; the will of the Lord shall prosper in his land; he shall see the fruit of the travail of his soul and be satisfied; by his knowledge shall the righteous one, my servant, make many to be accounted righteous; and he shall bear their iniquities. Therefore I will divide him a portion with the great, and he shall divide the spoil with the strong; because he poured out his soul to death, and was numbered with the transgressors; yet he bore the sin of many, and made intercession for the transgressors (Isaiah 53:5-12, RSV).

The fact that Negroes do not perceive themselves as the people chosen by God to be His suffering servants for the "transgression" of all God's people in America, if not elsewhere, is a positive rather than negative sign of chosenness. In this the Negro is markedly different from the Anglo-Puritans who settled this nation in the conscious belief that it was the "promised land" and that they were specifically "chosen people," in contradiction to the early beginnings of the people of Israel, whom the Anglo-Puritans decidedly attempted and failed so decisively to imitate. The record is clear: initially the people of Israel did not know themselves to be chosen of God. They had no choice. That they were the chosen ones is a declaration of faith made by the interpreters who in historical perspective have asked and found the meaning of the paradoxical and enigmatic life of the Jewish people. The Jews of ancient Israel became unfaithful only when they interpreted "chosen" to mean "specially favored" with the privilege of limiting the people of God to Jews. Then came their decline and fall, as with the Puritans from the beginning. The exclusiveness of Jews was a late misinterpretation corrected by Jesus Christ; the exclusion of Puritan minds has yet to be corrected.

Precisely because the Negro has not called his people "chosen," it is in keeping with the faith and Negro Spirituals to perceive them as chosen. The idea of "chosen" is a religious interpretation of a people's experience. Indeed, Negroes would not wish to be called—and would actively resist being—the "chosen people" were they consciously to understand and accept the biblical meaning of being chosen by God: inflicted, stricken, grieved, chastised, an offering poured out as "intercession for the transgressors." But just as they have neither known nor accepted it, this is their history. For it is through their experience that the presence of God in all our midst can be affirmed. Through their suffering "we are healed"—black and white together.

This journey is documented in the Negro Spirituals which parallel Israel's freedom *Movement*. The Negro has lost the experience of the Spirituals. Negroes once expressed their plight in Old Testament phrases, documented in such Spirituals as "Go

Down, Moses," "Oh Freedom! Oh Freedom!", and "Deep River." Although the Negro people have rejected the theology implicit in the Spirituals, these historical and theological documents are indisputable links with Israel. Indeed, Negro Spirituals can be counted as historical, biblical, theological, and philosophical sources of a new Israel. They may not be as impressive as the Old Testament, but then Negroes were not permitted to read and write and fashion their own "Negro consciousness." The authenticity of the Spirituals resides in their expression of the love of and drive for freedom and equality with and for all men. The inauthenticity of the Spirituals are those expressions of escape from this world without becoming "an offering for sin"—a life-denying rather than life-affirming motif which does not seek through fire, bloodshed, and war to be "realized eschatology." To the extent that this inauthentic motif is present it represents pseudoeschatology. Just as Israel desired to turn back from its perilous journey out of Egypt, so in the midst of the travail the Negro sought to turn away from this world. Others felt the urge and some were urged to depart for other countries. But, miraculously, escapism has been overridden by the will to freedom and equality through the "fiery furnace" of this land.

The inauthenticity of the Negro people as expressed in the Spirituals is parallel to the people of Israel at the point of the exodus. If the will of God for His people Israel demanded in their time of travail their departure from the land of Egypt through His mysterious ways and for His mysterious purpose, the will of God for His Negro people demands no exodus. For God has called the Negro people to an infinitely more complex and responsible task—not only of being released from bondage but of releasing its captors from their shackles as well. Slavery with eventual emancipation has too long been misconstrued as the end rather than the beginning to which God has called the Negro people of America. Slavery was but the means for in-extricably binding the Negro and the Caucasian. Without this binding the immeasurably more bruising work of releasing whites from their blasphemous bondage to whiteness and racial superiority cannot be done.

The great mission of the Jews was largely accomplished by ancient Israel. They were called to witness to the one God through the witness of their miraculous and paradigmatic life amidst their own nation and through intercourse with other nations. Though there be as many interpretations and ways to God as men have imagination, even the variety of religions in the world today witnesses largely to the one God. The increasing dialogue between world religions is centered upon mutual understanding and enrichment of the infinite ways of God to man via creation and redemption against an uncommon background of understanding. However interpreted, the dialogue is possible because of the common assumption of one God. As in the time of Israel of old, men still worship other gods but not without increasing judgment and awareness through a nearly universal affirmation—an affirmation which is most certainly dominant if not universal. If the mission of ancient Israel is largely accomplished, in principle if not in complete practice, the continuing chastisement of the Jews may be to the end of human time—for the nature of humankind is the idolization of other gods even while claiming to worship God. Their role as the "suffering servant" amidst a universal affirmation of God and worship of gods is both fulfilling and to be fulfilled, real and to be realized, a symbol of their continuing favor in God's purpose.

The great mission of the Negroes has yet to be accomplished: to witness to the one humanity of the one God here in the United States where groups reside in divisiveness. The dominance of the Puritan white folk religion in ecclesiastical and socio-politico-economic spheres, based on a preconscious white spirituality, is in evidence in British-tempered America as much as in Dutch-tempered South Africa. The oneness and equality of all humankind may be paid lip service by a minority here and there, but the preconscious whiteness dictates the practice and raises the barrier of sexual intercourse between God's imaginative creation of his people. God has called the Negro as the "suffering servant," whereby humankind the world over will consciously, not accidentally, voluntarily, not by force as in times past, affirm first in principle and then in practice a life of full human oneness

through the only biblical way of real knowing. Sexual together-
ness is in the Bible the fullest expression of knowledge and
union. The Hebrew people were called to abstain from other gods,
not from other people, with whom they have always inter-
mingled. But the mission of the "suffering servant" Negro people
also may not end in human time. There will be those who prefer
their own group not out of free choice but out of preconsciousness. As long as there are such men, so long will the Negro be
God's "judgment" upon their "sin" and "transgression." Whom
God bruises "for our iniquities," the Anglo-Puritan iniquity that
"turned every one to his own way," God will not let go to "see
the fruit of the travail of his soul and be satisfied" until "by his
stripes we are healed."

Just as God does not ask our permission to create us, nor
provide us with the choice of being born to this man and this
woman in that country and that time, so He does not ask for
volunteers as His "suffering servant." Were this not the freedom
of God which is as different from the freedom of man as *kairos*
is from *chronos,* God's time from clock time, there would be no
religious meaning to "chosen." If it had been up to the Jews they
would have asked God to do them no favors, and the same is true
for the Negro. The Anglo-Puritans "chose" themselves, and their
establishment has become disestablished in principle if not in
practice. The real difference between being "chosen" by God and
choosing to be "suffering servants" is the absence of choice; whites
who choose to suffer, as do some Christians presently, have an
escape hatch which neither Jews nor Negroes enjoy.

God affirms how interdependent we are potentially and how
enriched we would be were all indeed interdependent. Clearly
God affirms what white folk religionists and proud blacks do not
affirm. Interdependence is not a substitute for or an elimination
of the variety brought through many socio-cultural-ethnic groups.
But true interdependence, free and willing co-mingling, increases
the value inherent in unique persons and groups by making their
fullness an enrichment of rather than a barrier to all. All mankind
is in a state of deprivation and the Negro is the servant of
release from this bondage of human separateness—this depriva-

tion—being as he is externally the most deprived, though neither by his will or his doing can he undo the calling as "an offering for sin." Like the Jew before and with him, the Negro will receive no reward until all are healed. As a member of the Kingdom's brotherhood, the Negro is in all mankind as all mankind is in him; he too is being but is not yet fulfilled. As a sign of his unity with all mankind, the "suffering servant" Negro finds "they made his grave with the wicked and with a rich man in his death, although he had done no violence, and there was no deceit in his mouth."

If the Negro is the "suffering servant," God has called him not to make group differences irrelevant but to make them enriching for all mankind. So many white liberals have made this mistake, such as Will D. Campbell, who proclaims as the objective the irrelevance of differences, so anti-biblical and negative.[2]

Moreover, the Negro is called to be the servant whereby all nations, not just America, will be redeemed. If the Negro can gain group justice and opportunity in America without bloodshed simply because he is a minority and calls forth the American outpouring for the underdog, his mission will have only begun and not ended. The mission of the Negro must be to unify mankind through acceptance of group differences as blessings rather than punishment. It is doubtful that this mission can be fully realized without bloodshed. But even if it were, it would not be in those parts of the world where the Negro is in fact the majority such as the Union of South Africa. America is a part of the *whole* world. The Negro is a part of the *whole* of mankind. America and the Negro are parts of the *whole* Kingdom of God. Neither America nor the Negro can become partly *whole,* nor *whole apart* from humankind.

This is the point at which the non-violent movement becomes suspect. The non-adaptability of the non-violent technique to the urban, dynamic North which shapes America may be questioned. We will await the effects of Martin Luther King, Jr.'s Chicago endeavors. What cannot be questioned is the irrelevance of this

[2] *Katallagete, loc. cit.*

technique to South Africa. If it were not irrelevant to South Africa, then Martin Luther King, Jr., or even more plausibly his African counterpart, would be leading people there in the non-violent ways. Instead, Dr. King has avoided the confrontation of this problem by shifting his direction to demands for peace in Viet Nam.

This new "peace" tactic is a violent distortion of the mission of the Negro, a thorough documentation of the only partial understanding of the biblical message among those who seek to identify the Negro Freedom Movement with God's purpose for mankind. Surely it is presumptuous to believe that God has called the Negro to redeem mankind from war, nationalism, pride, and other human weaknesses.

A too narrow, if not non-biblical view of man has thus led to the idolization of non-violence and peace. On any reading of the history of Israel in the Old Testament, their mission was not construed as a disassociation from violence and war via non-violence. Those who would shrink from violence and war or lead people astray from the Bible in proclaiming non-violence as *the* way do not know the extent to which men will go to resist God for preferred gods. It was but a few years ago that six million Jews were exterminated, a horrible reminder of their unfinished mission. The limited "bloodletting" on the civil rights front is but a clue to its superficial penetration in America, not to speak of what threatens in South Africa. Rational idealism, the notion of scientific progress, the belief in civilizing and "Christianizing" have combined to repress the biblical truth about man and God. White folk ethics has invaded Negro folk religion at this point and partially resulted in black religion's being inseparable from white folk religion. Only those who take their stance outside the Bible and claim man has been transformed can believe blood will not flow as a mighty stream in South Africa, if not America, when the union of men above "race and clan" is demanded.

In the Bible, bloodshed, violence, and war are works of men which bring judgment upon them and the opportunity for God to be praised. God is no respecter of persons or deeds; He uses the evil and the soul of man for His purpose. Through war and blood the "chosen people" of Israel discovered their mortal enemies to be people whom God loved. It is not too much to say that only through violence, war, and bloodshed were the people of Israel able to lie down with those whom they once called the enemy and who became brothers and sisters in blood, culture, and religion.

Yet this is not a call for bloodshed, war, and violence. It is but a declaration of faith in God through an understanding of the history of his "chosen people"—a God who makes even the wickedness of man to praise Him. The point is, God is not like the Anglo-Puritans; He does not operate on a dual standard of opposing bloodshed in principle when it is unsuitable (Negro-white conflicts) and demanding its practice when it suits their purpose (Dominican Republic). God does not demand bloodshed, men do. God simply uses the folly of man.

Insofar as the Martin Luther King, Jr. non-violent technique dominates through calling men to bleed in social action for the purposes of a hamburger and calling them back from bloodshed in social intercourse, it is guided by faithlessness in God and distortion of the "suffering servant" mission. Moreover, King has followed the white rational line of white folk ethics which is steeped in white folk interpretation of the New Testament ignoring its unity with the Old Testament. It is true that the New Testament demand is *katallagete*, but the key to being reconciled is not the Apostle Paul but his Master, Jesus, whose unbreakable link is with the Old Testament understanding of redemption. Redemption is, in the Old Testament and in the death of Jesus Christ, incomprehensible apart from the offering of blood. Christ was the true sacrifice—not of materialism or ideas, but of his very life and blood. The Christian faith means nothing if it does not mean sacrifice. But as in the sacrifice of Christ, blood becomes an offering which is no more chosen by human will than is the choosing of a time to be born. When the time comes for blood in order to join human groups into a brotherhood it will be a sacrifice—not offered by man of his own free will but in the larger freedom of God—at the *Kairos,* the time God chooses.

The organized, calculated, technical, contrived civil rights movement has been and is doing a good and necessary work of relieving a laceration, though it confuses its work with major surgery, with all the risk involved in a malignant tumor which has spread throughout the body. Faith in man, not in God, is too clear too often—for the movement to be the *movement* or mission of God. The dominant voices of our time rejoice in Martin Luther King, Jr., a sure sign that he is not an Old Testament prophet. God has called a people, not a man, to be His "suffering servant." The "suffering servant" people is wounded, bruised, stricken, cut off out of the land:

> But this is a people robbed and plundered, they are all of them trapped in holes and hidden in prisons; they have become a prey with none to rescue, a spoil with none to say, "Restore!" Who among you will give ear to this, will attend and listen for the time to come? (Isaiah 42:22–23, RSV).

There is missing in white folk religion and white folk ethics the biblical grounding in the Old Testament without which the New Testament finds neither anchoring nor fulfillment. Genuine religion is absent, too, from white rationalists who take pride in the accomplishments of man, upon whom white folk religion feeds as a leech, while defiantly and foolishly ignoring genuine religion which is the spirit of every culture, the provision for its transformation. The illiberal response to real religion may be due to an unwillingness to disentangle it from admittedly profane and demonic pseudoreligions. It is a pity that the influential liberal in high and low places does not know the voice of God:

> I am the Lord, and there is no other, besides me there is no God; I gird you, though you do not know me, that men may know, from the rising of the sun and from the west, that there is none besides me; I am the Lord, and there is no other. I form light and create darkness. I make weal and woe, I am the Lord, who do all these things" (Isaiah 45:5–7, RSV).

For if the responsible leaders in public life discerned the politics of God they might discover the realistic political activity of God in the nations and become like Cyrus in the Book of Isaiah, commissioned of Him to "let the earth open, that salvation may sprout forth, and let it cause righteousness to spring up also." Without considering the political activity of God in human affairs, His freedom as the Creator is striven against by the freedom of man, which must operate within the freedom of God. Thus, the purpose of God is ignored as if the purpose of man could usurp it. God has called His human creations not only to subdue the earth but "to subdue nations before him," as well, and to be His shepherd who remains faithful to His word:

> "I made the earth, and created man upon it; it was my hands that stretched out the heavens, and I commanded all their host. I have aroused him in righteousness, and I will make straight all his ways; he shall build my city and set my exiles free, not for price or reward . . ." (Isaiah 45:5–7, RSV).

This faithlessness to God, who is engaged in the politics of men for a purpose is due to their lack of imaginative understanding and serious hearing of His judgment and promise:

> Rouse yourself, rouse yourself, stand up, O Jerusalem, you who have drunk at the hand of the Lord the cup of his wrath, who have drunk to the dregs the bowl of staggering. There is none to guide her among all the sons she has borne; there is none to take her by the hand among all the sons she has brought up.

> Therefore hear this, you who are afflicted, who are drunk, but not with wine: Thus says your Lord, the Lord, your God who pleads the cause of his people: "Behold, I have taken from your hand the cup of staggering; the bowl of my wrath you shall drink no more; and I will put it into the hand of your tormentors, who have said to you 'Bow down, that we may pass over'; and you have made your back like the ground and like the street for them to pass over" (Isaiah 51:17–18; 21–23, RSV).

The white liberal in politics thinks that through economic upgrading we can work out our problems of intergroup conflicts without deghettoizing the Negro and therefore the white, as much because of his fear of bloodshed as because of his belief in man's allegiance to law and order. This outlook affirms that the machinery is set up and it is just a matter of time for it to operate properly. This view gives countenance to the reality of Negro slavery, though it is given in the more humane term of the ghetto, in mind, body, and spirit—that he, the white, is burdened with the immense energies of keeping the Negro in slavery to the white preconsciousness. He neither discerns that the ghetto-slavery is against the purpose of God and though he be unwilling to change radically and give up the false securities of his pleasures to deghettoize himself and the Negro, God has called a people to break the social, psychological, cultural, economic, and physical chains. Nor can the white liberal understand the meaning of the "troublesome presence" of the Negro which does not require imaginative interpretation as does the Old Testament.

The white conservative and liberal in religion thinks, to put it in biblical terminology, that he not only has the task but actually is establishing the Kingdom of God on earth. He does not discern that the Kingdom has been established and the only question remaining is whether man is willing to give up his fiefdoms today and lose his pride, or resist tomorrow and lose his hide. "A man in white skin can never be free while his black brother is in slavery."

In religion as in politics, rational whites have taken false comfort and false hope in the civil rights movement as if it were being faithful to genuine religion and democracy, overlooking the truth that only insofar as the freedom of man is attuned to the freedom of God can there be discerned "righteousness and strength."

The civil rights movement's faithlessness is in its being the servant of man rather than the servant of God. The non-violent movement of protest simply tinkers with the old and dated pattern of Negro-white group relations and appeals to the consciousness of whites in the name of white folk religion, thereby relieving their frustrations temporarily instead of their guilt permanently, confirming their trust in human goodness rather than confronting them with the reality of the unbroken commitment of keeping the Negro in the new slave galleys—the ghettos. All of this in the name of religion is a religious travesty. That dimension of the civil rights movement which seeks fundamental change, for example the Student Non-violent Coordinating Committee, believes its task can be accomplished apart from God and genuine religion, ignoring the task of expunging the preconscious white folk religion structured in the socio-cultural fabric. Man is *homo religio,* and to ignore this is to ignore the fact that like an iceberg only one-tenth of him is obvious.

If we take seriously the establishment of the Kingdom of God as the field in which human forces are restricted, and the reality of God's political activity in history, no less the evangelical mission of Christian religion to accept the condition of human brotherhood through its life together with all men, we have the essentials by which to judge the actions and changes of men. The kingdoms of men are structured in the shifting sands of individual and collective pride and maintained by appeals to ego exclusiveness rather than inclusiveness. The Kingdom of God is His unfailing and eternal purpose of human oneness. The present apparent, not real, conflict between the kingdoms and the Kingdom is set in Negro-white group apartheid. The Negro is God's "chosen people" not merely to break through the barriers but in so doing to restructure human life on the bases of group acceptance of all other groups. There is no way for the Negro to be a fully accepted human being without whites accepting themselves and other human groups as co-equals. The question is not whether the King will reign, nor whether violence will flow in the world. The question is whether the people of God called Negroes can be faithful to their folk religion and still consciously accept their mission. Will the Negro choose to be what he is, "suffering servant," the source of power, or fatalistically acquiesce in suffering, if not exploit it for personal gain rather than group salvation. It is questionable whether the Negro will choose to engage creatively in suffering, not in the sense of white folk courage, but to accept his role in human time to deliver whites from the white mystique and the black mystique as well.

The power of the Negro, the black hope of mankind, is the Kingdom of God's imperative of freedom and equality personified in Negro folk religion's rejection by the kingdom of whites.

Black hope is not the utopian hope of white rationals who envision upgrading individual Negroes without full acceptance of the group, nor is it the utopian hope of white devils in South Africa whose religion they call a divine destiny to submerge the African. Though the secular optimism of this secular age may be used to improve the economic lot of a few Negroes substantially and many Negroes niggardly, these concessions are but eschatological symbols of the ultimate union which is inconceivable in the United States and South Africa but which is the ground of the Kingdom of God. The black hope is not dependent upon prospects and improvements; the hope is that present stirrings of human intergroup healthfulness may be realized in the future. The Negro people as "suffering servant" are an eschatological symbol in history of our ultimate need for and means to human fulfillment, the ground of black hope.

Negro folk religion has been forgotten by Negroes in their preoccupation with civil rights and black religion as the objectives of suffering egos, confusing these signs of the incidentals with the essentials of the "suffering servant." The value of the civil rights demands and gains is their positive contribution of sustenance in this world, the means by which God through men and institutions provides the Negro with the will to live, as God's "troublesome presence" for the purposes of human redemption. White folk religion and ethics militate against the Old Testament description of the larger freedom and purpose of God the potter on behalf of secular optimism's smaller freedom and purpose of man. Through the niggardly crumbs of the civil rights movement and the escapist comforts of black religion, Negro folk religion has prostituted its faith and hope by capitulating to white folk religion's purposive misconstruction of God, who Himself declares:

> "Woe to him who strives with his Maker, an earthen vessel with the potter! Does the clay say to him who fashions it, 'What are you making'? or 'Your work has not handles'? Woe to him who says to a father, 'What are you begetting?' or to a woman, 'With what are you in travail?' " Thus says the Lord, the Holy One of Israel, and his Maker: "Will you question me about my

children, or command me concerning the work of my hands?" (Isaiah 45:9–11, RSV).

Instead of perceiving the freedom and equality of some as the call of God to the freedom and equality for all, the Negro has been persuaded by some to seek material gain as the ultimate within the framework of white folk religion instead of the Kingdom of God.

The vulgar seeking of success and culture-religion, against which white liberals wax eloquent, is not seen in its more sophisticated form of immediate success in the bits and pieces of the denominational pronouncements and politico-economic-educational-social compromises by white ethicists. This realm is deemed the practical politics of men and is not questioned as to whether it patterns itself after the practical politics of God. Negro folk religion has become the partial captive of the immediate success-worship of white devils in blackface.

Here there is a parallel between the chosen "suffering servants" of Israel and the people called Negroes. From Moses and Aaron through the Babylonian captivity, the prophetic leaders of Israel were forced to contend with the idolization of the gods pervading the surrounding people and empires. This idolatry led to the worship of immediate success symbolized in graven images. The setting up of a separate nation with love of kings and wealth was denounced by the prophets of Israel, not as evil in themselves but as distractions from their mission to live faithful to God whereby all men would be God-worshippers. This mission of the Jewish people persists beyond the final destruction of Jerusalem in the Graeco-Roman period and the scattering of Jews throughout the world and in all nations—as well as beyond the confines of the present state of Israel. The mark of God in Judaism is symbolized today in the present urgency over whether they still have a mission and the continuance of the remnant which affirms it against the deluge of dissent.

The Negro people have failed to take seriously the experience of Israel and the relentless call of God, who is faithful to His purpose. Negro people wish to interpret freedom and equality in the context of white culture and wish it to be demonstrated

through their own rise in middle class representation. Thereby
Negroes shun their call to free the white preconscious here and
everywhere in order that all men may be free for the Kingdom.
They desire a stake in this country for the understandably human
purposes of personal satisfaction rather than for ultimate social
change which may bring more than a mere realignment of human
power. The fascination with immediate successes leads to the
comforting delusion of individual achievements based on the
assumptions of white rationalizations, which are themselves in
need of redemption. Immediate success not only fails to provide
for group equality but feeds the illusion of an escape from the
mission of suffering until all men are one. Occasional, strategic,
and limited suffering on the white property of this land may be
an imaginative creation within white presuppositions. It is not
the creative suffering of an entire people, which is the presupposition of the Kingdom.

The dominant white middle class, guided by the elite establishment of the "WASP" upper class, is the bearer of the ideas
which dominate America. The controlling religion therein is white
folk preconsciousness. The intellectual framework is the white
rational belief in progress through science. Fundamental to this
rationalism is the hope in the change of men through reason.
It is the acceptance of this western faith in reason which has
led to the white support of what is deemed the reasonable demands of the civil rights movement. And it is the acceptance of
this acceptance which leads some Negroes down the road of
immediate success as if it were possible for the whole group. If
a man in white skin can never be free from white kingdoms for
God's Kingdom while his black brother is in slavery to white
kingdoms, it is certain that some Negroes cannot be free from
the psychological-spiritual-social-educational-political-economic-
cultural slavery of white kingdoms while operating with their
presuppositions within the white kingdoms even for so noble a
cause as changing from within the kingdom of whites, if the
majority of Negroes are selected out.

The rational scientific religion of white men will not change
white men, who are the generators of these presuppositions.

Negroes and whites may know the cause of the passionate white preconsciousness, outlined in an earlier chapter. This knowledge of the cause of passionate white folk religion is a necessary but insufficient source of transforming it. The Negro people need and ought not to deny themselves the relatively frugal gains doled out by greedy, self-centered whites, even though they are ounces of white conscious offerings outweighed by the pounds of white wretchedness. These minuscule offerings should be gratefully received and more demanded as the gifts of God, rather than evidence of white good will or change in heart. They are to be seen as the mysterious workings through the civil rights struggles of the means to keep the black hope alive for the ultimate purposes of the Kingdom of God. As the children of darkness, Negroes need to be more wise in the Kingdom of God than the children of light are in the kingdoms of this world. The knowledge and gifts of white passions are white materials which the Negroes can use to change whites only if the ground of black hope is outside white ideology. If one can at best shift and rearrange white ideology from *within* white ideology, a passion outside white ideology is alone sufficient to bring about the change implicit in Negro folk religion. While working within as the black hope of change, the power of black hope must be outside white folk religion.

The only passion more powerful than white folk religion is the passion at work in white America's disavowed religion and democracy—the Kingdom of God. White America has consciously rejected or distorted this Kingdom in favor of liberal, inch-by-inch, middle road expansion on its own terms. Negro folk religion and the "suffering servant" Negro is the only hope left for the "elect" Puritan Calvinism in the United States and South Africa. Negroes constitute God's promised hope for white rebelliousness which deserves death and destruction. The "suffering servant" Negro is the depository of the life destroyed by white folk religion. Surviving the catastrophes, bound together by high visibility and faith in the hope of group acceptance, the Negro is a historical fact witnessing to God's active presence in human history. Ancient Israel was the foundation and Jesus Christ the chief cornerstone, establishing the Kingdom of God throughout the earth. These beginning and climactic remnants were both rejected in their fullness by white Puritanism in its taking over the exclusive theme from late Israel and working it out as a selective authoritarianism of immense theological-political-economic-national-ethnic dimensions. The black hope in the world has become a deterrent to the purpose of whites and a flywheel for the purpose of God to open Christendom's dam of exclusiveness and permit the mighty force of God's inclusiveness of all human groups to expand.

The Negro's seeming undeserved punishment is his opportunity to release all men from the sin of in-groupness. The "curse" of being a Negro is really the blessed symbol of God's paradoxical instrument as the means of His grace for all men. The inescapability from being black and its accompanying inhumane treatment by white humans is to be cherished and used for the purpose of God and not despised through the prejudices of men. This divine blessing in disguise of being the people destined by God, called out by Him, to be His Cyruses in human politics, cannot be cancelled by refusing to be obedient. God has chosen to use the suffering-color of the Negroes whether or not they choose to accept their destiny. But if this "suffering servant" people of God accept their mission they will have the joy of creatively working out with God His purpose of inclusive, intergroup interdependence in all things. Perhaps in this acceptance Negroes will not forestall but impede the next stage in human life when men can move beyond acceptance of God and groups to acceptance of the Kingdom.

Only through accepting their destiny and passion for the Kingdom of God can Negroes counter white passion. The black hope is the Negro's being in and of this world, enjoying all its pleasures, seeking more, and yet not being concerned with rejection or satisfied with the good fruits of human labor. For the black hope is in opening the eyes of men to the certain presence of the Kingdom of God in this world, unacceptable though it may be to the white mystique. The real hope of blacks is their inescapable presence in human affairs, the human fulcrum in white religio-social, cultural, temporarily established kingdoms by which they are to be changed with the eternal lever of the Kingdom of God.

With this passion for the Kingdom of God the Negro can grasp and be grasped by the meaning of life—his life and the life of all men. In living this passion there is inexhaustible courage through grace which flows from the Eternal's purpose to change white folk religion everywhere in the world. Toward this end there may be many opportunities presented by God—in violence or non-violence, war or peace, hate or love, segregation or re-segregation, prejudice or ignorance, discrimination or stupidity, work or play, private clubs or churches. Out of this passion the passion of whites can be challenged and transformed. The passion of the Kingdom of God frees the Negro to participate in all these aspects of life: the psychologists' concern for interpersonal relationships, the psychiatrists' desire for self-understanding, the sociologists' insistence upon fluid social structures, the educators' belief in education as cure-all, the theologians' affirmation of the churches as objective, the conservatives' commitment to individual heroics, the elite's curatorship of culture, the liberals' fixation upon the progressive goodness of men—and frees him from their delusions. By this passion the Negro can be grasped by a strength to meet personal defeats, disparagements, disadvantages, with group unity built upon faith and hope in the Kingdom at work in this world. Here there resides the impatience with white dominance and patience with the sure but slow fulfillment of the Kingdom in which his role in binding all men together may be rewarded in a new humanity. The Negro must live this passion of the Kingdom of God and oppose all other passions to it, for by design or choice the black presence is his fixed point in human history, God's black hope for all His human creations. Herein lies the source of authentic, creative "Negro consciousness."

God will accept nothing less than the freedom and equality demands of His Kingdom personified in the Negro. The Negro has hitherto been concerned with his own freedom and entrance into equality, an imperative individual and group hunger and thirst preparing him for the larger responsibility of gaining this goal through freeing whites. While the Negro is insisting upon "freedom now," he has not yet understood the price of freedom to be his responsibility of living this passion, chosen for him and all men by God. The Negro's suffering will be creative only when he accepts "Negro consciousness" and learns that his destiny is true freedom, which is not possible for some individuals or groups apart from all individuals and groups. Friedrich Engels once pointed out that "freedom is the knowledge of necessity." If the Negro people can soon accept the fact Negroes will always be black and objectionable to whites and thereby the necessity of their role as the "suffering servant" in the Kingdom of God, this knowledge will be the black hope upon which the freedom of all men is possible sooner than later. The individual exceptions of Negro-white friendships and marriages confirm the possibility for the freedom of groups beyond the curiosity of isolated persons. They highlight the urgent need and dramatize the hope.

Why God has chosen Negro people to be His "suffering servant" fulcrum to transform through acceptance of group differences divisive mankind into unitive mankind (the brotherhood of man dimension of the Kingdom) is no more fathomable than His choice of Israel to be His "suffering servant" to make known the fatherhood of God dimension of the Kingdom, or His choice of Jesus the Christ to reveal His Kingdom established for all mankind, or the delimiting or rejection of His purpose by the Church manifest through establishment of proliferated kingdoms with exclusive rather than inclusive dimensions. What is certain is God's presence in human history. God's purposive Kingdom is at work in people, involved with people irrespective of their heritages. The Negro *is* this certainty. As he cannot escape being black or once being enslaved (and therefore repudiated by whites), the Kingdom of God cannot be escaped.

Jews have suffered throughout the centuries in the purpose of God, through no choice of their own, and so continue even now to miraculously exist in the face of the most tragic suffering any group has known as witnesses of the fatherhood of God and the judgment of rebellious men. The Negro is the new people marked by God who cannot escape as other men do. They differ from Jews in being among the majority in the world instead of a minority. The failure of humankind to acknowledge the fatherhood of God was the opportunity of God in the people of Israel, whose community experience changed human worship from prayer to many deities to prayers to the One: "Hear O Israel, the Lord our God, the Lord is One." In Jesus Christ the work of Israel reached a pinnacle, in Him the old age of the fatherhood of God and the new age of brotherhood of man converged. Since the first century the fatherhood of God has been writ large in the head and heart of man, but the brotherhood of man has been writ only in the head of man. The brotherhood of man ideal guided the early Church in its conception of itself as the "third race" in which there was "neither Jew nor Greek, bond nor free." Down the centuries the institutional, political, national, ecclesiastical, theological, "racial" or ethnic rigidities forced out of the manifest Church "Jew and Greek," "bond and free." The manifest Church has been unable to hold in equilibrium Jesus Christ's revelation of the Kingdom of God as the fatherhood of God and the brotherhood of man. In strain and tension, the manifest Church split the difference and chose the fatherhood of God over the brotherhood of man (neither Jew nor Greek, bond nor free), thereby dividing itself in particular and the world in general. As a result of this failure within the Church manifest, a people has been chosen to redeem the Church manifest for the Church latent. But most of all to redeem the world in general for which the Church manifest throughout its past centuries of established power and in its present lack of power has failed in its witness to the brotherhood of man. The Church manifest has before it the task of extricating itself from the peripheral and trivial, but most of all to become what it proclaims—the Church latent.

It appears contradictory that God has chosen the most divisive mark of being Negro as His fulcrum for the Kingdom of God's *Movement* of Brotherhood. But the "suffering servant" has always been rejected, despised, stricken with sorrows and grief. It continues to be so with the Jew. Jesus Christ spent a great portion of His time with the outcasts and became Himself an outcast. In God's own mysterious way He chooses the greatest stumbling block to the powerful and the most unlikely to the elite to bear His redemptive purpose of reconciliation.

It is not possible to comprehend the choice of the Negro, for if it is God's way to work through people, the Japanese, Indians, and Chinese would seem more likely. It is a fact that the white preconsciousness takes its own white mystique so seriously that it carries it out in the world of human affairs to dominate. Japan, India, and China have been the victims of white expansion. They unleashed extraordinary endeavors to effectively control white aspirations of dominance. The technological-political-cultural-economic lag of the African continent behind the dominant western advance, even behind its extension in Japan, India, and China may be traced historically. But *why* rather than *how* human events developed into the pattern of the once rising and now descending western star is an enigma. Much the same limits the *why* of Africans being the only group in history to be first enslaved and then subjugated into a different or inferior human species because of their skin color. Some bases were suggested in Chapter I, but even they do not answer sufficiently. What can be said is that although the present dominant white preconsciousness disparages the Japanese, Chinese, and Indian people, the African, and particularly the American Negro, is not only the victim of prejudice but is also held in the lowest esteem and even contempt as well. Negroes are of all people the first rejected by practitioners of irrational white folk religion. Yet, God has chosen these outcasts to effect His high purpose of brotherhood. Given the experience of the Negro, he would be the least likely candidate for concern with brotherhood, by human standards, since he has been so long denied the experience of brotherhood. Yet he has the power to realize it. There is no precedent in human history of a people who while in slavery became everywhere and always ghettoized first because of economic gain and then genealogical structure. What other people have known the enforcement of the will of a small minority which became fixated on placing barriers of color without granting the indigenous majority an opportunity to be free, to acculturate or assimilate—as in South Africa? Historically, the systematic victimization of the African and the American Negro has been accepted as the punishment of the will of God. But this very belief sparks the reality so opposite, the truth of hope: these victims bear the marks of those blessed of God to do His work of love rejected by men more acceptable to each other but not to God.

When the chosen "suffering servants" of Israel became consciously the elected, their work was well done as a people. Then, their demise as spiritual leaders followed upon the claim of their exclusive corner on God. It first resulted in the fall of national Israel. However, the role of Jews as "suffering servant" continued through its apex in Jesus Christ, who broke the exclusiveness of Judaism and invited all men into the Kingdom of God. The Church manifest reversed the openness of Jesus Christ and returned to the select remnant notion of late Judaism which we are just beginning to see as its downfall now. If the Negro people can be saved from this pattern of being stepped upon and gather strength to put their foot on the neck of the oppressor, saved from turning rejection into oppression, it may be due not only to the fact that in group color preconsciousness of superiority is a white and not a black inclination, but to the new age in which men may be ready when forced to unite in practice their experience in principle. The peculiar chosenness of the Negro is for human group inclusiveness. The black hope lies not in bringing in full justice and equality in all human relations and endeavors, but in detribalizing human groups. In this work of detribalizing there remains a great gap between its realization and the fullness of the Kingdom of God among men on earth.

If the Negro people become conscious of their permanent blessing as the "suffering servant" of God to bring about the interdependence of all groups, perfect justice and love will not ensue but the time of intergroup communion may be hastened—no less the risk of black exclusiveness. But whether Negroes gain a group consciousness of their divinely ordained mission with its risk of black superiority or not, the black hope of all mankind is the fixed presence of this people as the witness that God will not leave man to be satisfied with his group preferences without conflict with the Kingdom of God.

CHAPTER VII
BLACK PROMISE

THE NEGRO CHURCHES may well be indispensable to the development of "Negro consciousness" and black hope. Thus they may be indispensable for the North and the new South, the responsibility of all our human persons, institutions and resources. This accomplishment will be impeded to the extent the distinction is not made between God's work of creating a new earth and a new heaven and the human work of creating a new North and South.

The emerging islands of integration in the seas of discrimination and segregation, North and South, are as isolated as they are superficial. Those engaged in the federal government's poverty program know the real possibilities it holds for economic improvement. What is impressive is the way the program bogs down in the mire of massive bureaucratic agencies and agents within the existing community structures. The insufficient funds which trickle down to the poor from the "solid citizens" in control provides enough paper success to feed the optimism of those who need individual successes and mathematical indices of progress to support their belief in relative upgrading, the myopia which obscures substantial change.

Churchmen involved in middle class ventures of desegregation of local congregations are encouraged by the changes in church segregation. There are ministers and laymen who take great pride in the accomplishment of bringing their white constituents around to the real acceptance of one Negro family. Others have worked in a moderate and temperate way, North and South, to move an entire congregation over a period of years to accept four Negroes out of a membership of a thousand, only to find the whole process undermined when influential members of the community threaten personally the key members of the church because of their public stand.

The exceptional cases of Negro upgrading in socio-cultural and church organizations are undoubtedly a step forward out of the past, but no more. What is not seen is that the present rate of upgrading, often perceived as minor miracles, is in reality a natural increment of the expanding middle class in our escalating society. There are technical difficulties in the way of even these minor concessions. But when one takes into account the predominance of whites over the relatively few Negroes in America, the step-by-step upgrading becomes insignificant. Indeed, Negroes comprise 15–20% of America. They could be rapidly and fully integrated and assimilated into this predominant white society-culture without even this event's becoming a major accomplishment, statistically speaking.

These minimal adjustments in churches and the socio-culture should lead Negroes to question rather than accept the presuppositions of white folk theology. Historically, Christianity has made a distinction between the Church and the world, denying the reality that the Church is in the world and the world is in the Church. What has been deemphasized is God as creator of the world and His purpose for the world being worked out in the Kingdom of God. This Kingdom is to be witnessed to by the Church—reconciliation—in the world and whether this witness be in the churches or not does not finally matter. White folk theology has claimed that the Church is in but not of the world, rather than the Church being in and of the world. This dichotomy has been the basis of distinguishing between the Church and the world, the basis for the separate existence of the Church in the world. Actually, the Church as the servant of the Kingdom of God has no special prerogatives. Its manifestation can only be in the world, not in the churches which are only subsidiaries of the world.

It has been granted that the Church is sometimes manifest, sometimes latent, but inevitably bound up with the churches, the local edifices, memberships, organizations, national and international ecclesiastical structures comprised of denominations. Despite heroic endeavors in monasteries, exclusive Protestant communities, missionary compounds, national and international charities, the criteria of success in church institutions are the same as for non-ecclesiastical institutions. The number of persons added each year and the fiscal increase of the institutional enterprise is indistinguishable from church institution to business institution. Admittedly, the institutional dimension of the Church is supposed to aid and abet the purpose of increasing the Body of Christ. The problem is that the organizational operations of churches, so necessary for any human objective, get in the way of and become severed from the purpose of reconciliation. While the organizational sides of the churches parallel other institutions whose business it is to organize human resources for human objectives, the real failure of the churches is in putting these human resources to use for the manifestation of the brotherhood of man in the spirit of the Kingdom of God. Church institutions would do well to recognize they differ *de facto* in no objective way from other institutions or businesses in and of the world.

The reason these church institutions exist and duplicate what is best done by other institutions is the assumption they are the exclusive agents of reconciliation of the divine extensions of the Body of Christ in ways which are not the same for non-ecclesiastical bodies. It is assumed that reconciliation is the special province of churches. Their failure to be reconciling agents does not disclose God's purpose to reconcile the world and the churches, not just the churches. There is no doubt that church institutions do good things and often have the lead over other business organizations, but business organizations do the job better once they are made aware of their responsibility. In the area of Negro-white group relationships there is the clearest evidence that the churches are not the Church and even that the Church is best manifested in worldly institutions. The Church provides the discernment of the Church at work but not the guarantee of its presence in the churches. Insofar as the Church is in the churches, it is in the world, for the churches are in and of the world just as the world is in and of the churches. This is obvious in both the institutional criteria for success and the persons who manage ecclesiastical and non-ecclesiastical institutions. The same people are often in both institutions. In our time we are witnesses to the most radical and permanent reconciliation taking place in the world of which the churches are a part rather than in the churches which are a part of the world. The world or non-ecclesiastical forces have taken the lead and are far more inclusive in their organizations than are the churches. Moreover, the inclusiveness of the churches only follows the pattern of the world rather than providing it with an image to pattern. The Kingdom of God determines the inclusive brotherhood of man pattern of the churches and the world.

This truth which the Negro knows in experience should lead to a reconsideration among Negro churchmen of the Church as distinct from the churches. The Church came into being as a witness through the localized churches or congregations to the spirit of Christ which established the Kingdom of God. This spirit of Christ, reconciliation, has been interpreted to be the unique province of the institutional churches. This interpretation leads to the claim of the exclusive presence of the Kingdom of God demand in the churches, supported by the fantastic organizational achievements of the ecclesiastical institution. But this interpretation is not founded in the Bible—the Church, the Body of Christ, the engagement of reconciliation, is not a permanent provision of the churches but a demand of the Kingdom of God upon all men which need not be dependent upon nor wait for the churches to be the Church.

In reality, the Church as the people who will to do the will of God's Kingdom is the living presence of God in the reconciliation between man and man through the spirit of Jesus Christ. The Church as the people of God is not the churches, nor is it institutions or the men within the institutions. It is possible for men of the Church in institutions, ecclesiastical or not, to use their organizations for the purposes of reconciliation without falsely claiming these institutions to be identical with the Church.

The confusion of the churches with the Church began when

the visible and established churches became significant identification marks in contradiction to the spirit of the Kingdom of God
in the hearts and minds of men, the presence of which is the Body
of Christ. The Church, the witness of the spirit of Christ in the
lives rather than in the institutions of men, has been particularly
obscured since the Holy Roman Empire through its seeming
churchly or Babylonian captivity in the dominance of Roman
Catholicism and Protestantism of the West. Especially is this
true of their ecclesiology which sets forth the churches as the
earthly embodiment of the Kingdom of God. The presence of
the Kingdom of God is in the hearts of men who live by this
spirit of the brotherhood of man—this is the visible Church.
Sometimes this Church is in the churches; more often it is in
the world. The sign of the coming Kingdom is in the present
sporadic responses of men who live in this spirit, however tenta-
tively, and not in transitory institutions created by men.

The distinctive biblical teaching is that the Kingdom of God,
the presence and fulfillment of the Fatherhood of God and the
Brotherhood of Man, is neither identical with or dependent upon
the churches. Churches are human institutions expressing the
operational procedures of human pride. The promise of God is to
the churches in the world as to the world in the churches: "For,
behold, I create a new heaven and a new earth." The establishment of this promise in the world through Jesus Christ is not
understandable apart from the Kingdom of God which is being
and is to be realized. The rebelliousness of men is not dissimilar
whether they function in ecclesiastical or non-ecclesiastical institutions and this reality provides evidence for the New Testament teaching that the new order, the order of God, will not be
established upon the kingdoms of this world. The New Testament
faith is that world renewal will follow world destruction. This
biblical promise is not sounded in the successful churches which
dominate America, largely because the criteria of success are human institutions rather than the Kingdom of God. The fact that
out of the freedom of God nature was created and man was set
forth with freedom and reason to control the natural realm for
the purposes of the Kingdom of God—this fact and the obvious

success in the natural realm is not perceived against the failure in intergroup relations which is also the task of human freedom and reason. It is the presence of Negroes which places the successes and failures of churches in bold relief against the background of the Kingdom of God. Negroes are the black promise symbolizing the biblical truth of the destruction of human enterprises prior to human renewal.

The failure of white dominated ecclesiastical institutions in intergroup relations and the failure of Negro dominated ecclesiastical institutions in institutional successes may be experience enough for Negroes to cease patterning white ecclesiastical organizations and to take the refreshing approach of recognizing their churches and denominations to be most valuable as secular institutions. Realistically, Negro institutions qua Negro institutions are inferior to the dominant ones because of obvious disadvantages which are highlighted in their inability to draw upon the full resources of the majority white society and power structures therein. There is no way for Negro institutions to make up for the generations of deprivation. But Negro ecclesiastical institutions will continue to exist, and as such their promise lies not in the area of obtaining the full compliment of knowledge and skills to compete with white institutions on the business level, but in realizing their inferior status (because of the inferior status of Negroes) and thereby accepting the secular function of deghettoizing. Negro institutions only exist because of ghettoized Negro people and can exist meaningfully only if they meet the basic need of Negro people—deghettoizing; to be distinguished from deNegroizing.

Clearly, the white institutions which dominate the society, ecclesiastical and non-ecclesiastical, know how to and do achieve success in the organizational, technological, theoretical, and business spheres. The inability or unwillingness of this same dominant white society to achieve success in intergroup relations provides the opportunity for Negroes. Such a contribution requires Negroes to participate fully in the successful institutions of this world in order to gain their full share without setting up further competitive inferior institutions or simply perpetuating colored duplications, through using their institutions to propel Negroes into the mainstream. Such a thrust would not only advance the deghettoizing demands but contribute substantially to the need for intragroup and intergroup acceptance.

The Kingdom of God is not dependent upon the responses of men to be realized. That it will be realized fully following the destruction of this world is the biblical promise symbolized in the exceptional upgrading of singular Negroes and the ghetto scars of all Negroes.

"Then comes the end, when he delivers the Kingdom to God the Father after destroying every rule and every authority and power" (I Corinthians 15:24, RSV).

This biblical promise and Negro experience provide the pragmatic direction for Negro religious institutions. Obviously, the successes of white institutions have neither advanced the Kingdom of God nor have they been shared equally with the Negro; at best they have illuminated the demands of the brotherhood of man. Reason dictates to the Negro that the ecclesiastical double-talk of churchmen leads not to substantial changes and may well be hindrances to the brotherhood of man demands of which the Negro is the black promise. Freedom provides the Negro with the opportunity of using religious language and rituals taken over from whites for the purposes of deghettoizing the Negro and the whites which is the singular concern of Negro folk religion, rather than to use religious language to keep Negroes and whites in ghettos.

Since the Negro masses are both cut off from the theological-ritual-liturgical forces of dominant whites and in segregated churches and institutions, which are indifferent to these intellectual forms, what has been generally a negative or defensive posture can be a positive and offensive one. Indeed, Negroes can be among the avant garde secular institutions in ecclesiastical structures. Since Negro masses are so dependent upon churches and religious expressions, perceptive Negro ministers, laymen, and bureaucrats can channel this natural affinity and emotional attachment toward the objectives of Negro folk religion through using rather than abusing the power of community which is presently pure potential for deghettoizing.

In order to meet the needs of the Negro, which are the demands of the Kingdom of God, Negro ministers, laymen, and denominational institutions require as Negro forces a conscious rejection of white theological and ecclesiastical doubletalk and a conscious acceptance of their black promise. This conscious direction is not to be interpreted as a withdrawing of the exceptional or "show Negro" from white institutions but the means whereby there can be institutions of quality in which whites and blacks mutually participate, rather than white and black institutions in which these groups mutually exclude each other. The inclusion of the Negro in the society is the demand of the Kingdom for the health of whites and blacks, but is dependent for extensity upon black cohesion in the present for the fullness of black dispersion throughout the society with equality in the future and as a whole.

Toward this objective Negroes will be helped by discerning the activity of God and making His pattern their own rather than the activity of churchmen. Man is a political animal and the major political activity of God in human affairs is in the demand for and resistance to the brotherhood of man. The clearest expression of this demand and need is the Negro-white apartheid groups in the United States, no less South Africa. The single most important human issue is not peace or the absence of war—the destruction of this world by man is within his freedom and is not a deterrent to the Kingdom of God which is in the freedom of God. The presence or absence of war and peace is no guarantee of human degrouping. The fundamental issue is the deghettoizing of the entire Negro group. For the singular restriction of the Negro to the ghetto is the visible reminder of the less obvious ghettos in which all are victimized.

Negro ministers are in a peculiar position to see and heed the truth that the degrouping of all groups whereby the richness of all groups can enrich all receives the greatest impetus and strain in Negro-white group conflict. Therefore, Negro ministers are in a unique position, ministering as they do to the ghetto, to see that this issue takes on a universal dimension. As ministers they have the biblical perspective to place this human warfare of deghettoizing against the only background which makes its ultimate imperatives durable and meaningful, the cosmological warfare which the biblical faith marks as the final encounter of good and evil ushering in the Kingdom of God at the end of human opportunities. In dealing with the suffering people upon whom he is dependent for his professional function and livelihood, the Negro minister in a special position to experience, understand and interpret the role of the Negro "suffering servant" in this human warfare. He can know that in this singular human issue whites who join with Negroes in this warfare are sufferers as well, but their suffering is one chosen by them which can be renounced, while the suffering of the Negro is not of his own choosing and cannot be escaped.

This experience means the Negro minister can proclaim reasonably and freely, without feeling guilty about the ecclesiastical vested interests he has been denied, that in the deghettoizing struggle the Church and the world are inextricably one—about the same task of reconciliation through the requirements of an urban and secular ethos. Without the Church (the concrete occasions of Negro-white group reconciliation demanded by the Kingdom) and the world (the concrete opportunities to express and structure Negro-white group equality) the perceptive Negro minister will know there is no possibility for the "suffering servant" people to participate fully in the socio-culture, typified in white ecclesiastical churches which are more often than not bastions of relief from the Church and the urban-secular world. The Negro minister can assert with real authority that the Church is in the world and the world is in the Church! This good news will be liberating for the "suffering servant" and therefore the Negro minister can proclaim—Let the world be the world! Let the Church be the Church! Let them be one in deghettoizing the Negro and stripping away white preconsciousness.

The Negro minister, alert to the urban-secular dynamics which structure society, perceives the world primarily engaged in the legal, educational, political, economic structures which can result in reconciliation of groups. At their best, the churches are working on this level and with this thrust. The Negro minister, alert to the Kingdom of God demands of intergroup interdependence, perceives the Church as primarily engaged in an inclusive life of fellowship, social-cultural-spiritual intercourse, demonstrable beyond formal spheres which does result in reconciliation. He sees the world saying to its Church dimension that real deghettoizing is visionary apart from intimate Negro-white group life together. As the natural leader of the "suffering servant" people the Negro minister is specially situated to hear the world saying to the Church and the Church saying to the world that apart from our demonstrated interpenetrating actions reconciliation does not exist, for reconciliation is not good feeling but dynamic good living; whether in the intimate or organizational spheres of the ecclesiastical or non-ecclesiastical structures of the world.

Through the tenets of Negro folk religion and the experience of the "suffering servant" Negro people, the Negro minister may know the Church is reconciliation and reconciliation is the Church, to which end the worldly organizations or churches are specifically intended to promote. Whether 'reconciliation takes place by the initiatives of these ecclesiastical bodies or other non-ecclesiastical bodies, whether reconciliation takes place in these churches or outside of them, is of no matter to the Church. That the Church, or reconciliation, takes place in the churches or outside them is the singular purpose of the churches, and where they fail in this they have lost their primary purpose for existence. The Church is not concerned to question how or where its life of reconciliation takes place because reconciliation is reconciliation, rooted as it is in the Kingdom of God. Where churches are concerned to take the credit, baptize, or determine reconciliation they are not the Church. The life of the Church is reconciliation without restrictions.

In the world as in the churches the issue of degrouping, deghettoizing is equally demanded. The insightful Negro minister is aware that this means the "suffering servant" Negro people, in America as in South Africa, is the *sine qua non* of social change beyond social action. Being as he is, the Negro is a stumbling block in the world and the churches. No fundamental social change of group separatedness can take place without the Negro changing in status. He is, in a white dominated society, the underdog representing the blackest threat and promise for full group acceptance.

What the Negro minister has yet to realize is this: if the Negro is the key to world and church transformation there can be no change without the Negro precipitating the change. Moreover, the Negro must be the precipitant in change beyond that demonstrated in the civil rights movement, in the realm of socio-religio-cultural intercourse as well. Up to this point the Negro has been the catalyst of shifts in the economic-educational-legal-public utility peripherals—but not in the fundamental spheres of social intercourse. This failure provides the opportunity for the black promise residing in Negro ministers and their congregations: a promise that is to be distinguished from the civil rights movement which has taken place in but has not been of the life of the Negro institutions.

The Negro minister has yet to analyze sufficiently the society as a whole from the experience which is his own. The white folk religious life pervades America and makes this preconscious religious society a segregated one. In this religiously racist society the clue to social intercourse is white congregations. They are country club structured. Their pattern is worldly exclusiveness, white for whites, representing the worst features of the world. The equally exclusive but potentially creative black congregations for blacks represent the single greatest potential for de-grouping and reconciliation. This is because of their possibilities for heightening "Negro consciousness," situated as they are in the geographical and emotional center of the disadvantaged Negro people. Heretofore, Negro ministers and their congregations have not interpreted their role as the "suffering servant" in the Kingdom of God perspective. Rather their interpretation of suffering as deprivation has resulted in a defensive, escapist inferiority complex. This interpretation is characteristic even in Negro congregations which have been the epitome of insularity, best described as a gift and the high visibility as the guarantee of congregational participation. But the suffering shared in common has to be interpreted as an opportunity for responsible, offensive "suffering servant" people.

It is precisely this dilemma of black promise in Negro congregations which can make the remnant conscious of their mission, the black hope.

Negro ministers have to be awakened to the fact that they minister in their congregations to the single most powerful and untapped resource for reconciliation, degrouping, and deghettoizing which can deliver us all from the bondage of Negro-white group separateness. The natural response of mass Negroes to Negro congregations is presently the most formidable power in the emerging powerful Negro communities of the urban centers. But how long this tradition of natural affinity will last may well depend upon its use. It is this experience which undergirds the opportunity for Negro churchmen to operate on the principle that religion is not the Church, though religion, like politics, *is* in the Church and the churches. As an instrument of the Church, one people's religion is another people's politics. Unlike ministers in white churches who question the purpose of their ministry (which in effect is a business operation offering the fringe benefits of comforts at birth, marriage, personal crises, and death), the Negro minister has been a less successful businessman. The key to the white ministry has been a successful business and being a nice guy with obvious marks of sincerity. The key to the Negro ministry has been a stimulating preacher who knows how to give the people the spiritual injections they have traditionally sought, success being determined by the number of people attending and how much they contribute to his person, rather than whether or not a successful business operation is administered. White ministers have had success as businessmen in churches and may find this venture meaningless; therefore, they seek ways to make the churches meaningful. It is the exceptional or fringe Negro minister who has qualms about his ministry; for in the Negro community he is still a very significant figure in ways which the white minister cannot match. The personal advantages and opportunities of exploitation which has given the Negro status in a segregated community in the past may not be sufficient, or present, in a society which continues to upgrade Negroes, even on so sparse and selected a basis as the present.

In our rapidly changing society the fact that the non-ecclesiastical dimensions of the world provide more healing than the ecclesiastical dimensions raises serious questions about the ministry in white congregations and provides the greatest opportunity for the Negro ministry. The reason Negroes should be in the ministry today, as well as why there is need for more ministers of the best quality, is that in the present Negro ghetto the Negro has unprecedented power to realize freedom and equality. This objective of the Negro people has been dreamed of for so very long. Moreover, the Negro minister being the natural leader of the ghetto is potentially the most powerful force for the consolidation of Negro people. For the first time, in this urban-secular ethos, being a central figure in the Negro community the Negro ministry is a position of power to effect the aims of the Negro people as a whole, and not just for personal advantage, as in the past. This newly created center of power is not due to activity on the part of the Negro ministers. It is due to the shift from rural to urban centers, from South to North, and the traditions of the people carried with them in this period of dislocation and quest for better opportunities. It is true that the Negroes who move from the South in large numbers are the lower class Negroes, who do not enjoy the economic advantages of the middle class Negroes who remain in the South, just as the movement from rural to urban centers of the South is by the lower class and not the middle class. But these masses are both religiously attuned and numerically powerful. The time has come when the historic function of Negro folk religion can and should regain its dominant role over black religion in Negro congregations. Negro ministers can and should take the initiative again and bring this power together in concern for the health of the whole community, "black and white together."

Among the reasons given for Negro ministers not using their congregations as centers of power for deghettoizing the Negro has been first the unawareness of the inescapability of suffering as blacks because of being black and consequently not perceiving the "suffering servant" role as a way to suffer creatively in hope rather than in despair; second, the unawareness of the congregations as secular institutions responsible for intergroup changes; third, the recent shift to a dynamic urban-secular directed society; fourth, the fear that the congregations would not support the minister in social action for social change; and fifth, the lack of education among Negro ministers. Thus there have been precious few Negro ministers who have lost their pulpits for reasons of being too involved in social change. This lack of ministers being too much in the avant garde of social change and thereby not losing their positions, particularly in stodgy middle class congregations, may be as much an indication of the ministers being behind the people as a lack of boldness to lead the congregations. In the South ministers will be threatened by the white power structure more readily than the power structure in black congregations. Increasingly, laymen of middle class status are aware of what lower class Negroes unconsciously feel: that there is no escape from being black. This is impetus enough for the Negro minister who requires added encouragement to lead or be led.

Just as the Negro cannot pull himself up by his own bootstraps, so the whites of the Church and in the churches and the world, engaged in deghettoizing, cannot pull the Negro up or into his responsibility. The Negro cannot help being the "suffering servant," but he can resist its demands. Whites desperately need Negroes in action to strengthen and encourage them in their theological or human based struggle to change the old patterns of white preconsciousness in white congregations and white society. The Negro needs whites to change his old pattern of black defensive exclusiveness. Whites at work in desegregating churches and neighborhoods know theologically or humanistically what the Negro knows experientially: that the times demand degrouping. Specifically in the sphere of desegregating churches, whites have taken the initiative and chosen to be the "suffering servant" while the Negro has accepted without joint action his suffering. The time has come for Negro ministers and congregations as Negro institutions to act.

The potential of Negroes in separate congregations and denominations cannot be seen if one begins with the assumption of significantly different features from white congregations.[1] It must be recognized with President Harry V. Richardson of The Interdenominational Theological Center that

> despite the lack of distinctive features, what we call the Negro church is well established as a separate institution or group of institutions, and bids well to remain so for a long time.[2]

However, the following significant facts can be stated without fear of contradiction:

> The church has traditionally been a formative and controlling influence in the life of the American Negro, not only in spiritual matters but in other areas as well. It is by far the largest institution the group has had, having today better than twelve million members. It has served as an instrument of expression and action in civic, cultural, and educational concerns.[3]

It is true that the "Negro church" in urban areas has been shown by recent studies not to be serving the "depressed urban masses," nor has it yet developed "an effective program of serving the indigent masses in inner cities." It is further true that "church service declines as economic status declines," and this is compounded by the startling fact that "92 per cent of the men entering the Negro ministry each year are professionally unprepared." [4] One cannot expect these "untrained leaders" to develop the "intensive service programs necessary for the development of a handicapped people" unless they are inspired and motivated by a cooperative mission with experts which transcends their ability and selfish interests. It is toward this end that we feel impelled to write. After all, there are "between fifty and sixty thousand

---

[1] See my *Black Religion: The Negro and Christianity in the United States* (Boston: Beacon Press, 1964).

[2] Harry V. Richardson, "The Negro in American Religious Life," *The American Negro Reference Book,* John P. Davis (ed.) (Englewood Cliffs: Prentice-Hall, Inc., 1966), p. 412.

[3] *Ibid.*

[4] *Ibid.*, p. 413.

churches and forty to fifty thousand pastors" which form the basis for great possibilities.[5] But this historic institution can no longer live off the capital of the past or the mere patterning after whites. It must play a needed part in the lives of its people if it is to continue with respect and support.

What the Negro ministers and laymen are required to perceive is the absence of an effective power structure in the total Negro community for the good of the entire group. Given the centering of the fragmented civil rights groups in ministers and church buildings, the obvious potential is incontrovertible. The most readily available key to a cohesive power structure in the Negro community is the fusion of the Negro congregations which dominate the life of the Negro ghetto. Herein lies inactive the real health and strength of Negro congregations, the natural centers though not as yet the real centers of power.

The weakness of Negro congregations are inadequate educational-personnel-curricula-facilities, financial resources, intellectual seriousness, imaginative planning, experimentation, and loyalty between congregations. The absence of these foundations increases dissipation and proliferation via personal ambitions, rivalry, and exhibitionism. Of course it would be foolish to overlook the poor educational opportunities of all Negroes, reflected in poor professionally trained ministers. These deficiencies in dependent Negro congregations of white denominations are also reinforced by dependence on white organizations and the lack of opportunity to participate in decision making processes at the national and regional levels. In effect, these white institutional Negro congregations have been allowed to go their own way without the stimulus of competition. This absence of pressure to keep pace in the midst of obvious socio-cultural disadvantages resulted in independent Negro institutions and congregations' equally objective deprivation. For these reasons the long range goal is to bring equality to Negro religious life in these areas of deficiency and to enrich white congregations via the spontaneous spirited joy and fervor of the Negro through their mutual involvement in

[6] *Ibid.*

degrouping. But the attainment of all these resources for the entire Negro group requires total socio-cultural equal opportunity and therefore cannot be the present, singular, or major objective of Negro congregations. Indeed, this socio-cultural fulfillment can only result from the intercourse which will be the byproduct of Negroes first concentrating upon gaining communal unity, the source of power together for a common advance demanding total inclusion in the total society.

There is no simple or automatic process whereby Negroes can be brought together for the purposes of concentrating their power to gain the worldly and Church objectives. The knowledge, experience, and dedication of ministers and laymen who now participate in the urban-secular changes of society may be spur enough to lead in socio-religio changes along with the educational-economic possibilities. Changes in these areas or deghettoizing will be as extensive as the Negro community is united, imaginative, and forceful. Whites can and will include Negroes only to the extent Negroes are willing to bring the power of pressure relentlessly to bear.

Deghettoizing is a two-way process in which Negroes and whites must give and receive, challenge and respond, speak and listen. The disadvantages of the Negro congregations and ministers are undeniable. What they lack in knowledge, skill, and organizational know-how they may make up in fervor and desperation. It is obviously much easier for whites to be in the avant garde of integration even in the isolated instances of churches. In fact such action on the part of the majority can be a demonstration of superiority and magnanimity, for the few Negroes who do attend white congregations are easily placed in the category of exceptions. The functional inadequacy of Negro congregations does not only mean a few if any of the most dedicated and extraordinary whites will naturally attend without persuasion, but it means, as well, the qualitative difference between white and Negro congregational life poses a threat to Negroes, especially if whites attend Negro congregations. Yet, the presence of whites in Negro congregations and Negroes in white congregations in more than token numbers is as essential in this sphere of life as it is in education, employment, and housing. Indeed, without the presence of whites and Negroes in real communication, sharing the possibilities for Negroes to upgrade their organizations and whites to break the barriers of exceptions, the chances for equal enrichment are nullified.

Thus, it is not possible for Negroes with all their deprivations to wait until they are equal in quality with the more advantageous whites before taking the initiative in integrating churches. Since churches represent the most obvious instances of group separation, with the highest amount of guilt, Negroes need to begin now to accept their deprivation. Out of this sense of need to gain advantages they can work for unity of groups in congregations which will in and of itself increase the necessary upgrading.

Within their own lives and structures Negroes must be about reconciliation within churches as in the larger society simultaneously, to not only demand Negro-white group unity but witness to it as well. In the larger socio-economic-educational-political fields, as in the churches, Negroes need awareness of their "suffering servant" or instrumental role in degrouping. To gain the objective of deghettoizing requires the unified diversity of Negro ministers and laymen of all congregations in each community. Such unity within and between myriad varieties of Negro congregations is only conceivable out of the awareness of their common closeness as "suffering servant," which transcends their denominational differences.

The unity of all Negro congregations as a power base in each community and between communities across and throughout the United States can only come about where the denominational differences and variety of successes and methods are accepted structures. The unity of Negroes through the natural power center of churches must be on the basis of respect for and acceptance of ecclesiastical differentiation. For the Negro's purpose is not like the ecumenical movement to witness to a unity of theology, polity, doctrine, and liturgy, an advanced and sophisticated movement predicated on the equal opportunity of whites; rather, the unity of Negroes is for community power to break down the barriers of the ghetto. The ecumenical endeavor may be a happy byproduct. The numerical, financial, ritual, class differences of Negro institutions must not only be disallowed. They are necessary gathering centers and therefore resources to be tapped as demonstrations of their inescapable role as "suffering servant." Negro ministers and laymen so aware will undoubtedly be the minority in each congregation but this minority of different classes is the indispensable remnant which can mobilize a larger group for responsibility. This means disinterest in black religion or culture religion, disinterest in the motivations of people attending religious worship, disinterest in the variety of memberships or number on the rolls, disinterest in personality cults. However primitive or sophisticated, emotional or intellectual the religious mode or tone of the services, these are of little consequence compared with ministers and laymen channeling these varieties of expression beyond individual release or inspiration to community unity and power in political life together. Instead of passive acceptance of and delight in suffering, what is needed is for all Negro churches to develop ingenious ways of making the climax of each congregational gathering a call and commitment to creative suffering servanthood in the face of the inevitable common suffering of Negroes regardless of their ecclesiastical differences.

It is in the life of the churches themselves that Negroes have their greatest weakness and strength; there they must pull together toward the common objective of deghettoizing. The churches are the most strategic places to develop the awareness of total deprivation of all Negroes, their inclusion in society requires involvement in all dimensions of society. This will mean an obvious threat to all Negro ministers. But in their cooperation together the realization may come that their security in the ghetto at the expense of keeping all Negroes in the ghetto is too high a price. Here is the possibility of courage to meet the demands of ministering to the people at their deepest needs. It may be difficult for many ministers and laymen to accept the reality that their parishioners need God the least at eleven o'clock on Sunday mornings, but they may respond to the reality that this hour offers the greatest opportunity to meet the real needs of the people throughout the week and that this is Godly. The way is that of uniting the sacred and the secular, the religious and the profane, the chosenness of "suffering servant" with ego strength from being black, fervor with direct action, spirituality with political power. If Negro churches are to be the Church, reconciling agents of the Kingdom of God on behalf of the brotherhood of man, Negroes must unite across denominational lines as the "suffering servant" to ensure that whites are in Negro congregations and Negroes are in white congregations, in substantial numbers, in every community where there are Negroes and whites.

The initiative requires the Negro to be a responsible "suffering servant," aware of his role as the fulcrum of the Kingdom of God in the process of degrouping and committed to the Kingdom of God above the kingdoms of this world. To this end he must be willing to sacrifice the security of minorities within the minority for the health of the whole minority and consequently the majority.

The process of deghettoizing of churches as a positive thrust, rather than the loss of members through white initiative or the gaining of white members by their own boldness, means the Negro will be becoming a mature if deprived churchman, involved in the decisions instead of bowing to them. This process demands long range and imaginative planning to formulate both the objectives and the methods for the number of whites and Negroes to be engaged in churches dominated by other groups. The threat of losing the best members will have to be faced in the light of deghettoizing.

The long range planning can produce hitherto unknown experimental ministries among Negro institutions through the cooperation of ministers and churches supporting in common with local congregations and national denominations Negro missions to whites as there have been white missions to Negroes. Indeed, it may be necessary to begin with experimental ministries to discover what needs to be done throughout all Negro congregations.

This cooperative, experimental ministry among all Negro denominations means the hard work of locating Negro based churches in strategic urban areas of the North and South where they will be in a position to minister to whites and Negroes. To so locate Negro based churches in strategic areas outside the ghettos requires hard cash, which is best available in an inter-denominational venture in degrouping. The basis for missions to whites would not be on the theory they need to be saved from hell for heaven, but they need the wholesome healthfulness which comes from degrouping and the Negro needs the same salvation or healthfulness. In addition to strategic locations, financial co-operation, and organizational imagination, the selection of the right minister or ministers is imperative. The Negro minister engaged in mission to whites, not only to demonstrate the readiness of Negroes for total inclusion but the necessity thereof, will need to be extraordinarily confident, resourceful, bold, and dedicated to the responsibility of the "suffering servant." To ring doorbells in white neighborhoods where hostility abounds takes one kind of courage. To impress whites with their need to be "show whites" or "a fool for Christ" takes another kind of courage.

These missions to whites will further require the ability to work with white ministers and white power structures to discover those whites who are ready for this venture and to discover the means whereby the advantages can be brought to bear upon those whites to be made ready. Simultaneously, the same kind of venture in the Negro community will be necessary to elicit those Negroes who are ready and can be made ready.

Mission churches to whites provide the opportunity for recruiting Negroes and whites best qualified to determine the educational plant needs, the curriculum of quality, the personnel to teach, the worship program and the necessary social program all of which are to be integrated for the purposes of realizing the brotherhood of man.

One of the key tasks of these mission churches would be to deal directly and openly with the sex themes which church groups avoid. The fears and uneasiness about sexual relations between Negroes and whites will need to be set forth in open and vigorous discussions and their results transmitted to Negro and white churches and the society as a whole. It is clear that in a society dominated by white preconsciousness the South American pattern of intermarriage and miscegenation cannot be *the* way to deghet-toizing the Negro, although neither the Negro nor the white can be deghettoized until intermarriage is a live option which can be freely chosen or rejected by Negroes and whites. White and Negro sexual relations take place on the lower class fringes and among the marginal men and women of middle class stations for the most part. In an expanding middle class society, as Negroes increasingly gain the advantages of the society, they tend to marry Negroes as whites do whites. It is a question as to whether this pattern of group intra-marriage is a natural result of an expand-ing middle class society or an unnatural result of the black and white mystiques which pervade. The answer lies not along the route of demanding intermarriage but through the process of degrouping, a means to which and the result of which may well be intermarriage of Negro and whites in substantial numbers to re-flect the total assimilation that is deghettoizing. This may mean that deghettoizing can no more take place in society without sufficient numbers of intermarried Negro-whites willing to take the offensive against a white preconscious society than churches can be the Church without Negroes and whites. One thing is cer-tain, wholesale intermarriage for the purposes of miscegenation would be a violation of marriage. It would also be visionary to plan for or wait for this process. Moreover, deghettoizing is not the same as intermarriage, it is more. In the process of deghettoiz-ing intermarriage can occur naturally, but in the process of inter-marriage deghettoizing does not naturally occur. Further, full intermarriage of all Negroes with whites would not result in com-plete deghettoizing, any more than complete deghettoizing would result in full intermarriage. Intermarriage has to be faced as a good and healthy free choice and possibility, a positive rather than a negative relationship. It is a challenge to white precon-sciousness. If in America this impossible possibility were to take place it would be little more than a shrewd maneuver of the majority and in this light would have to be seen in the context of South Africa. Miscegenation may be a demonic form of deprecat-ing the value of group differences through group dominance which is unwilling to accept the values of groups without divisiveness of groups. Insofar as intermarriage is a weapon in the total arsenal trained upon deghettoizing the mission churches are obligated to seek its meaning and power.

The experimental churches or Negro-based missions to whites are the secondary objectives of which Negro institutions should strategically engage in for the degrouping of churches. Their work may be unique, but their procedures can and ought to be those of each Negro congregation. Toward this end Negro seminaries may well provide the resources and give their life for the people rather than for ecclesiastical institutions.

As significant as degrouping churches is, it is only one thrust of the Negro church based power and not the most important one. Degrouping of churches is necessary both for those Negroes and whites who are ready for social intercourse now and as a symbol of and means to the completeness of deghettoizing.

The least threatening and most pervasive task of Negro church power is to bring about degrouping in education, housing, economics, and culture whereby all Negroes can gain the good things of this life if they so choose. This objective leads some to the mistaken conclusion that Negro churches should become community or day care centers engaged in ameliorative but peripheral social work and recreational programming. This is not the task of the churches primarily and should be engaged in only insofar as it furthers the "suffering servant" mission of Negro-white reconciliation.

One of the most dangerous programs for Negro ministers, especially in the South, and at the same time one of the most helpful programs for the Negro people is the Equal Opportunity Act. Since in many communities Negro ministers are natural leaders, the opportunities to administer this program on a non-sectarian basis is presented to them.

Ministers are not giving proper leadership in most instances to the "suffering servant" people if they function as social workers, recreation leaders, day care administrators, educators, or poverty program agents. Nor are ministers properly engaged among the remnant if they are mere spokesmen for the spiritual and not using the spiritual as a means of setting forth the suffering of the Negro—leading the people to see they cannot find God through escape to the churches since God is not in religious services but at work in the world of deprivation where they must find and respond to Him in the hard ways of the brotherhood of man.

The primary task of the churches and the Negro ministers is to cooperate and pull together in each community to form the power base to deghettoize the Negro and realize the good life of freedom and responsibility for all Negroes. This means churches are required to be totally involved with the world in the daily and risky business of politics.

Negro churches are the only natural communities universal enough to command the loyalty and respect of the majority of the Negro masses. They alone are so extensive as to form unity in political power. The great weakness of the Negro community is the absence of consensus and concerted action, divided as it is by apathy, personality conflicts, and divisive forces culled out by various forms of compromises. Despite weaknesses of the churches by any objective criteria, the affinity of the Negro masses provides them with the greatest potential strength. To mold this potential into reality the Negro churches would be emphasizing and reaffirming the Negro folk religion of freedom and equality, the original purposes of their creation.

For the churches to become political power bases of real effectiveness they would first need to see their real power source and the presence of no comparable alternative for deghettoizing. This discernment may best come from charismatic leadership of Negro ministers. The difficult task will be in permitting a minister to be the spokesman, and/or a selected group of ministers with real persuasive power and influence, since the minister is generally the central figure in each church. Beyond the immense problems of each minister gaining the support of his laymen and each minister supporting each minister is the formidable task of each congregation supporting each other. The route taken to solve these problems will differ in each community, depending upon the charisma, temperament, and calibre of the ministers in particular and the laymen in general. As a guideline here the Negro community has the experience of American Jews and Irish

Roman Catholics, though these former immigrants did not have the yoke of Protestant proliferation through the dissipation of freedom which plagues the in-migrant Negro.

Whatever techniques are used to raise up and support a spokesman, the real issue centers about unifying Negroes from the various churches around a personality or personalities. Here a great deal can be learned about what to and not to do from Adam Clayton Powell. The minister who is the political spokesman must have the kind of drawing power Powell has and, beyond this, a dedication to deghettoizing the Negro people which transcends personal ambition. The risk of personal ambition's taking over will have to be run. The key to control, ensuring that the minister is the spokesman for the people, lies in political power being based in churches which gather weekly and thereby can constantly express and demand the will of the people. It will be no mean trick to keep the power in the churches rather than in personalities circumventing the churches, or building up separate organizations of power. But in keeping the power through the checks and balances of myriad churches the inevitable conflicts of interests and opinions will have to be managed for the larger objective of community control.

Such an organization may lead to the election of political representatives in the Congress and on the state and national levels. Even more important than the election of Negroes to office, or whites who represent the Negro, is the task of a concerted and unified community-based power structure to see that the needs of the Negro are met on the local level on a continuing basis, week after week, not just concern with elections. For this purpose the churches are indispensable as the weekly gathering points for information and its dissemination.

Occasionally—or frequently, as the case may be—the Negro minister who is the spokesman may be elected to office. This should be the case only insofar as he is the best person or if a better person is not available. The primary function of the Negro spokesman and minister is not to be elected but to be the voice of the people, to formulate its mind and articulate it in such a way as to unify the community around concrete and real issues of vital concern. The leadership needed is not for the purpose of the Negro minister's becoming the politician, social worker, school teacher or administrator, board chairman, or poverty program agent. The leadership needed is to see that the qualified persons who represent the mind of the community do indeed function in this manner in their role of expert.

As the remnant of the "suffering servant" people, the black hope can be the black promise through ministers mobilizing churches into powerful political communities which not only respond positively to federal, state, and local forces for deghettoizing—but increase their effectiveness in each local community through initiating and directing the change. When compared with white ecclesiastical institutions the Negro institutions will necessarily be inferior, but if the criteria is shifted from effective *business* organizations to effective *political* communities, Negro churchmen and churches will have a unique contribution to make to both Negro and white groups of a superior quality. The process of intergroup interaction may raise the standards of Negro congregations, but the real and imperative gain during the continued existence of Negro ecclesiastical institutions will be the pride with which Negroes can participate in Negro congregations for the purpose of the whole community and disinterest in the inadequacies which are after all inconsequential in the fundamental task of degrouping or reconciliation of groups. The realization of their indispensability for the unification of the Negro community is meaning enough for Negro ministers and churches to purposely exist as agents of change, while in the process changing from necessary dependent institutions to interdependent ones. For as the Negro is amassed to speak and participate in the society with massive unity, the impact upon degrouping will force deghettoizing in education, employment, culture, housing and social forces as well as religion.

The civil rights movement has been largely a confrontation between middle class Negroes and whites. Since the theologians and other academicians engaged in this confrontation are middle class and do the writing and speaking about this venture, they naturally see their confrontation as a real breakthrough and therefore think of it as far more significant than it is. The optimism of white liberals is fixated about the economic escalation of a few middle class Negroes. What the churches' task of deghettoizing the Negro in this society means is that better employment and education, sometimes housing, does not deghettoize the Negro who gains from these benefits and that the real task is not occasional summer skirmishes but year round daily sustained efforts to bring all Negroes into the society. For this "suffering servant" mission churches can be expendable.

The absence of this necessary indigenous Negro leadership and unity in each urban community, no less the small towns and rural communities, is evident in the swing of Martin Luther King, Jr., through the selected cities of the North (Chicago, Cleveland, Newark, etc.) in the summer of 1965. Were there real leadership his non-violent approach would be seen as irrelevant in the North, as in the South, to the basic political power needs. The response to his whirlwind tours indicates a felt need for real means of achieving the goal. Clearly, this kind of evangelistic pep talking cannot be tolerated as a substitute for political unity and action. Obviously, Martin Luther King, Jr. cannot be the leader in each community, however much he dramatizes the need for leadership in every Negro community.

Yet, the fundamental note of community responsibility which Dr. King reiterates cannot be ignored. The problem is how to translate this into real action and power beyond moral admonishment. The way set forth here is via the churches and their leadership. In the process of cooperation and communication they will develop the Saul Alinskys to carry forth the opportunities of the Adam Clayton Powells. The fact that America is gaining in riches while the non-technologically oriented nations are gaining in poverty has to be seen in the light of white America becoming richer and black America becoming poorer. The responsibility for this discrepancy is in part in the Negro community which has been passive rather than active in this time of great opportunity. The occasion for the simultaneous assault upon depovertizing and deghettoizing the Negro is here in the fantastic affluence of the society and the stricken conscience of its affluent white leaders and structures. What is missing is the organized and intense power of Negro communities to politic. It is the responsibility of Negro churches and churchmen of all denominations to centralize and throw the political weight of the Negro "suffering servant" behind sustained, long term efforts for full participation in every dimension of life. They have inherited respect and support which they should now earn. Other groups will be at work concentrating upon the technical specifics. The expertise of the NAACP, Urban League, SCLC, federal, state, and local economic-housing-employment programs will be as far reaching as the force of Negro responsibility in each community and between communities.

Previously, Negro churches and churchmen could feign powerlessness and ignorance, concentrating only in spiritual escapism. It may have been the case that the way to power and action was inconceivable. Today the technical skills of public and private agencies are present to respond to demands. The Negro community North and South no longer have alibis to delay the completion of a new North and South. Negroes can no longer tolerate being ghettoized without directing its unprecedented power in urban communities toward deghettoizing and the transformation of society. The churches must be the embattled lobbies for equal participation to end the separation of Negro-white groups.

The black hope which lies within this black promise is not a new heaven or a new earth but the enjoyment by all of this good universe and all of its human possibilities in the time between the new earth and the new heaven. The knowledge that God does not require our help to do His work and will not do our work for us is motive enough to be men and therefore responsible. It is the work of the Negro to refuse to let others take from him his rightful share and the transformation of this human realm which cannot but result from our creative efforts and not by default. The Kingdom of God, the full realization of the fatherhood of God and the brotherhood of man, will come in God's own time (*kairos*) and not our own time (*chronos*). Herein is the knowledge that God's intention for all to live in His Kingdom in no way conflicts with the joy of gaining earthly goods, among which is economic well-being and the enrichment in this time between the times of a life which freely accepts group differences. The Kingdom of God is not for Negroes who are the "suffering servant" people of this age, whites are also the creations of God who will inherit this Kingdom. If whites enjoy the riches of the kingdoms of this world by the route of superiority which excludes the Negro group and the riches of the Kingdom of God as well, whose fault will it be if in this time of new and adequate resources the Negro does not make the "suffering servant" people irresistible and thereby lose the riches of the kingdoms of this world—which they can gain by their own initiative—for the sake of the Kingdom of God which they will inherit without merit?

In this urban and secular age, where technological rewards abound, a minority of Negroes have gained in comparable degree with the majority of whites and yet remain ghettoized. It is the responsibility of mature Negroes to ensure these opportunities for all Negroes and with the experience that the technological transformation is no substitute for human transformation, use these resources to confront Negro and white groups with each other in every realm of life without which Negro and white ghettos of abundance will emerge as warring rich and blockaded encampments in the United States and the world, each threatening and eventually destroying the other. There is hope and promise in the Negro "suffering servant" people through the remnant within the churches, calling into being a new North and South whose reality is not identical with nor dependent upon the new heaven and earth, the divine initiative, but upon human challenge and response to human possibilities. The way is difficult beyond comprehension, laden with misunderstanding, fear, failure, violence, bloodshed, the force of freedom acknowledging necessity. The hope and promise of the Negro may be insufficient, but without his acceptance of being chosen the certainty of death confronting us all will not be transformed in the ultimate meaning of Negro-white reconciliation, the certain reality of the fatherhood of God and the brotherhood of man which is the Kingdom of God.

CHAPTER VIII
BLACK POLITICS

THE INSTITUTIONAL CENTER of the Negro community is the Negro church. The riots in the northern and urban communities cannot be understood as sanctioned by the Negro church or stemming from its agitation. As the dominant social institution of the community, the Negro church condones in no way the destructive violence which erupts in the warring madness of a Los Angeles, Chicago, or Springfield in the summers, as in other cities of our past and future. The Negro church continues to be for the present the heart of the Negro community in the South where riots do not occur as in the North, partly because the vicious segregation of the South has provided the Negro there with the opportunity of owning businesses in particular and property in general so that the Negro underdog has a stake in even a segregated economy. This outcome of a thoroughly segregated society augurs well for the future of Negro-white relations in the South together with the thus far largely southern-based civil rights movement which demonstrates the insufficiency of economic well being for the privileged few who have functioned in the past, consciously or not, to keep the majority of Negroes in tow.

These dilemmas of Negro-white segregation and class separations within the Negro community have resulted in the migration to the North of the lower class Negro at the bottom of the heap who has the least stake in the society, seeking in the North the opportunity denied in the South. While the South has permitted Negroes to advance economically within the Negro community, the process has been ingeniously selective and promotes the survival of the fittest. The North has not condoned a dual system, preferring to operate on the basis of including exceptional Negroes into restricted areas of its economy, a process which has allowed a fewer number of Negroes to advance in business and the ownership of property than in the South. Since there is not a sufficient number of Negro businessmen in the South to include the lower class masses they act as inhibitors and are of sufficient strength to aid the in-migration of the masses to the North. The even less numerical strength of Negro businesses in the North results in an absence of control of the Negro masses, providing the possibility for the only outlet of a frustrated mass in riotous destruction.

Negroes are of sufficient numbers in the North and whites of sufficient deference to the democratic creed to prevent the return of Negroes to the South or a segregated southern pattern in the North. The only way out of the ghetto is that of full inclusion into society. The question is since whites will not rapidly move in this direction by their own initiative, how can the pace be quickened? Presently, despite their adoration of property, whites are even more concerned to preserve preference for whites and willing to take chances on the destruction of property they so dearly love—presumably on the basis that there is enough financial power in the economy to rebuild the destruction of property, whereas the inclusion of Negroes fully into the society is irreversible. In the long run, barricading Negroes in ghettos will not prove an adequate deterrent, but, as the Los Angeles riots of August 1965 revealed, they provide a postponement of the inevitable which is less of a sacrifice than equality. This is the antireason of whites which is no more to be condoned than the emotive response of Negroes through riots. To rob a people for three generations of full economic equality, which not only means poverty at the lowest levels but an equally weighted poverty at the highest levels of becoming big businessmen and at the middle level of becoming middle class businessmen—to so rob a people for so long and then attempt to compensate by emergency measures of poverty programs is the height of preconscious irrationality. It is equally a preconscious irrationality to give men a taste of the goods of society and deny them full measure or allow them to be full partners in the society. Obviously, the Negro male is not allowed to compete equally in business with the white male because the Negro male is not accepted equally and therefore cannot gain the natural clientele of the general public. With the availability of lower class jobs rapidly receding, these situations tend toward the disintegration of the Negro family and the desperation for material goods, which takes the form of re-robbing what has been robbed. Negroes engaged in riotous vandalism may not be comparable to Robin Hood, but neither is their status, for a Robin Hood could be accepted in the larger society from which he chose dissent as Negroes cannot now be in this society. People tend to respond irrationally if they are treated irrationally. The new technique of rationally formed rights and equal opportunity programs are based upon the preservation of the irrational white preconsciousness, which is the real objective of riotous irrationality.

Heretofore, the function of the Negro church has been that of a haven. In effect it has served as a cut-rate social outlet, selling itself for quantity rather than quality, offering cheap white medicine in colored doses of several hours of relief for a week-long headache. Without the Negro church's false offering of second class status—a substitute for first class equality—there would have erupted more riots on a larger scale in more communities. Let us prevent their irrational occurrences in future summers by better means than that of hiring more police to protect the status quo. The 1965 and 1966 Los Angeles riots might well serve notice that the old technique of the Negro church at the heart of the community is no longer strong enough to combat disadvantages, weakened as it is by strengthened desire for real freedom with and for equality. In the absence of freedom with equality, material goods gained in any way possible and the gratification of destruction is the next best thing. Indeed, the time is short for the Negro church as the heart of the community. There is no question about its demise. What is at stake is the terms on which it will cease and desist as a Negro qua Negro institution of courage, power, wealth, and strength with meaning.

The history of histrionic black politics in churches can no longer be tolerated by the Negro church unless it desires to abdicate its opportunity for creative responsibility in providing the Negro a base in each community for a means to bring about the permanent power and wealth momentarily felt in a riotous war. The one value of the Los Angeles riot worth nurturing beyond the inextinguishable reality of powerlessness and poverty is the actual power of the Negro community. Nearly a quarter of a billion dollars in destruction resulted from the negative concertedness of Los Angeles Negroes in 1965–66. Would not the amount of power and wealth generated through a Negro community in concert toward positive goals—sustained, strategically concentrated, and with a permanent, community-based political machine—would it not be greater than that of a riot?

The responsibility of the Negro church in the process is inseparable from the opportunity through its engagement of the Negro masses. It has the task of neither controlling riots for the well-being of the white ownership of property nor of providing a means of escape from suffering via the route of religious services which culminate in the ineffective if spirited "waiting for Godot." The spiritual outpouring of the masses may well be needed for a long time to come and moreover may be instrumentally effective if this spirit in churches becomes, like the spirit in the civil rights movement protests, a source of strength—this time for political action beyond protest.

To be quite candid, Negro churches may not be the imperative required to gain the political power increasingly sought by other Negro organizations; but one thing is clear—a perceptive Negro church can hardly miss the truth that insofar as these other organizations are effective, the need for the Negro church will decrease proportionately. It is also clear that if the Negro church releases its hold on the Negro masses in return for the support of existing power structures that in the long run cannot but bring the personalities and institutions power and health which now exist only because both take advantage of the disadvantaged—the process will be speeded up immeasurably. Herein lies the opportunity of the Negro church in black politics which is also its responsibility for the Negro masses. The Negro church began as a movement for freedom and equality and although it has slipped into the ameliorative role of a social-cultural institution, it is not yet clear that it cannot reaffirm its original function, especially in view of its present dysfunction with respect to the substantive issues which confront its people. In truth, there is no other live option.

If this option is to be a living one, the leadership of Negro churches will have to be led indigenously, no outside Negro institutions of social uplift will be able to bring this about. Some ideas may have to change among the presidents and staff of the two National Baptist Conventions, as well as bishops and officers of the several Methodist Episcopal Churches—no less the less populous Negro ecclesiastical institutions. If the imagination is lacking to envision the present need of Negro churches for religious and even sacramental support for the political unity of its masses, the desperation of the masses may fill the leadership gap. It would not be too much to ask of Martin Luther King, Jr. to spend his energies in reshaping the intent and content of directions within and among the national Negro ecclesiastical leadership which affects the local churches. This would be no substitute for direct action in local communities. Confrontation of both institutionally-based Negro church leadership and the masses is necessary for the indispensable changes called for in objectives if not methods. It should not be surprising to find, were such a radical move undertaken, the real leadership and motivation within the masses themselves and therefore the greatest possibility for realization of the mass based Negro church. A pincer movement within the Negro church would ultimately result in the destruction of the Negro church based on the present non-voluntary, Negro-white ghettos. Yet, a pincer movement would be based upon the constructive task of releasing the masses and their leadership from barriers to their involvement in the process of change, without which involvement there can be no change. The value of this pincer movement outweighs all of the blood, sweat, and tears it demands. For the Negro mass is amassed at the bottom of society and nowhere is their presence identifiable more regularly than in the Negro church. It cannot be reiterated too often or too strongly that despite the frustrations, the white community will move no faster than the Negro community forces it to move through power, which is potentially within the Negro church—though by no means exclusively.

As an institution, the Negro church has long ago lost the respect and support of secular leadership organizations and leaders in the Negro community, despite the fact that a number of Negro churches support the NAACP. Negro ministers who join in a movement such as the Southern Christian Leadership Council demonstratively withdraw from the institutional Negro church. Clearly, the way in which King has used the Negro church in detachment from it has not only won respect from Negro leadership outside the church but clearly illuminated the untapped power potential in this community center. If Negro ministers and the masses can be directed to engage in political power, their objective will not be to elicit the respect of intellectuals, though this would be an inevitable outcome. In any case, despite the antipathy between non-ecclesiastical Negro leadership organizations and the Negro church, or for that matter the failure of the Negro church to be true to its inception resulting in the increasing number of other organizations, these organizations need all the support they can get to organize the masses into a powerful political force for change. The support of Negro churches would be most welcome.

In the preceding chapters the moral and theological bases for Negro churches' involvement in politics have been laid and in such a manner as not to be in conflict with or contradiction to the function of the church. Together with the moral requirement to meet the needs of Negroes through a positive acceptance of the masses and their capacity to engage in the challenge of change, the theoretical, theological, moral, and political groundwork is unmistakable.

Given this theological and theoretical basis for moral action and change, the next step is to gain the moral commitment to responsibility. This calls for skill and knowledge for redirection within the institutional Negro church. Whatever tactics are used for this purpose (e.g., appeal to tradition, conscience, suffering—disclosure of sham through shame, opportunity for advancement of parishioners lost—education), "pragma" rather than dogma must be the rule.

Beyond the moral situation, a radical theological perspective, and an institutional commitment, a practical method is required. This practical method the Negro church cannot provide. It can indulge in practical politics wholeheartedly out of experience in ecclesiastical politics which have been less moral than these times require and certainly more exclusive and circumscribed. There is a sense in which the Negro church may lose face in practical community politics insofar as it works in concert with other organizations. This loss of prestige can be turned into face-saving through several significant functions the Negro church is in a position to contribute. *First,* the Negro church is the most natural means for the regular gathering of the largest number of Negroes in the community. To contribute the people in concert is its primary task in the new demand and opportunity of black politics. *Second,* the Negro church, aware of its role in the process of fundamental social change, can bring to bear upon white pre-consciousness its contradiction of the biblical faith through relentless efforts in social integration of churches and communities. The position must be that of the impossibility of a church's being Christian without the demonstrated presence of Negroes and whites which requires the removal of discrimination in housing, which is possible only with equality of income, which cannot be gained without equality of social acceptance. In any planned effort within the Negro community for a direct attack upon social inequality there will be an ample number of Negroes to carry forth the main burden of politics through cohesion of Negroes in Negro churches. *Third,* real commitment of the Negro church in politics will earn it the right of its inheritance, the populous center of the Negro masses instrumental in the cooperation of all Negro organizations for the advancement of the people. This cooperation through political union would not interfere with the different functions of the various organizations (e.g., NAACP—litigation; Urban League—economic opportunity; Student Non-

violent Coordinating Committee—youth development; CORE—
enlistment of non-church–based masses; churches—cohesiveness
of church-based masses), but would mean a united political front.

Thus, in the new politics, of necessity and moral rightness,
a real function of the Negro church would include mass cohesion
on a broad base to provide a center for the mass-centered and
issue-oriented politics of independence. The clearest model for
such political unity is in the Mississippi Freedom Democratic
Party (MFDP) which not only uniquely demonstrates the powerlessness of black politics South and North, so far, but the real
possibility therein were it supported fully by the institutional
Negro church.

What is now needed (and the Negro church must support
if it is to be responsible to its oppressed masses, who are not
needed in a society of abundance and therefore are passed off as
"drags") is the real organization of the community. Although the
Negro church has been the titular head of the Negro community,
it has not engaged in its mobilization for power; rather, it has
done little more than open its doors through which the masses
have flocked with little if any nurturing. Thus the Negro church
has not been involved in community mobilization and is without
the essential skills and techniques for this fundamental operation.

Indeed, none of the old line Negro organizations is in position
to provide more than support in this area of community mobilization and even the more recently developed SCLC is at best
equipped for short term organization of a select community for
the more emotional force of protest. The Negro church and other
Negro organizations which are committed to the Negro masses
will need to learn mobilization through cooperation with other
movements.

A good beginning for community organization would be to
utilize the techniques of Saul Alinsky and his Industrial Areas
Foundation. Alinsky, well-portrayed in Charles Silberman's *Crisis
in Black and White,* is the highly respected and paid community
organizer, well known for his strategy of mass jujitsu in Chicago's
TWO (The Woodlawn Organization). The IAF has branched out
into many communities where mobilization has taken place as

often outside formal social structures (in low income neighborhood house meetings for example) as within structures calling
upon IAF consultation or direct involvement. Alinsky is a firm
believer in grass roots democracy via the masses, insisting that
theory be tested by its pragmatic value rather than building a
theory which is then taken untried to the field. While he does not
respond favorably to ecclesiastical institutions as such, he works
well with and for religious community organizations which request
his leadership and may for this reason praise churches extraordinarily on occasion:

> The biggest change I've seen in the twenty years or so that I've
> been involved in social action is in the role the churches are
> playing. Back in the 1930's an organizer might expect to get
> some help from the CIO or from a few progressive AFL
> unions. There wasn't a church in sight. But today they have
> really moved into the social arena, the political arena. They
> have taken over the position organized labor had a generation
> ago. They are the big dominant force in civil rights.[1]

It may be necessary to wait for Alinsky's forthcoming book
on the subject to learn of his "rules for revolution." But the Negro
church, and the other Negro community organizations with
which it must cooperate if the Negro community is to turn its
potential into political power, can learn now from Alinsky how
to build "a strong, disciplined, vital organization which will maintain its form and force over an extended period of time."[2] Alinsky
aptly criticizes the civil rights movement for relying on the single
issue of civil rights instead of building community-based organizations on many issues including "housing, jobs, schools, con-
sumer prices, representation and power at the decision making
centers, health, crime, and every other aspect of life that affects
the welfare and future of the local people and their children."[3]
The art of organization is the alliance of groups with varying

---

[1] Saul Alinsky, "A Professional Radical Moves in on Rochester," *Harper's*,
July 1965, p. 52.
[2] *Ibid.*
[3] *Ibid.*

interests which can be supported in agreed upon priorities while working for common objectives of the total community.

Such development of a community into an organization depends upon concrete and immediately realizable goals. Stemming from these successes is the unity necessary for the middle range and long range goals of more abstraction. To build such an organization in community after community requires sophistication, manpower, money, stamina, intelligence, experience, and compromise. These never are in abundance in any community with commitment to the grubbiness of politics. A beginning in the large urban communities can be seen with the IAF, the Northern Student Movement, Students for a Democratic Society, and the Student Nonviolent Committee. These groups are a good beginning, but they are not enough, leaving as they do too many communities without organization and those with organization without enough cohesiveness upon which to ground astuteness.

This process could be more effective if Negro churches would sponsor leadership schools throughout the country directed by Saul Alinsky and his teams of organizers, as well as other proven groups, to which ministers and laymen would be sent for the express purposes of learning the tactics of organizing a community. To learn how to project grievances into public issues instead of riots is the key to Alinsky's success, which needs to be mastered and extended into a formidable political power.

Community organization is basic, but its purpose must be for practical black politics. In the South the MFDP has shown the way without community organization on the strength of not being represented. This experience of the MFDP is insufficient in the North, and even now in the South with the voting rights bill. Together with community organization there must come an awareness on the part of the masses not only of their frustrations but of their power to turn these defeats into gain, perhaps even with the "ace" of riots as the ultimate threat, comparable to the wildcat strike in the labor movement. Since it takes more than leadership to organize a community and to build the community into a political power, it is a question as to how the Negro masses can gain the awareness and commitment needed now.

While in cooperation with other groups in community organization for black politics, what the churches can provide is the drumming into the Negro masses of their sorry plight in such a fashion and with such consistency as has previously been the case in making the masses feel better than they are or providing the suggestion of future reward. If such a constant confrontation with their unfortunate lot were combined with the opportunity to translate their frustrations into ways of securing the necessary transformations of society, the cruelty involved might not bring immediate compensation via solution of social problems but it would aid in the realization of the plight of the Negro masses, which is the precondition of community organization for political power on a nationwide scale.

When the trust in ministers and churches is taken into consideration, along with the deference to religion, there is a force for black politics which does not require a political ideology to be acquired by the Negro masses. What is needed are ministers and laymen who can be trusted and will instruct the fellowship in the realities of sophisticated city politics in unsophisticated ways. Most of all the masses require inspiration to create the only power for real change—their collectivity in mutual trust against the preconsciousness of white middle class society which favors a few Negroes in order not to accept masses. To make the transition from social centers through community organizations to political power structures does not mean an independent political party detached from the Democratic or Republican Party. It does mean an independent political movement within the parties, an alignment of the ghettos for a viable political movement. The rallying cry of the pulpit must be that this is a racist society, inciting not to riot but to political concert for purposes of changing the local power structures in each community and therefore the economic forces which respond positively to legislative changes, in lieu of root changes required to eliminate the profound social evils.

Direct engagement of the Negro church in politics will result not only in a broad base but the much needed injection into the movement of black politics the hope based upon the Kingdom of

God which cannot be shaken by despair. Despair is the inevitable result of hope based upon human beings and institutions. Based on the brotherhood of man demand, black politics will be informed by a faith more sustaining, if not more instrumental, than an ideology. Ideologies do not necessarily lose their ground for hope; they are more often than not illusions of grandeur. Faith in the demand of the brotherhood of man permits the alignment with all groups seeking the equality of the Negro. Such faith deploys political bickerings via the commitment to the Kingdom of God that requires all human groups to work together toward its requirement and seeks its spirit in realignments beyond every crushing defeat. It is this faith the Negro church can offer instead of ideology—better still, a faith against which to evaluate ideology and with which to inform it.

If the Negro church will enter the arena of black politics as an institution in each community, whether by leadership from the top or coercion from the bottom, it will together with other groups in large measure determine whether the Negro will remain half slave and half free. It is a serious question: Can the Negro be deghettoized within a democracy or must he remain a victim of ghetto? If the latter, it means that the United States will be following the pattern of South Africa, and in this event it is only a matter of time: thus, the imperative of the Negro church reasserting its role. Whether or not time has run out and it is not now possible to bring about the fundamental social change needed for the Negro to be equal is not now certain. It is certain that if the Negro church does not assume an active and cooperative role in the guidance of the masses toward a designed destiny, the immense task of mass reaffiliation in other groups may be too costly and too long for the realization of the democratic Creed.

We are now beset by the alternatives of political power: to shape the political and economic confluences of the North and thus of the South toward equality *or* spontaneous riots which lead to a police state. The history of America attests to the vigorous role of religious institutions in mobilizing immigrant people for strength in union. In 800 A.D., Charlemagne turned to the church for the political unification of the empire. The "suffering servant" people of Israel did not differentiate between the community of faith and the community of politics. More than any other institution, the Negro church has the ear of the Negro masses. It is the masses which set the pace for the Negro group by their sheer dominance. The exceptional Negro is feared neither in the white North or the white South. It is the black horde which whites fear, and in keeping back this vast majority they inevitably deny full equality to all Negroes. The last chance for the Negro to be accepted lies in the arena of politics dominated by the masses. The last chance for the Negro church to be effective lies in its exercise of influence to form with other groups a mass political base. The last chance for a democratic America lies in effective black politics, lacking which violence will pour forth from Negroes and they will be overwhelmed by a greater violence and there will result a police state with "justice and freedom" for neither whites nor blacks.

If the future of Negro-white relations depends upon the Negro's gaining power via politics, black politics cannot be concerned with power for power's sake. Political power for blacks means a voice in the decisions of the community and the opportunity for negotiations with the white power structure for the good of the community. There is no community good if it is not good for the Negro, and there is no good for the Negro which is not good for the community. The present emphasis in human relations, which the swing toward politics clearly manifests, is upon changing behavior. To change behavior and therefore social structures, it is generally assumed by social scientists, eventuates in the change of attitudes. It is not a question of changing either white attitudes or white behavior but both. It is an illusion to assume that when whites are forced to sit down with Negroes and negotiate their attitudes will change toward the Negro, who will be seen as an equal, just as the illusion once was dominant that attitudes must be changed to bring about a change in behavior. Of course, there is a difference between civil rights negotiating from pressure and power politics as the basis for negotiations. Politics is the way of democracy. But politics does not change human nature. Nothing would be more foolish than for Negroes to expect from concerted power a sudden change in behavior and attitudes. Power can change social structures, but not the human beings who are structured in social groups. Only through political power will Negroes increasingly share in the economy, but this is not to be equated with equality. The real value of black politics is in providing the Negro with a new image based upon real power which will allow him to take the offensive in both the change of social structures and social living. This is evident in the Negro middle class, marked as it is by the same unacceptability as the lower class. Without the result of social equality, the gains of political and economic equality are of no ultimate value. Today, the immediate objective must be political unity of Negroes, the means to economic well-being. About this there is no question. The long range goal of social equality may not be possible in a racist society dominated by white preconsciousness. Yet, the Negro will be as frustrated to-morrow as he is today if he aims for political and economic power and assumes that in gaining both he gains social equality. He must ultimately aim for nothing less than social equality, at which he must work with the same vigor as political and economic power.

The Negro church in its engagement in politics for blacks must turn to those with expertise in community organization, economics, and politics. In attracting and gaining the allegiance of the masses of Negroes, the Negro church is responsible to and for the masses. No less than instilling in the masses a fervor for politics equal to religious fervor, the Negro church must also make them aware that ideologies, methods, strategies, and plan-ning, though absolutely essential, are not absolutes. They are the necessary tools of democracy. The Negro church must be a school in the democratic process and one of its first lessons should be to make clear that economic and political power can be achieved and earned, while social equality is a birthright which can neither be achieved nor earned, though it may be denied. It is because the Negro has been denied his birthright, social equality, that he does not have political and economic equality. The reverse is simply not true. Only a change in Negro-white group relations will bring about social equality. To place confidence in political and economic power as the means to social equality is but to be taken in by a more sophisticated and updated interpretation of the old line that when Negroes prove themselves they will be accepted. Many Negroes have proved themselves according to any objective standard—none has been accepted.

In this next stage of Negro-white group relations, the Negro church must challenge the even now dominant mood which offers the motivation of political and economic equality. This mood takes the tact that the Negro must develop a class consciousness among the masses, which is tantamount to an ideological warfare between Negroes and Negroes as well as between Negroes and whites. The Negro church cannot avoid fellowship with those who take this line and should not for they are often the source of tactical astuteness. The Negro church in working with ideologists must work with the Negro masses, reminding them that all Negroes suffer from segregation-discrimination and this is motivation enough to engage in community politics for blacks. The Negro cannot become a tool for those who wish a radical reconstruction of economics via an independently-based Negro political movement. To become so would not result in the gaining of the birthright the Negro has been denied. If the present democratic system and free enterprise system are flexible enough and sufficiently responsive to power for the well-being of most whites, the fact that there are poor whites and Negroes may mean changes occur too slowly, not that the necessary changes cannot occur within the system. The poverty stricken white and the poverty stricken Negro do not share the same plight. That the Negro has a movement going for him which other poverty-stricken groups do not have is a fact. It does not follow from this he should become a foil for those who wish to eliminate poverty by the militancy of the Negro. The movement of the Negro will aid this democracy and this economy to improve the lot of its own people and the people of the world. But this is not what motivates the Negro; the history of the Negro church is a singular reminder of this fact. What motivates the Negro is that he is an outcast and therefore his objective is to radically change, not simply reconstruct or reform or renew, the fundamental value of white preconsciousness. It is not certain whether this change is possible until every method within the limits of democracy has been tried. The remaining method to be tried is the mixing of what so many have been taught to avoid: religion and politics. In the past they have been tried separately by Negroes, a key difference from whites. Their value is in the power which comes from a people working in concert. Nothing less than the tangible rewards of religion in politics is sufficiently cohesive for the Negro to unite for the long, long attack upon white preconsciousness. If in the process there are transformations of traditional operational procedures, and some Negroes receive exceptional opportunities, or all Negroes are raised economically along with their white brethren—these are but nourishments for the substantive task.

The solution to Negro-white group conflicts is not lacking because knowledge is unavailable. There is more than enough information. The conflicts persist because of a conflict of interests and opinions within and between white power structures and Negro groups. Thus, the function of the Negro church in black politics is to bring about unity among Negroes whereby the disagreements as to how social equality can be achieved will be subordinated to the unity for its achievement. A unified Negro body in each community can affect even more the daily and long range decision making processes of local governments than those at the national level. In the domestic sphere, national policies reflect the conflicts of interests at the local level. Each community in urban America is governed by the process of politics, the varying ideas, opinions and interests. Both elected politicians and appointed bureaucrats engage in politics. The engagement of the Negro church in politics would not be for group power politics alone—to which elected politicians are peculiarly sensitive. It would be an engagement for the purposes of establishing an image or presence which affects administrative decisions. Politicians respond to overt pressure of groups, particularly at election time. Administrators or bureaucrats are subject to politics in their decisions more out of concern for effective implementation than for favors or a mutual exchange.

The unity of blacks in politics means that the Negro church is concerned equally for the politics of politicians and the politics of administrators. Administrative decision makers are influenced not only at the time of decision making but prior to this in what is to form the content of decisions. What is allowable in the thinking stage, the planning board stage, the proposal stage is a matter of politics—that which is allowable or determined either by voting bloc power or special interest groups. The unity of the Negro through the church means not only the pressure of voting bloc power but the presence of a special interest group. The advantage of black politics is a united front on both political bases, a counterweight to conflicting white ideas and interests with respect to the inclusion or exclusion of the Negro special interest in each decision of the community. The Negro has to be concerned about all community interests. The plus factor of white politics is the special interest of the Negro group for the neglected dimension of social equality. Toward this total concern the Negro church can contribute the solidarity of the masses which will not sell out for mere economic or political growth where this jeopardizes the opportunity for social equality, or merely postpones consideration of social equality.

In capitalizing upon the role of politics the Negro will need to disavow bickering and cherish conflict. The fundamental principle to be advocated is that the special self-interest of the Negro for social equality and all of its subsequent economic benefits is in the public interest. The fact that the Negro is not a social equal is a political reality. The Negro must be determined to change this political fact of inequality. To do so requires the control of conflicting political interests and modes of achievement within the Negro community whereby the Negro group becomes a moral force of revolutionary significance. Thus, the added role of the Negro church is not only to pay lip service to the principle that the masses can make decisions for themselves, but also to provide this possibility through not allowing black politics to become so machine-like as to make the machine a higher priority than the people. Such vital concern for the masses requires the Negro church to be a permanent political organization, voluntary through and through. What the Negro church has that any political group requires for maintenance of strength is prestige for masses, their involvement in an organization of congenial people who are committed to increasing the good of their fellowship and the community. These are the natural strengths of the Negro church and imperatives for non-ecclesiastical as well as ecclesiastical politics.

With this strength the Negro church can function as a mediator with other Negro organizations, forming a cooperative which initiates programs for the pressing immediate and long range needs of the Negro. To be effective as a mediator does not mean the Negro church needs to be the initiator of political programs, it can give or withhold its sanction and therefore exercise enormous influence—particularly with its hold on the masses. Its positive role is in building personal ties of support through building up a strong family bond so that there is a sense of personal commitment to the well-being of relations. Beyond the strengthening of personal and family ties among the masses, the Negro church has a responsibility of engaging the middle and upper middle class Negroes whose destiny vis-à-vis equality is tied to the breakthrough of the masses.

It is a formidable task, unifying Negroes despite the numerical urban strength and the visible gap between their hopes and deferred attainments. An unprecedented maturity is essential to develop a singularity and prevent schisms through the push and pull of those militants who demand black politics be reform politics, machine politics, independent or nonpartisan politics, or politics of alliances. While unity of the Negro is basic everywhere, the tactics must reflect the peculiarities of each community, each issue, and each stage in the overall objective. What is necessary in each situation is not a matter of knowledge or general principles, it is a matter of experience and intuition. There are a small but sufficient number of Negro and white citizens able and willing to provide the necessary resources for effective political action, given the unification and commitment of Negroes.

It is true that family disorganization, the economic instability of the male, limited education and skills are marks of the masses which are the extraordinary heritage of the Negro, compounding his desire for security above his sense of community. The basic securities of adequate education and attractive employment and homes must be provided. Yet the achievements of these fundamental conditions will not automatically yield loyalty to the Negro family and community. The heritage of second class citizenship, which results in both destructive frustrations of the male Negro lashing out and apathy, can be countered only by a sense of common unity that transcends individual and family disorganization. This the Black Muslims have taught us. The evolutionary process of providing the Negro male job status and family loyalty need not be a deterrent to a revolutionary Negro group unity. The alienation of the Negro male and the atomization of the Negro family we will have with us for decades, however many emergency measures are unleashed to upgrade employment. The disunity of the Negro community need not follow.

To the extent the Negro community continues to be divided it will be so because an historically divisive Negro church, seeking first personal and then institutional loyalty, fails to meet the opportunity of emphasizing its unitive powers for the larger interest of the total people. In such an event, the Negro church at the center of the masses who are the Negro community will be an unredeemable imbalance of immorality, decadence, selfishness, irrelevance, irresponsibility, and unmitigated corruption. It will then earn its despise and hasten its demise.

The opportunity of the Negro church to which the masses has given blind allegiance is to unify them wherein lies the real possibility for overcoming the influence of the destructive elements within the Negro community as well as outside of it. The emergence of political orientations within an increasing number of civil rights movements are possessed with either the position that the Negro masses must become class conscious and thus oppose blacks and whites of the middle class or that the Negro masses must be siphoned off into the middle class in the hopes that a small number of Negroes remaining in the masses will not be detrimental to an expanding middle class. The Negro church cannot become a party to any divisiveness. It knows that all Negroes are in the same situation of statuslessness, a condition that cannot be corrected by disunity but *may* be through unity. The fact that some Negroes enjoy more economic rewards than others does not mean they have a monopoly on courage, community interests, and the willingness to improve their lot and those of their children where the opportunity is clear. Though tagged as the group interested in welfare as opposed to middle class interest in status, it was the lower class Negro who braved, for the most part, the lines of jeering whites in the desegregation of schools. At bottom all Negroes desire economic security, but the absence of equal economic gains is as inevitable in the Negro community as in the white community. Clearly, various economic levels do not necessitate division of the Negro group, given a good and even high rate of living for those at the lower levels. It is clear that the small middle class Negro group is dependent upon the rise in opportunity of the lower class Negroes. The further up the economic scale the masses rise, the middle class rises proportionately further. A dedicated Negro church will give itself for the unity of the masses not only as a basis for their improvement but as a basis for the unity of all Negroes. For a unified, militant, and skillful lower class is the necessary condition to bind all Negroes together.

The singularity of the Negro masses would form an attractive body which the middle class Negro need no longer fear. Having overcome *internal* hatred, all Negroes could then accept the hatred expressed by whites and make political use of this hatred. In the drive for social equality, hatred is a necessary basis for Negro-white relationships, and though it is neither inevitable nor an acceptable basis, it is a concrete one to be affirmed. Hatred is not idealistic, it is realistic and therefore pragmatic. Since the white community is based upon an irrational presupposition, the rational use of irrationality may prove the most permanent basis for a relationship, which is after all the essence of politics.

Social equality may elude the Negro as surely as equality of economic well being between Negroes. The function of the Negro church is not to be deluded by but increase the broad base of political unity to unite the Negro through economic well-being and prevent him from being satisfied. It is the voice of the Negro church which must be heard loud and clear. Whether or not the Negro can win or be given his birthright, his primary motivation must be not to allow whites to have any security in their birthright until *all* groups have their right. The task of the Negro is not to change the minds and hearts of dominant whites. The task is to change their world. They must seek first the Kingdom of God and then all else will be added. This is not only black politics, it is good politics, it is the demand of the Kingdom of God—the rudimentary principles and practices of the politics of God.

INDEX

DATE DUE

11-27			
2/13/7?			
GAYLORD			PRINTED IN U.S.A.